# Ain't That a Shame

## SANDRA S. FRENCH

iUniverse, Inc.
New York   Bloomington

Ain't That a Shame

Copyright © 2010 Sandra S. French

iUniverse books may be ordered through booksellers or by contacting:

iUniverse
1663 Liberty Drive
Bloomington, IN 47403
www.iuniverse.com
1-800-Authors (1-800-288-4677)

ISBN: 978-1-4502-5110-5 (pbk)
ISBN: 978-1-4502-5112-9 (cloth)
ISBN: 978-1-4502-5111-2 (ebk)

Printed in the United States of America

iUniverse rev. date: 9/10/2010

For Morgan and Fraya

# Contents

## Introduction
## It's All in the Game

Contrary to what many people believe, the fifties weren't totally cool, even in a normal place like the comfortable suburb of Buffalo, New York, where I grew up. Hot on the heels of World War II, the smoke-filled indoors air of my house and of most homes in the neighborhood still reeked with a fear of alien invasions and all-out nuclear war. Recurring nightmares of mushrooming atomic bomb clouds haunted my sleep, and I looked askance at anyone who struck me as different.

Like most kids I knew, I worked hard to fit in. I earned excellent grades at school, and I enjoyed a fairly active social life. Despite the fact that several boys fawned over me, as a teenager I earned an impeccable sexual reputation by devising a clever scheme for fending off unwanted kisses. Some kids called me a prude, but that didn't bother me. I suppose a psychologist might have diagnosed my attitude as a phobia, or fear of kissing, but my parents never took me to see one. Our family doctor came to our house; he knew enough to keep all of us healthy. Besides, anyone in our family could afford to be choosey about doling out favors.

The first chapter is set in 1958. I was a senior in high school then, and that's when Peter French, our new pastor's kid, or PK as I called him, invaded my life. To put it bluntly, I hated the guy. He was alien to everything I stood for and admired. Yet that PK managed to screw up not only his life but my life too, and I let him get away with it.

*The PK*

## Chapter 1
## HEARTS OF STONE

His hand reached out toward me, and before I realized what he was doing, he set something in my lap. A Christmas present? I stared at it in disbelief. He had no right to give me anything. He meant nothing to me. He wasn't a member of my crowd. He was a nobody: an unattractive, foul-mouthed PK who seemed determined to trick me every time I let my guard down. This was one of those times; I hadn't seen it coming. He ambushed me with a Christmas present! When he steered his car in the wrong direction, I should have insisted that he turn around. I blamed myself, but I also cursed Miss Maxmillian for making me promise to be polite to him. She knew that I hated everything about Pete, but she still wanted me to act as his mentor. I couldn't agree to that, but I promised her that I'd try to be civil to him. I was a good girl: I was careful about my promises, and I always kept those I made. The way I saw it, making a promise was the same as telling the truth. Lies, even white ones, could cause me trouble.

This story is the truth, exactly as I remember it, although I changed most of the names and put words into people's mouths. After all, I can't remember precisely what I or anyone else said all those years ago. I can't even quote the exact words people said in a movie that I saw only a week ago, but I can get the gist across.

That's what I've done here. The dialogues that I've created convey the gist of what we said to each other. For example, on that fateful Christmas morning, I don't know precisely what I said to Pete after he gave me that gift, but I certainly recall how annoyed I was. However, I also figured that since he had bothered to get me something, I'd better stifle the noisy protest I wanted to raise and come up with an uncharacteristically demure objection instead.

"What's this? You shouldn't have gotten me anything."

"Don't act so stupid, baby. Open it. It ain't no big deal." That's how sloppily he always talked. I wouldn't make that part up.

"Don't call me baby," I said.

"Open it, baby."

"Okay." I shrugged my shoulders. What could I do? I attacked the wrapping. It was a small, velvety-looking box. A ring box? It couldn't be.

"Go on," he urged. "Look inside."

I hesitated.

"Like I said, it ain't no big deal. Come on, open it."

Slowly I opened the box, took one look at the ring, and exclaimed, "Oh, no!"

That happened at shortly after one o'clock in the morning on December twenty-fifth, 1958, providing further evidence that my senior year wasn't going according to the way I had planned it. For as long as I could remember, it had been my goal to become the first female in my family go to college. That much of my plan was still in the works: I had received a written notice of early acceptance to Gettysburg College in Pennsylvania, a big step for a girl who had spent her entire life in a small village northeast of Buffalo. I had worked hard to earn that acceptance; I was justly proud of my top-notch grades, and I felt entitled to enjoy my senior year. When school opened that September, I was dead sure that nothing, short of Buffalo getting bombed by Moscow, could possibly ruin my year.

Looking back on the way my life had gone up to that point, I wonder why I bothered to plan things so carefully. I even went so far as to pick out the guy that I was going to marry after college. Perhaps I was just too young or too full of myself to allow any wiggle room for more surprises. At any rate, it wasn't long after the first day got under way that the unexpected happened. Two new guys showed up in Advanced English. Right away I noticed that both of them had a good deal in common with my future husband Paul. The three of them were handsome, excellent students, and members of the right crowd. Each guy obviously admired me. Sadly, as it turned out, each of them caused me grief. One of them nearly cost me my life, although he never knew it. None of them, however, caused me as much trouble as that lying son of a preacher did.

I met Pete's dad at his initial service at our church. Dr. French was good looking for a minister, and he was so charming and amiable that when he introduced me to his eldest son Pete, I was both shocked and appalled. Unlike his dad, Pete didn't appear to be the least bit classy. He wore an ugly pair of Coke bottle thick, horn-rimmed glasses, his skin looked pale and imperfect, and his green tie didn't match his blue suit. He used gobs of Vaseline to paste his hair to a point in the back of his head. Some kids called that style a ducktail. Others called it a DA, short for duck's ass. I didn't approve of that term any more than I approved of Pete flaunting the first DA that I had ever seen on a boy living in Snyder. To top it all off, the jerk made it obvious that he couldn't care less about me. No boy had ever reacted to me that way. It was incredible.

Later on, when we couldn't avoid talking to each other, Pete didn't so much speak to me as snarl at me, abusing the beauty of the English language with repulsive words and contemptible grammar. Naturally I did my best to avoid him. I could usually spot him a mile away because he wore basically two different sets of outfits: mismatched suits and ties to church, and black shirts with dark pants to school. Black was the perfect color for someone with his disposition. I had never a met guy who was so gloomy and disrespectful to me.

I expected guys to tease me; that's not what I'm talking about. When Paul, Cal, Ken, or any of the other boys in my crowd made fun of me, I teased them back. They tolerated my playful comebacks with good humor like the gentlemen they were. But for some reason, Pete seemed to take pride in the fact that he wasn't like them. In fact, he held himself aloof from everyone at Amherst High. I could count the people who got along with him on fewer than ten fingers: his elderly grandmother, his little brother, and two or three fellow delinquents, including a frightening Negro who lived in Buffalo's inner city. The numbskulls in our church youth group, the Luther League, seemed to admire Pete too, but no one in that bunch of ninnies had so much as a lick of good sense.

I seldom saw Pete in school, but when I did, I ducked for cover. Pete didn't walk through the halls like the rest of us; he prowled through them, looking like a caged cougar with a cigarette tucked behind his ear. Cigarettes were forbidden in school, but he didn't seem to care. He just skulked along, peering straight ahead, ignoring the normal kids who passed him. In my opinion, his high and mighty facade was just that: nothing but a big pretense. His disgusting appearance and fake posturing were enough to revolt a well-brought-up, reasonably popular girl like me, but I also sensed that he was hiding something. I was as curious as the next girl; I identified with Nancy Drew, Sherlock Holmes, and the other detectives in the mystery books I devoured. Yet I sensed that whatever Pete was up to was something no stylish sleuth would bother to investigate. He wasn't as weird as the two perverts I had encountered, but he was up to something that wasn't aboveboard.

I only agreed to be nice to Pete because two adults, my school counselor and my new pastor, waylaid me into it, and it was not my place to argue with grown-ups. But I was right about him, and I knew it. Any attempt to be polite to him would just be a waste of my precious time. Pete was no ordinary delinquent-slash-truant either. One minute he'd be spouting outrageously complicated theories, attributing them to writers only he had ever heard of; the next minute he'd be hoodwinking old ladies and nincompoops by masquerading as a veritable lion of generosity. In short, he was too clever by half.

Being polite to him stretched my considerable capacity for self-control; I never knew what to expect next. I certainly hadn't anticipated Pete's offer to escort me to the midnight Christmas Eve service. As a rule, I didn't accept last-minute offers from boys, but I agreed to go with him because the rest of my family was attending the earlier service, and I wanted to go to the later one. A respectable young lady couldn't go out alone in the middle of the night; she required an escort. So the trade-off I made to get to that service was to suffer the embarrassment of being seen with that disgusting pastor's kid. Don't get me wrong. I was no fool. Before agreeing to his offer, I made him promise to act like a gentleman and take me back home right after the service was over.

When we arrived at the church, the nave smelled of warm candles and pine. Everyone greeted us cheerfully, and I belted out my favorite carols with unbridled pleasure. Pastor French's sermon was short and heartwarming. All of that was good. But when we were driving out of the parking lot afterwards, Pete didn't turn his car in the direction of my house.

"Where are you taking me?" The shrillness of my question embarrassed me. I squeaked out "please," before continuing more calmly in my normal voice. "Remember that I promised my parents I'd be home directly after the midnight service. And you promised to take me right back."

"Take it easy, will ya?"

He pulled his car over to the curb near a street lamp and dropped the present into my lap. When I opened it and saw the ring, my shock must have been obvious, even to a guy as socially clueless as Pete was. Open mouthed, I stared at a huge red rhinestone heart set in gold mounting with two tiny golden bows carved on either side of it.

"Ya don't like it?" He sounded crushed.

I shut my mouth, sat there quietly for a couple more seconds, and then calmly replied, "Of course I ... like ... it." He searched my face as if he didn't believe me. I studied the ring again, holding it up so that the facets of the red stone reflected the glow of the street lamp. The ring was pretty, in a bizarre sort of way. "It's ... it's quite special," I improvised.

A heart? A rhinestone heart? Panic was setting in.

"That's a genuine gold setting," he said proudly. "You like it then? Really?"

"Of course. I ... I just don't know what to say." He had no right to give me this.

"Try it on," he insisted. "I think it'll fit."

I slipped it on the third finger of my right hand. Darn, I said to myself. It was a perfect fit. Now I'd probably have to wear it once in awhile. I scoured my brain for a polite, reasonable excuse for refusing to accept it.

"It does pose a slight problem," I finally muttered.

"Ya always lookin' fer problems? Even on Christmas?"

"No. That's not fair, Pete. It's just that ... you do understand, don't you? To some people, it could symbolize ... something. It's shape that is ..." I floundered uncomfortably.

"What're ya tryin' ta say? Spit it out."

"Well, someone might ask me what it means, exactly."

"Yer still makin' no sense."

"Sorry. I'm trying be as clear as possible, but it's not easy."

"Heh. A bossy dame like you should have no trouble makin' yer point. Yer not afraid of me, are ya, baby?"

"Don't be ridiculous," I scoffed. "It's just that, usually when a girl wears a ring a guy gives her, especially one that's heart shaped, it means ... it could signify that she's, well, going with him."

"Geez! We ain't never even had no real date, fer Christ's sake. Hell, I just meant ta give ya a Christmas present, it bein' Christmas mornin' now and all. Ya said ya like rings. I found a pretty ring that I figured a girl would like. That's it. It's simple, ain't it? Why d'ya gotta ruin it?"

Despite his swearing and terrible grammar, I thought it was a good question—one that I had often asked myself. Nobody I knew was as talented as I was when it came to ruining things where boys were concerned. I had already broken more hearts than any other girl I knew. Usually it wasn't my fault either. I wasn't responsible for the fact that I was born with the good looks I had inherited from my two grandmothers and the brains I got from Grandma Chrystene and Grandpa Schall. I also inherited Dad's good luck. If that hadn't been true, I probably would have been dead before then.

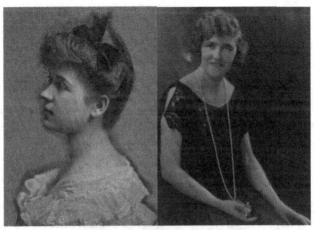

*Grandma Chrystene*          *Grandma Schall*

*And Me*

## Chapter 2
## TOO CLOSE FOR COMFORT

I had had misgivings when Mike asked me to ride over to the rock quarry with him. My initial instinct had been to say no. "Why would I want go there with you again?" I had asked him suspiciously. "The last time we went there, you caught a big, black water snake and kept dangling it in my face, trying to get me to pet it. You know I hate snakes."

"I was just kidding around, Sandy. Why do snakes bother you so much anyway? They're cool. Look, I promise that if I catch one today, I won't even tell you. I'll keep it in my dungaree pocket where you won't see it, okay?"

Could I trust Mike this time? It had taken me forever to get the picture of that wiggling black creature out of my mind.

"Come on, Sandy. You like to go to the quarry, don't you?" The tone of his voice had turned uncharacteristically sweet. "Remember the time we caught fourteen tadpoles? And the pretty fossil you found? You liked that a lot, didn't you?"

He was right. I had enjoyed exploring the old town quarry with him before. It was a neat place, even if it was dangerous because you had to be careful not to step on loose rocks. If you lost your balance or tripped on a stone, you could slip and fall into a crevice or a deep hole and break an ankle or, worse, your neck. You might even end up in one of the pools of rotting water full of snakes and other creepy crawlers. I imagined most of them were poisonous.

My younger brother wasn't any braver than I was; he just never thought about the dire possibilities like I did. He only wanted to climb around the quarry and hunt for reptiles, using the bigger rocks in the ponds as his hunting posts. I can still picture how Mike looked when he was going after a water snake. Intent on his prey, he balanced precariously on the edge of a slippery rock, ready to grab it. The creature moved quickly, but Mike was quicker. He reached his hand into the water and grasped the loathsome thing before it saw him coming.

Unless it was pollywog season, I avoided those excavation pools. I searched around in the dry areas, sifting through the loose stones scattered at the bases of the pit's big boulders, hoping to find something to add to my treasure. There were many places in the huge quarry that I had yet to explore, including some narrow crevices I had spotted higher up on the cliffs. I was after fossils or rocks that had unique, colorful patterns. I took the best ones home and put them in the back of my underwear and sock drawer. After I brought my fern fossil home, I looked up fossils in our encyclopedia. I read about rare dinosaur-age fossils kept on display in science museums, but the encyclopedia had a picture of a fossil like mine. The caption identified it as common. I didn't agree. None of my friends had one.

"Did you ask Mom if it's okay for us to ride our bikes over there this afternoon?" I asked Mike.

"Yeah. She said she didn't care, as long as I didn't go alone, but Mark, Dave, and Bruce are somewhere else today. How about it, Sandy? Will you go with me?"

My brother was determined, Mom needed me to keep track of him, and most importantly, I wanted to go.

"Remember, you have to stick to your promise about snakes, Mike. If you so much as show me one, I swear I'll never go there with you again."

"Sure. I promise. Let's go."

"In a minute. I need to stop in the bathroom, and I'd better tell Mom I'm going with you. Get out my bike for me."

That was summer vacation of 1952, and I was eleven. Mike was only nine, but he rode his two-wheeler faster than I could, so he arrived at the pit's edge first. He abandoned his Schwinn against a jutting boulder and took off down into the deep quarry on foot before I could ask him where he intended to hang out. I carefully set my blue bike on its kickstand between two tall rock formations, not far from the boulder that propped up my brother's. Gingerly, I navigated over the rocks and down into the depths of the quarry. I spotted Mike several yards away on a rock near a pool of water. He looked safe enough, so I began to climb up a ledge leading to the top of a high embankment. I intended to keep an eye on Mike while I was up there searching for rocks for my collection. The ridge I walked on was narrow, and the going was rough in places. I stepped into a cranny to look through a pile of loose pebbles, but I found only one that I liked. It was streaked with crossing purple and red lines forming a plaid pattern. I tucked it into my dungaree pocket, thinking I'd probably throw it away if I found something better.

It was a beautiful July day with no rain clouds in sight. We had the whole afternoon, so I could take my time going up. I told myself that even if I didn't find a fossil, it would be worth the effort just to sun myself on the grass at the top of the rocky cliff. I continued to climb carefully, testing the rocks I stepped on to make sure they weren't loose. Occasionally a sparkle from one of the stones at my feet attracted my attention. Wouldn't it be something if I were to find a crystal? After stirring through some stones with one foot, I moved on. Suddenly I felt uneasy; I sensed that I was not alone.

Someone was standing on the cliff above me. This seemed odd to me, because Mike and I hadn't seen anyone anywhere near the quarry when we arrived. I looked up, curious to see who it was. There was a man up there, someone I had never seen before.

Judging by his face, he looked around Dad's age, but that was the only similarity I could see to my father. He had stringy, unkempt brown hair that was blowing around in the breeze. His blue eyes seemed set in a glazed stare, almost as if he were half asleep, and his thick lips were shaped into an unreadable smile that felt halfway between friendly and mean. I stopped in my tracks.

"Hi," the man said. "Come up here, pretty girl, and see what I have."

I didn't move up toward him, but I had been taught to be respectful and polite to adults, so I responded to his greeting with a less than enthusiastic "Hi."

Then I saw what he was holding. His pants were unzipped, and he was holding his male thing. It looked huge, not like the little things my brothers had hanging between their legs. The man must be a freak, I thought, and my stomach began to hurt. Mom had taught us that it was wrong for anyone to show his or her private parts. We weren't even allowed to show ours to another family member—not on purpose anyway. This man was not only putting his on display, but the thing was abnormal. It was too big, and it was sticking out. I couldn't imagine how it had ever fit into his pants. Why was he doing this? I didn't want to look at it. Who would? I had to get away from him, and fast.

My feet almost slipped off the ledge as I struggled to back up against the cliff while maintaining my footage on the narrow ridge. I knocked a big stone over and heard it hit the floor of the quarry several feet below with a dull thud. Gripping a stone that jutted out of the cliff tightly with one hand, I carefully swung my body around so that I was in position to start back down.

"You're not going to leave me, are you?" The man whimpered like a disappointed toddler.

I didn't look back; I just scrambled as fast as I dared down the narrow, craggy path. I wished that I could make my muscles move as well as my friend Barb's did. I knew I was taking a chance, climbing down so fast when I was such a klutz. One false step could send me over the edge.

"Don't go away," he pleaded.

It wasn't polite to ignore the commands of an adult, but to me this guy was not normal. He was a sideshow creep. I held my breath to listen for his footsteps behind me, but I couldn't hear anything. Was he still up there, or was he following me? When I had nearly reached the foot of the rock mound, I shouted to Mike.

"Mike? Come here, will you? Mike? Michael? Robert?" I called out Mike's middle name like that on purpose, so maybe the weird guy would think I had two men with me. Maybe he hadn't seen Mike at all, so he wouldn't know he was just a kid.

Mike didn't answer. After I landed on the floor of the pit, I spotted him over where he had been when I had started my ascent. I shouted his two names again.

"I'm busy," he growled. He was balancing on a stone at the water's edge, hunched down, ready to grab something in the water.

Gasping for breath, I cried out, "Mike, listen to me. I ran into a freaky guy up there. His thing was out. It was too big, and it was ugly. This is no joke. We need to get out of here. *Now!*"

Mike looked up at me for the first time. He couldn't understand what I was trying to tell him, but he could tell from the tone of my voice that I was scared. I looked back up toward the top of the cliff. There was no sign of the man, but that didn't mean he was gone. He could have snuck down somehow and be hiding nearby.

"We need to get out of here," I yelled. "Now! *I mean it, Mike!*" My brother got the message. He jumped off his rock, and we both hightailed it to our bikes and lit off as fast as we could pedal. After we had gone a couple of blocks, Mike waited for me and signaled to me to stop.

"Why did we have to leave the quarry, Sandy? What did you see?"

"Just ride home. I know what I'm doing."

He arrived home first. When I rode up, he was trying to lift the garage door in order to put his bike away. "Put mine away too, Mike," I ordered him, dropping my bike on the grass and heading for the side door. Out of breath, I ran into the kitchen where Mom was peeling potatoes at the sink.

"There was a man at the quarry, with his big thing out." I gestured at my crotch.

"*My God!*"

Mom's reaction surprised me. I had never heard her say the Lord's name like that before.

"He didn't touch you anywhere or hurt you, did he?"

"No. I got away from him as fast as I could. I rounded up Mike, and we hopped on our bikes and rode right home."

Mom dialed the phone. I could see her finger shaking as it spun around the dial.

"Harry?" she yelled into the yellow speaker's end. "A pervert exposed himself to Sandy at the quarry." I could tell that Dad was bellowing questions at her through her plastic receiver. "No, no." Mom's voice sounded shaky. "She got away. Okay. Yes. As fast as you can. Please, hurry."

Mom hung up saying Dad was on his way. I hadn't expected him to leave work. I didn't want to have to tell him about that freaky man. He might get mad at me. Dad sometimes got angry if he had to leave his work or a meeting with someone because of one of us. I needed to go to the bathroom. When I came out, I was shocked to see Dad already in the kitchen, talking intently to Mom. A stocky, uniformed Amherst policeman stood between my parents. The cop looked angry.

As town councilman, Dad knew all the town cops. They were his drinking buddies, and he always kept extra beers in the refrigerator for them. The cop's expression changed when he saw me.

"Hello, Miss Schall," he said, smiling kindly. "I'm Sergeant Wilson, remember? The councilman here tells me you had a run-in with a bad guy. Mind if I ask you a few questions?" What could I say? He was an important adult, and I was only a kid.

The officer probably handled the questioning as sensitively as he knew how, but I was too mortified to be of much help. He asked me to tell him embarrassing details about the strange man: how he looked, what he said, what he was wearing, and, worst of all, what he was doing. "I didn't see him for long, sir."

"Please speak up, Miss Schall."

"Officer Wilson needs to hear your answers," Dad said sternly. "This is important, Sandy. Don't whisper. Speak up."

"Sorry," I said louder. "I just ran off when I saw his ... when I saw what he was doing."

"He was exposing himself to you? Showing you his private parts?"

"Yes. And they were big. Something must have been wrong with him."

"Uh, hum. Was his car parked nearby?"

"I never noticed a car. I'm sorry."

"What was the pervert, uh, the man, wearing? What color was his shirt?"

"I'm not sure. I think it was checked. Blue and white?"

"How tall was he?"

"Normal height, I guess. I couldn't tell. I was looking up at him. I'm very sorry, sir."

My answers were wrong. I felt as if I were flunking a test. My stomach hurt, and I was so confused that I wasn't certain anymore of the color of the man's hair. Sergeant Wilson asked me if it was red, and I said I didn't think so. Later, after the cop left, I got mad at myself for forgetting that it had been messy and brown.

I had no inkling of the danger that I might have been in. All I understood was that people weren't supposed to behave the way that man did. His body was freaky like some fat lady's at a circus but much worse. Obviously, Dad and the officer thought that he should be in jail. I wanted to help them catch him, but I couldn't, and I felt sick in my stomach. The two men left the kitchen and went out in the hall where I couldn't hear them whispering. I guessed that it was about me. All too soon they returned.

"I'm finished with my questions for now, Miss Schall," Officer Wilson said sternly. "Thank you for trying, but I'm afraid you haven't given me much to go on, but I'll try to find the suspect. Meanwhile, I don't want you to go to that quarry again, either alone or with anyone else. It's not a safe place for anyone, especially children. It's not a playground. Do you understand me?"

"Yes, sir."

"I agree with Sam, Sandy. I don't want to hear that you and Mike have been anywhere near that place again." Dad's voice sounded unusually harsh. I could feel the tears rising. I was tempted to argue that it had been Mike's idea and that Mom had given us permission to go, but I knew enough not to. My place was to stay respectful and silent.

Mike was lurking behind a door; I got a glimpse of his angry face. He probably blamed me for spoiling his favorite hunting grounds. I didn't care. Mike was usually angry with me about something. What bothered me was my feeling that I had disappointed everyone: my parents, the police, probably the whole neighborhood. To my surprise, however, no one spoke to me about the incident again.

I learned a lesson from my narrow escape. A couple of years later, after Claire had told me the facts of life, I was walking home alone from school when an unfamiliar man pulled up near me in his car. His window was open, and he called out to me to come over. He said he was lost and needed me to give him directions, but I could see from a yard or so away, through the passenger window, that he was exposing himself.

"Just a minute, sir," I said sweetly. "Let me come around to your side."

I walked behind his car and memorized the numbers on his license plate before bolting over to the other side of the street and scooting home. This time I called Dad myself, described the stranger in the car who was exposing himself, gave Dad the numbers on the car license plate, and told him the color of the car. Dad wanted to know the make of the car too, but I couldn't tell one make from another. All I knew was that it was an old car. He thanked me and said he would tell his cop friends right away. In less than two days, they had the guy in jail. It turned out that he had been on the police Wanted Persons roster for some time. Once he had nearly killed a girl.

I felt like Nancy Drew. She was a sensible character—fictional, but sensible. She would have agreed with me that both of the perverts I ran into were rare, grotesque specimens of the male sex. Most men—like my dad, her dad, my pastor, all the policemen, the neighbors, my favorite movie stars, and all the boys I knew at school—were normal. In fact, no one remotely like those two perverts has ever approached me again. But they left me scarred, and they probably contributed to what my classmates referred to as my prudish, suspicious nature.

## Chapter 3
## TEARS ON MY PILLOW

My very first walk to school lasted forever. The boys walking behind me called me names: Chubby, Tubby, Kindergarten Baby. When I finally got to Amherst 18, I followed the other kids through the big doors, went left as I had been instructed, and walked into the smelly classroom. Then my nervous stomach turned foul on me, and I threw up all over the floor.

I didn't blame the boys for my mess. I was bigger than they were; that made me different. The boys couldn't tolerate different. I understood that; neither could I. As far as I knew, everyone who lived in Snyder felt the same way. The village of Snyder was a suburb of Buffalo, New York, in the town of Amherst. We lived on Harwood Drive, a neat little cul-de-sac branching off Harlem Road, near the center of the village. Its blind end swung around a grass-filled, curbed circle with a lonely tree sticking out of its center: the arrow in the bull's-eye of my universe. I lived there for the first eighteen years of my life.

America wasn't officially at war in April of 1941 when I was born. Mike, however, was born a couple of years after the attack on Pearl Harbor. We lived with our parents and grandparents in a two-story shingled house among similar homes of middle-class nonprofessionals like my father, mostly factory researchers and small business owners. The war was part of the language we were learning. In that sense, we are war babies. In another sense, we weren't. Happy Harry, our dad, wouldn't risk his handsome neck to fight, not even against "those dirty Japs." I can only imagine what I might have heard from my playpen:

"Oh, Harry, I'm so afraid you'll still get drafted." That would be Mom, whining.

"There's no need for you to worry, Marie." My father's smooth voice could calm a banshee. "Dad says our work is important to the war effort. He knows more about everything than that bastard FDR does."

"If you two can't say anything sensible, don't open your traps." Grandma could get a bit testy. She and Mom argued a lot.

"Mother, go read a book or something." Mom tried to push her mom around, but Grandma was stubborn, and she was smart.

"Marie, FDR is working to keep us safe. Buffalo's steel mills are necessary for making plane parts and other war materials, so it's possible that the Axis might want to drop bombs on us, right here."

"You can be so damned depressing, Mother."

Grandpa Schall owned the Buffalo franchise of the Cleveland Tram Rail Company that designed and made conveyors and monorails used to maneuver heavy war equipment in factories. He had friends in high places that he finagled into arranging exemptions from the draft for his sons, arguing that both Dad and Uncle Jim were integral to his business. In Uncle Jim's case, it was true, but Dad just drew up the final proposals of what Grandpa and Uncle Jim had designed.

Mom was at home most of the time. She couldn't afford to hire help with housework or for nursing her parents' illnesses and taking care of Mike and me. She complained to my sick grandma about having to chase my little brother around and having to do her chores "with very little help from anyone." She was a grumpy Cinderella who dressed herself every morning in a housedress and apron and set her hair in oiled strands, curled and secured with metal bobby pins and covered with a headscarf. She hand washed the dishes and toweled them dry; rubbed dirty garments over a metal corrugated washboard; washed diapers and clothing in a large, iron double sink; cranked the handle of a wringer attached above the sink to squeeze out the rinse water; and hung everything up on clotheslines with wooden pins. It's no wonder that she valued her cigarette breaks with neighborhood women, as well as her beer, her afternoon naps, and her evenings out with Dad.

When Grandma was well enough to take care of us, Mom and Dad went out on the town to drink and dance with their friends. On Sundays, they both went to church, not to pray, but to see people. Dad did business and political networking, and Mom received solace from other mothers coping with young children and older dependent relatives. She paved the way for my church affiliation by teaching me how to pray: "Now I lay me down to sleep. I pray the Lord my soul to keep. If I should die before I wake, I pray the Lord my soul to take. Amen."

I don't remember when I figured out that the part that went, "If I should die before I wake" didn't bode well for me, but I do remember that I usually hopped up quickly from my prayer, grabbed my doll, jumped into the bed, hid under the covers, and worried about the bombers flying overhead.

My first vivid memory is of the gray afternoon in late September of '43 when Mike was thrust into my life after Mommy had been alarmingly missing for two weeks. I was thrilled when she reappeared at the door, beaming proudly, and leaning on Daddy's arm. He looked so handsome and cocky, standing behind Mom in his long, belted trench coat and dark brown fedora. Then I spotted what Mommy was carrying close to her bosom, and my heart took a dive. She said, "Look, Sandy, the stork gave you a baby brother." But Mike didn't seem like a present: he drew everyone's attention away from me. My folks made a big deal about their blue-eyed, golden-haired boy, but I thought Mike's narrow blue eyes looked evil. They weren't round like my green ones.

One day Mom pointed to a magazine photo of a chubby

six-month-old. She giggled at the caption: "Before you scold me, Mom, maybe you'd better light up a Camel." Mom smoked Camels or Lucky Strikes all the time: during her pregnancies, while she nursed, and whenever she wanted to. Grandma's pleas for her to stop were as useless as a wake-up call in a graveyard.

"Marie, if you don't care about the fact that your smoke makes me miserable, at least don't blow it into the babies' faces."

"Lay off me, Mom. You know damn well I'm too old to have to put up with your bitching. Go live somewhere else if you can't stand a little smoke."

"That's cruel, Marie. You know very well that I have nowhere else to go. And watch your tongue around the children."

"They don't care if I smoke. And they certainly can't understand what I'm saying."

"Sandy understands more than you give her credit for. Little pitchers have big ears. You're going to have to stop swearing, or she'll start swearing at you."

The household was a frustrated, three-generational codependency. War restrictions added to the foul tempers. My parents resented having to use rationing books to buy measured supplies of food, clothing, and other necessities. Alcohol wasn't rationed in America, but grain was, so brewers made paler beer. My parents drank more to make up for the thinner taste.

Mom and Dad thrived on attention; each had been the younger of two children. At six feet, Dad was tall for his time. He had thick, wavy, black hair and dark brown eyes, and he radiated an aura of self-assurance. He knew that his keen sense of humor and flair for telling jokes could charm anyone. Although he had refused to take piano lessons when he was a boy, he had a natural ear for music that enabled him to plop down on a piano stool and play ragtime, mainly hitting the black keys, something he did for beer during the Depression. Grandpa took advantage of Dad's terrific eye–hand coordination in his business. It's what kept his son out of the army. Dad passed his art gene down to me.

Mom had no outstanding gifts, but she was willful and

opinionated—characteristics I grew to admire in a woman. She was medium tall, a full-busted, dark-haired, pleasant-looking woman, with wide red lips, a gape-toothed smile, greenish brown hazel eyes, and soft olive skin. Born in Buffalo, she was a spoiled late child of a loveless marriage. Perhaps because her parents' union had been a business deal, not a love match, I found it difficult to tell how she felt about men. Sometimes she'd declare them impossible; other times she'd brag about knowing how to "strut her stuff the way men like it done." But she loved my father; I never doubted that.

Mom told me that, although her mom had never loved my grandfather, she did love some guy with ugly yellow teeth. Appearances meant a good deal to Mom. My grandfather died before I was old enough to know him, and I never knew that guy with the yellow teeth, but I loved Grandma Chrystene. She was comfortable to be around: well padded and caring. She wore patterned dresses and aprons like all the ladies on our street. She was both kind and clever, and I hold her responsible for sowing in me the seeds of feminism. Speaking of seeds, in the summers during World War II, she planted a backyard victory garden: neat rows of vegetables and one extravagant, radiant row of purple and yellow pansies and daisies. She told me the Latin names of everything she planted, and she let me help her pull weeds and water plants.

Grandma read to me every night. One of her favorite stories was *The Little Engine That Could*, about a brave little engine that succeeded in pulling a heavy train up a steep hill. She told me to think of myself as that little engine. I could do anything I wanted if I worked hard enough. She told me I'd be as good as anyone, man or woman, someday. She taught me to recite the ABCs, and she gave me my first box of Crayolas and large sheets of butcher paper to draw things on. Coloring between the lines of coloring books was too easy for a girl with my talent, Grandma said.

Back in 1907, when my Uncle Hony was born, she had to wear long, cumbersome skirts that touched the ground. She wound her long hair on her head and attached big hats to it with hatpins tipped in shiny stones or porcelain beads. Recently I bought some vintage hatpins at an antique store along with a ceramic hatpin holder that looks like a fancy saltshaker. They remind me of her and of the Easter bonnets Mom pinned on my head when I was little.

I missed Grandma Chrystene badly when she became confined to her bed. A few months after I turned four, she disappeared from my life. I wept from missing her, even when Mom told me she was happy in heaven. Later I learned that she died of lung cancer. Ironically, Mom had a much longer life than Grandma did; although, by the time she was in her eighties, she had Alzheimer's. In one of her rare lucid moments, Mother whispered to me, apropos of nothing at the time, "My smoking caused Mother's death. I should have told her I was sorry."

Grandma must have had high hopes for Mom when she was born. She gave her the middle name of Belva in honor of the suffragist Belva Lockwood, a female lawyer who ran for the presidency of the United States in 1884 and 1888. After the Great Depression hit, however, the only education my grandfather could afford for Mom was secretarial school. Eventually she landed a position as assistant buyer in the drapery department at a downtown department store. She told me that "a really cute queer" ran her department. She also called him a fairy.

"He was a little person with wings?" I asked incredulously.

"No, dumbbell. But he floated around, like this." She strutted on tiptoe, arms extended, her wrists hanging limp, mocking her gay friend. The way she talked about her old colleagues made it made painfully clear to me that my arrival, six years after her marriage, had been the ruination of her contented career. I felt badly about that; I loved my mother. Pete was the only person I knew who ever claimed that he never had a mother, at least, not one that he remembered. When he told me he didn't shed a tear when she died, I knew he wasn't normal.

## Chapter 4
## MONEY HONEY

*Harry and Marie in 1932*

When I was little, I visited the elegant New England-style home of my Schall grandparents, located in a posh neighborhood of Snyder, every Sunday afternoon. They hired maids, gardeners, and a Polish cook who served their meals on Grandma's imported Haviland. In the warmer seasons, I loved to wander through their glorious garden. When I stopped to peer into a mirrored globe that sat on a fluted pedestal, I found myself staring at a funny-looking, curly-haired elf dwarfed by misshapen irises, gladioli, and other giant blossoms.

Dad's older brother James fell in love with "the wrong sort of woman," a Roman Catholic girl. My parents taught me we were Protestants because Catholics worshipped some rich guy in Rome.

They had another gripe against Aunt Bea: she came from Irish stock. My dad called her a Mick and informed me that Micks were always very poor or they were rich crooks, and all of them had quick tempers.

Once I asked Pete what the "C" of his dad's middle name stood for.

"My granddad's name was Chauncey. It's an Irish name," he answered proudly.

I was trying to be polite to him again that day, but he never made it easy. Aunt Bea may have been Irish, but she was easier to get along with than Pete was. I liked Aunt Bea.

Mom, however, talked about Aunt Bea as if she were a Celtic witch who had cast a spell on Uncle Jim. He clearly loved her, for he fathered nine Roman Catholic kids. I worshipped my cousin Judy, who was closest to me in age, blonde and pretty. Mother never complained about my visits with Judy to Grandma, because Mom was a social climber, and I guess she figured that Grandpa Schall held her ladder. He had graduated in 1907 from Yale University. She told me that Yale men made good money and went places in the world.

Judy and I dressed up in Grandma's clothes and pretended to be princesses. Grandma played along with us, but she said we didn't need to pretend; we had noble blood. Her European ancestors had been royalty who lived in castles before they came to America. She often boasted about how she had beguiled Grandpa with her blue-blooded beauty when they saw each other at school. They were high school sweethearts, but Grandpa was too sensible and ambitious to seek her hand in marriage right away. He went off to Yale, and they weren't married until a year after he graduated.

Grandpa's young family moved to Niagara Falls, a city built around factories, where he found work. Later on Dad took us kids to see his early home and visit the falls. Those roaring, horseshoe-shaped, rainbow-making cascades of waterpower enthralled me, but I didn't relish bucking the crowds of honeymooners that lingered along the rails, and I felt sorry for Dad, whose face turned green. Looking down from great heights made him sick.

Grandpa eventually moved to Buffalo, where he literally forged his career as a hands-on industrial engineer. I can still picture him as he was in his heyday: a striking, dark-haired man with a prominent nose and a dark moustache. I remember the sweet odor of his pipes and cigars. His ancestors had immigrated to America from Eastern Europe. A kid on our street called Grandpa a Jew, but I knew that was a lie. My family didn't approve of Jews. They don't worship Jesus. Dad told me Jews were smart, but they were also sly, tricky, and they couldn't be trusted.

In many ways, Grandpa and Grandma resembled Victorian Brits, and they taught me to think that way too. Grandma said she had never seen Grandpa without his clothes on. We all adhered to the rule that physical exhibitions of affection were beneath family dignity. The only way I could tell that Grandpa liked me was how he asked me about school.

"Have you learned anything yet in first grade?" he would ask me sternly.

"Oh, Grandpa," I giggled, "I told you before that the *Dick and Jane* book is already too easy for me. I get bored, so Mrs. Perkins lets me take my crayons out of my desk and draw pictures."

"Be careful, Sandy. Your head is getting too big."

"Oh, no. Really?" My fingers fumbled through my curls as I groped my gigantic head.

He laughed. "When I say that you have a big head, I mean you act as if you think that your brain is bigger, and therefore better, than the brains of others. It's not good to let anyone know that you think you're better than he is. Even if it *is* true," he said, winking at me.

When Grandma played with Judy and me, her face glowed with pleasure, her blue eyes often gleamed through her glasses mirthfully, but occasionally she turned sullen, and an ominous voice emerged through her rouged lips. "Enjoy your beauty now, girls. It won't last."

She kept losing bits of herself: her hair, her vision, her ability to hear well. Her real teeth were all gone. Once she took her false teeth out to show us. I didn't want to touch them, but Judy did; she wanted to be a nurse when she grew up. When Grandma brushed our hair with her ornate silver brush, she warned Judy and me that before we knew it, it would start falling out. "If you two ever do grow up to be as pretty as I was, enjoy it while you can. Soon you'll turn old and ugly like me."

I didn't think Grandma was ugly, and I don't believe that she intended to make me worry, but she did. What if I grew up ugly? I'd have no chance for happiness then. Besides, Grandma had something that I never got: a middle name. Hers was perfect too; it was Valentine. When I asked Mom why I didn't have a middle name, she casually replied, "Your father and I decided that when you get married, Schall will become your middle name." I wanted to ask her what made them so sure that I'd want to get married, or that someone would ask me to marry him, but wisely, I stifled it. I wasn't allowed to question adults.

On warm Sundays, Grandpa often drove us out to Greenfield Country Club, which sat above a well-groomed golf course in the hilly outskirts of town. He, Dad, Uncle Jim, and their business friends played golf there. The club restaurant, restricted to the use of its elected members and their guests, overlooked splendid gardens sloping above the first green. After a maitre d'escorted us to our seats, Grandpa made us wait while he adjusted Grandma's chair, before he seated each of us. Like an elegant thoroughbred mare, Grandma nudged her sons' fillies to sit properly with one arm in our laps, keeping our elbows off the table.

Our grandparents ordered grown-up cocktails and wine that smelled sweeter to me than the beer that my parents favored. The meals were luxurious; they started with appetizers, such as sherbet or fruit cocktail. Grandpa dictated our orders to a white waiter in a green uniform, and Negro men dressed in red brought the food to us on trays held high over their heads. The waiter stiffly ordered the Negroes to place each plate or glass where it was supposed to be, as if Negroes couldn't do anything without proper direction. Apparently, Negroes weren't good at anything, except heavy work.

I savored every bite of those Sunday feasts: vegetables, fruits, and all. The desserts were heavenly: pie or cake with ice cream, or butterscotch or chocolate ice cream sundaes with whipped cream. Afterwards, Grandpa drove us back to his house, where Judy, Grandma, and I listened to Jack Benny, Mary Livingston, and Rochester on the radio. Grandpa slipped quietly off to his library to read his books and listen to classical music. Jack Benny was a very funny man, but his raspy-voiced Negro, Rochester, made me wonder. Why did he seem so much smarter than Mr. Benny?

Grandma's sister Eleanor frequently popped in at Grandma's house. We called her Tanta, after a French or German word for aunt that she taught us. Tanta used to be every bit as lovely as her younger sister was when they were young. She said she had enjoyed more than her share of suitors. What she never explained to us, however, was why she suddenly took off to Europe, traveling by herself at a time when unmarried women didn't travel alone. When we were teenagers, Cousin Aggie told me that Tanta snuck off to Europe to have an abortion. She never had any children because God punished her by making her infertile.

Sometimes I caught Grandpa watching her from a defensive distance, as if she were about to spontaneously combust, taking the family reputation down in flames. I suppose that, in his eyes, she was a tainted woman. But I enjoyed my great aunt's wit and teasing nature. She usually entered talking, flinging her hat, scarf, gloves, and purse onto an empty chair.

"Oh, shi—" Then, upon noticing me in the room, "Sugar. Did I forget to bring that magazine I wanted to show Kitty?"

Kitty was her nickname for Grandma. Sometimes she greeted me in French.

*"Je suis heureux de vous voir, ma petite niece."*

"What was that, Aunt Tanta?"

"It's French for 'I'm happy to see you.' Remember, Sandy,

saying 'aunt' and 'Tanta' together is redundant. They mean the same thing."

"I wish I could understand French," I sighed.

"Well, get cracking, old girl. You're smart enough to learn anything. Now, how about some gin?"

Grandpa glowered at his sister-in-law.

She glowered back. "Howard, don't try to silence me with one of your black stares. I'm teaching her the card game."

"We all would have preferred it if you had just stuck to Old Maid, Eleanor."

Tanta had married a farmer who died from the ravages of tapeworm. Before his death, the couple lived in a farmhouse in the hilly countryside near Arcade, not far from Buffalo. I loved to visit Tanta's farmhouse. It was usually redolent with tantalizing aromas. She learned to prepare sauces when she was in France and Italy, and she grew spices in her garden that Mom had never heard of. Mom didn't care for her cooking, but whenever Tanta offered a spoonful of sauce to me, I found it quite tasty. I tried to convince Mom to try it, but she said her own recipes required enough work, and she was not about to plant a spice garden.

Tanta's barn sheltered a few chickens, a couple of cows, hay, and plenty of manure. To my suburban nostrils, it smelled unpleasant. Unconcerned about appearing ladylike, Tanta would sit down on a stool, hike up her skirt, and milk the cows, pulling their teats rhythmically, causing milk to squirt noisily into a pail. She tried to teach me to milk her cows, but I couldn't get the hang of it, no pun intended. Milking them seemed too intimate to me and somehow disrespectful.

Tanta's country home was a welcome change from my usual hangout. The Harwood cul-de-sac constituted what might currently be termed a day care center without caregivers. Kids were let loose within its boundaries to fend for themselves or to go down fighting, and parents felt secure that their kids were somewhere within shouting distance. Scrapes, bruises, and cuts were routine; parents dismissed them as growing pains. All forms of verbal abuse were common, short of swearing, of course. Any child who used a swear word could expect a brutal spanking. Mom hurt my feelings when she called me stupid or messy or told me I was getting in her way. I followed her example and doled the same sort of abuse to kids that annoyed me.

The only two girls around my age, Shirley and Rosemary, were a happy, harebrained couple that treated me like an intruder, bullying me until I fought back. Our barbaric confrontations evolved into shouting and punching matches, and I gave as well as I got. My pluckiness earned me some respect on the street. A second grade girl, however, scared me about school by telling me how hard it was, with all the rules about how to act and move in straight lines. She said I'd get paddled if I stepped out of line even once. I knew about spankings. Mom had spanked me with the bristle side of a hairbrush when I slapped Mike after he said something mean to me. She tossed me across her lap and hit my fanny hard, repeating, "You're never right. Obey your parents." Since teachers were always right at school, I decided to obey them.

During the war, some fathers on Harwood Drive, such as Rosemary's dad, got drafted. He made it back, missing one finger. Bruce's father never did make it back. Most of the Harwood fathers, however, had war-related jobs like my dad did. Dr. Jeb Ryan, from across the street, was a scientist. When I wondered why he didn't carry around a black medicine bag like Dr. Irwin, Mom explained that not all men called doctors practiced medicine. Dr. Ryan was a highly educated man who worked on developing ideas for new super-powerful secret weapons.

Everyone wanted the war to end. I hated the wailing sirens that meant we had to stop playing and run indoors to help the grown-ups pull down the shades. We waited in the basement until the all-clear siren rang. It was scary. News about friends dying in battle caused my parents great sorrow, but I never heard them blame the Germans. They hated Japanese people, and they hated President Roosevelt. Grandma Schall said something unforgettable about

FDR: "FDR is the devil incarnate. I'm sick and tired of hearing him talked about all the time. Mark my words, when that man finally leaves office, people will forget he ever lived, just like they forgot President Hamilton." She never understood why people laughed at that.

I was four years old when the Nazis surrendered to Harry Truman and Churchill. My parents and grandparents told me General Eisenhower was the greatest hero of the war. In 1952 and 1956, both Dad and Grandpa Schall campaigned vigorously for Ike. I vaguely remember how on V-J Day in August of 1945, we kids put on red, white, and blue outfits, decorated our trikes and bikes, and paraded up and down our street, waving American flags, blowing horns, and banging on pots and pans with large spoons. In the evening, there was a boisterous neighborhood picnic on tables spread across three backyards. Parents made gallons of lemonade for the kids and bought as much beer as they could afford. Everyone kept hugging everyone else, and the adults sang loudly into the night.

Later, when I read historical accounts of the war years, the unspeakable things that the Germans did to the Jews shocked and horrified me. My parents had never told me about the Holocaust. They claimed they knew nothing about it when it was going on. It might have been true. Television, then in its infancy, did not cover the news, radio reports were infrequent, and movie newsreels were old when they reached the theaters. I do remember, however, that my parents called Jews "hebes," "kikes," or "yids" and insisted they were different from us. I was insulted when, due to the ethnic ambiguity of their appearance, a schoolmate asked me if Mom and Dad were Jewish. I had a long way to go before I could appreciate the irony of that question.

World War II turned out to be a bonanza for the Schall family business. Eventually, Uncle Jim accepted a more lucrative position with a larger industrial engineering firm in South Carolina, and my father and grandfather became the sole partners in the Schall Company of Industrial Engineers. For a few years, their company was one of the leading industries of the Niagara Frontier. Dad invested his share of the wartime profits in the purchase of the last two vacant lots on our street, on the corner of Harwood and Harlem. Determined to build the biggest house on the block, he hired an architect to draw up blueprints for a ranch house, and in the spring of 1946, his new lots crawled like anthills with busy construction workers.

My fifth birthday celebration came and went, and kindergarten loomed closer. I was a nervous wreck, just like my mother, who was so absorbed in her own health problems that she took no notice of my worries. She wasn't feeling well, especially in the mornings. When she wasn't throwing up, she spent a good deal of her time looking for Mike, sending me out to find him, and making excuses for his behavior to the neighbors. I did my best to ignore him so I could worry about making a good impression in school.

Dad said it was naughty of me to go around looking so worried. "You have much to look forward to, Sandy, and you're being a bad girl when you mope around. I'll let you in on a secret weapon against disaster. Just imagine the worst thing that possibly could happen. Then whatever does happen will never be as bad as that, and you'll be happy. It works for me every time."

Unfortunately, I could think of thousands of things that could go wrong, especially after Mother took me shopping for school clothes. She had to choose dresses for me in a size larger than the one usually recommended for girls my age. When I tried them on and looked at myself in the store's dressing room mirror, I whined, "The other kids will call me fat and ugly, and they'll be right."

"Don't be ridiculous, Sandy. You've just got big bones," Mom said unconvincingly. I think she was just trying to say the right thing, but her relationship with shape, form, and color was often erratic and iffy. The file she kept in her head for color was labeled "Household Decorating." Her "People Decorating" file was primarily based upon various shades of tan. In her mind, bland looked good on everybody. She bought me the finest beige, brown, taupe, and mushroom outfits that money could buy. I didn't dare argue with her, even though I didn't count tan as a color, and I didn't believe God did either. Tan never showed up in his rainbows. I thought it made my olive skin look even more yellow. Dr. Irwin tested me periodically for jaundice, so he must have thought so too.

After I recovered from my embarrassment about getting sick to my stomach on the first day of school, I quickly learned that kindergarten was nothing like my nightmares. The rules were simple to learn, and the teacher chastised the boys for teasing me, so they left me alone. My hand was constantly in the air ready to give the answers, and to my surprise, none of the other kids could draw pictures as well as I could.

When I was six years and one day old, Mom went away again and came back carrying Patty in her arms. This baby turned out to be a pretty, happy, little thing. She didn't fuss as much as Mike did, although he was a lot older than she was. The five of us moved into our new home the following June. That house was a monument to Mom and Dad's one-upmanship. The biggest home on Harwood, it was also the only one with a double garage. Both our Buick sedan and our new Chevrolet woody wagon could enter it from Harlem Road.

I lived at 8 Harwood Drive until I went off to college. Its plan followed the new one-floor design; that is, the living space was all on one floor, although it utilized the spacious basement too. It had several entryways, but the one most people used was the side front door. The formal entryway was a thick, pillared, knotty pine front door. The garage entry was plain and casual: a wooden door with an outer screen. A back doorway led off the kitchen to the screened-in porch looking out upon the double-lot backyard. We ate supper on a wooden picnic table there in the summers.

Pete called the house gaudy, but he obviously had no taste. I, on the other hand, understood that things could be both chic and colorful. Mom decorated the interior of our house in beautiful living Technicolor. The center of family activity was a bright yellow, vinyl-lined kitchen with a sienna red linoleum tiled floor. The new Westinghouse refrigerator was yellow. Stairs ran from a door off the sunny kitchen down into the green basement. If you took a right turn out of the kitchen, you were in our turquoise blue living room. Walking straight back from the kitchen, you passed through a maroon and white wallpapered dining room to the baby pink, manganese blue, and daisy yellow wallpapered bedrooms and blue- and yellow-tiled baths. During her tenure in the drapery department, Mother developed a taste for flowered drapery fabrics like the ones she chose for all our windows. Her modern furniture had brightly colored upholstery. All three pink, blue, and yellow bedrooms had twin beds, covered by bright spreads that more or less matched the wallpaper and drapes. Red brick chimney places surrounded by knotty pinewood shelving and mantels were the focal features of both our living room and the basement recreation room directly beneath it.

Like many other suburban couples, after the war Mom and Dad bought new appliances: the washer and dryer in the basement and a dishwasher in our kitchen. They replaced our old push-pull sweeper with an electric Hoover. Mom hired a cleaning lady, a full-bodied, hard-working mother of nine named Queenie Mason, who came to Snyder on a bus from the inner city two or three days every week. Queenie was the first "Negress," as Mom called her, that I had ever spoken to, and her poor grammar annoyed me, but Mom said all Negroes talked like Queenie did. When I met Pete I learned that some white kids talked that way too.

The Hoover that Queenie pushed and pulled over the carpets sucked the dirt up noisily when I was trying to study, and the large woman groaned audibly when she lowered her heavy body to the kitchen floor to scrub the linoleum tiles with her big brush, her dark arms dripping with smelly sweat. Mom said she worked so hard because her man was lazy and uncivilized like most Negroes. He had deserted Queenie and her children; in Mom's words, it was "typical Negro behavior." Queenie's oldest children had to drop out of school so they could care for the younger children when Queenie was at work. I wondered how they would ever become civilized if they didn't go to school. Mom told me they didn't want to be civilized, so I shouldn't worry about it. She fed Queenie hot lunches of soup and sandwiches, but only after she fed us first. She didn't allow Queenie to eat at the table when we ate there, and she permitted Queenie to use only one of the bathrooms, the small, half-guest bath near the side front door. I never used that bathroom because I didn't want to catch black cooties.

Mom's last "accident" was Jerome. When Mother was pregnant with Jerry, she told me that another baby was growing inside her because the stork had planted another seed. I found this mystifying. How did such oddly shaped birds accomplish that feat of planting seeds in mothers' bellies? Did it involve their large beaks?

*8 Harwood Drive*

## Chapter 5
## IT'S A SIN TO TELL A LIE

The year Jerry was born was momentous for me, but not because of him. I learned about white lies, I ended a family tradition, I met my lifelong best friend, and somebody called me beautiful. The tradition that I had ended started when I was about two and a half. Grandma Chrystene read Moore's "'Twas the Night Before Christmas" to me, and I loved Moore's poetic description of Santa Claus so much that I begged her to read it repeatedly, until I memorized it. My recitation of the whole poem from memory convinced my parents that they had a genius for a daughter, which made sense: I belonged to them. Wanting to impress the neighbors, Mom invited them to hear me and costumed me in a bright red holiday dress. My performance created such a sensation that my parents decreed it an annual event.

I ended the tradition myself about six years later when I discovered my parents' white lie. My Sunday school teacher had taught me that all lies were bad. That seemed obvious. If people went around telling lies all the time, no one would listen to anyone. But she confused me by saying that occasional white lies were not only right, they were necessary. The term "white lie" was new to me.

"Aren't all lies bad?" I asked. She replied that white lies were harmless minor lies, useful when you didn't want to hurt someone's feelings by telling the truth.

"It would be kinder to tell someone that you liked her outfit than to admit you think her dress looks terrible, especially on her. Does that make sense to you, Sandy?"

"So, a white lie is not the truth, but it's harmless?" I asked, trying to wrap my mind around the concept.

"That's right, Sandy. If it makes someone happy and doesn't hurt anyone, it's okay to tell a little white lie, as long as you don't make a habit of it."

I figured out that the tooth fairy was a white lie when Mike hollered about not being able to find his lost tooth to put under his pillow for the tooth fairy. I spotted Dad winking at Mom when he told Mike that his coins would be under his pillow in the morning. Dad must be the tooth fairy! Then, that December, I heard something on the radio that clued me in to the fact that Dad played Santa Claus too. So Santa was a white lie? This one hurt; I loved Santa Claus. Why hadn't Mom and Dad trusted me enough to tell me the truth before I had to discover it for myself? That year, after being introduced by my mother for my annual recitation, I stood up in front of neighbors, family, and friends, only to discover that the inside of my head was as clean and white as the newly fallen snow that covered our lawn.

"Come on, Sandy. What are you waiting for?" Mom urged, annoyed by my silence.

"I'm sorry. But I can't remember how it goes," I said in a weak voice.

"Excuse us, please," Mom said to the audience. She hauled me out into the kitchen and asked sternly, "Are you trying to embarrass me in front of all those people?"

"Please, Mom, I can't do it. I've forgotten the words." I began to cry.

"I'll just have to tell everyone you're sick," she sighed. "Go to your room. I'll deal with you later."

I never recited the poem again, but each December I had to

steel myself against Mom's humiliating reminders of how I *always* let her down.

"From the time you were two and a half, you could recite "'Twas the Night before Christmas," word for word. You lost your memory when you were eight. Remember?"

I was dealing with so much personal stress that year, what we used to call growing up, that I was very lucky to find a friend willing to share my anxieties. Recently I asked Barb for her first memories of us. She e-mailed: "You were a pudgy little thing, and I was skinny with lank hair and glasses." In other words, neither of us was the class beauty. Our closeness developed from the fact that we were both good at our schoolwork and we both liked to draw. Our third grade teacher marked off a section of the front blackboard on which we could draw princesses and animals with colored chalk when we had completed classroom assignments before the other kids did. We sat next to each other on the girls' side of the cafeteria at lunchtime and chatted intimately. Barb empathized with my mortification when I got teased for my looks, since she had to deal with "four eyes" jeers. The kids taunted me with an unappetizing chant: "Fatty, fatty two by four, can't get through the bathroom door, so she did it on the floor, ate it up and did some more." That gagging image circled my visually oriented brain like an albatross.

Our family physician, Dr. Irwin, finally came to my rescue. After one of my regular checkups at his office, he pulled Mom aside, out of my hearing, and instructed her to put me on a diet. Mom broke the news to me in the car on our way home that day.

"I'm afraid that you've let yourself get too heavy, Sandy. Dr. Irwin says you're overweight for your age and height. It could damage your health."

"Oh, no! Will I have to take some medicine?"

"No. You need to go on a diet. I suppose I'll have to make you separate meals." She shook her head and heaved another sigh. The doctor had placed a great burden upon her shoulders. "You'll have to stop eating second helpings in any case."

"Can I have bigger first helpings then?"

"Certainly not," Mom said firmly. "You must eat less food and take in fewer calories: less potatoes and bread, more fruits and vegetables. No more double sandwich lunches. He wants you to buy cold lettuce salads and cottage cheese in the school cafeteria and eat nothing but Jell-O for dessert."

"But I'll be hungry all the time! Did he tell you how long I'll have to stay on this horrible diet?"

"For as long as it takes to get you down to a normal weight. Look, it is not going to be easy for me either. But I'll do whatever it takes to spare you from being unattractive. Good looks are absolutely essential to being successful and popular. You want to be popular, don't you?" It was a rhetorical question.

"Do you think I'm ugly, Mother?"

"Of course not," she protested weakly. "But you have gotten a bit … chubby." She sighed again. "It's for your own good, Sandy. Nobody wants an unsightly figure. Boys from good families like to be seen with pretty girls."

This didn't sound right to me. Why did I need to be attractive to boys? Boys were nothing but trouble, but food was necessary, and I enjoyed eating. It was worth arguing for. "I always eat what you give me or what you tell me to eat, Mom. Besides, you have second helpings and desserts, and you're not fat. Why am I different?"

"I don't want to talk about this anymore, young lady. We're following the doctor's orders, and that's all there is to that."

When we got home, I looked in the mirror. I hated the girl staring unhappily back at me. She was nothing but a chub ball! No wonder kids teased me. I cried for a while, I sulked for an hour, and finally, I made up my mind to go on this diet, even if it killed me. I'd prove how strong I was. Nobody would make fun of me again.

After one day of what felt like starvation, I knew I would die of the shear torture of watching others eat. If I died, everyone would be sorry, wouldn't they? I wasn't sure. To Mike my suffering was a payback for the fact that Mom and Dad compared his poor grades unfavorably to mine. He mocked the sounds of my growling stomach and ate my forbidden food in front of my face, with revolting relish. Shame and determination kept me from eating back at him.

My grandparents were no help. Grandpa wasn't interested, and Grandma continued to offer me candy and second helpings and looked hurt when I refused. It seemed to take forever for me to lose more than a couple of pounds. Just before I was ready to give up and eat myself to death instead, very gradually, my clothes began feeling looser, and the scale numbers began to drop. I became hopeful. The girl in my mirror looked thinner. And did I dare to hope? Was she pretty?

I continued to grow taller, however, and Mother told me I'd never lose my "big-boned appearance." But she seemed happy to buy me bland new outfits two sizes smaller in girth than the ones I had previously worn.

The first person to make me believe that I had really accomplished something was my uncle Hony. Mom described her older brother as an "ex-ladies' man." He had been a happy bachelor with many girlfriends until long past the time when other men his age had large families. He, Aunt Betty, and my younger cousin Jane lived in another suburb of Buffalo. When they first visited us after I had lost a good deal of weight, my uncle looked me up and down with the discerning eye of an artist who prided himself on his knowledge of the female form. Then he smiled his winning smile and proclaimed, "You're beautiful, Sandy! You could be a movie star."

A girl never forgets the first compliment she gets from a man like that.

"Hony, don't give Sandy any ideas," Mom complained. "You'll make her conceited."

Dr. Irwin told me to get more exercise, so I used that as an excuse for cycling over to Barb's house several blocks away. I liked visiting Barb's large, well-appointed home, and her mother Irene fascinated me. She wasn't like other mothers. For one thing, she usually wore pants, and she moved with an athletic agility that was surprising to see in a mother. Teachers came to Barb's house to give Irene piano and painting lessons. Until I met her, I thought only kids took lessons. Irene suggested that Barb and I could benefit from the Saturday painting classes for children offered at the Albright Art Gallery. We were okay with that, so Irene floated her idea to Mom, but both of my parents seemed to be leery of anything she suggested.

"Irene has a lot of crazy ideas," Dad said. "Did you know that she comes from a reformed Jewish family? And that she's a Democrat?"

"No, Dad, Barb and I never talk about things like that."

"That woman tried to run against me for my position on the town council. She didn't have a chance against me, of course, but it's the principle of the thing. Irene is too uppity."

Barb's father Klaus probably saved our friendship. He was a charming, cultured, good-humored man with a German accent, a successful businessman from a Lutheran family. Dad thought of Klaus as "an okay guy." It was because of him that my parents allowed me to sleep over at Barb's house occasionally, and that they eventually conceded they could see no harm in my attending the art gallery's Saturday painting class for kids.

Even back then, before it had its hyphenated Albright-Knox title, the gallery was an impressive building with a white marble exterior, tall classical columns, and a grand rotunda, located in downtown Buffalo not far from Delaware Park. Our parents took turns driving us to and from the museum, where our class met weekly in the basement. The teachers there viewed art differently from the way the art teacher did at Amherst 18. She gave "A" grades to Barb and me for drawing realistically. The Albright teachers, however, wanted us to express our feeling and emotions on paper. Older kids in our class just splashed around colors in designs resembling nothing I knew in the world, yet the teachers complimented their work. Barb told me that Irene sometimes painted like that. Since we were free to do whatever we wanted to, Barb and I continued to paint realistically, complimenting each other as usual.

One weekend, when it was her turn to pick us up, Mom decided to tour the gallery with Barb and me. To all of us, the huge masterpieces by Pollock, de Kooning, and Rothko looked as if a little child had painted them. They made no sense like the older paintings in the gallery did. After we dropped Barb off, Mom railed against Irene's poor judgment in touting the gallery, declaring those modern paintings to be "nothing but pure junk."

Barb and I joined the same Brownie troop, and that summer we went to Girl Scout Camp Seven Hills, located in Holland, New York, near a lake in the hilly farm country. Mom sewed labels into my bluebells, shirts, and shorts. She drove me to the camp, told me to be good, and said she would miss my help with the little kids, but I didn't feel sad when she left. I was eager to explore the area and take swimming lessons in the lake. Barb, however, was homesick. She hunched down on her cabin cot and cried. I told her she was being stupid. A counselor urged her to telephone Irene, who wisely ordered her daughter to get out and play baseball. Barb's natural agility was as powerful as new butterfly's wings in succeeding to raise her out of her cocoon of separation anxiety. She soon proved herself to be far more dexterous than most of the girls at camp. When it came to sports activities, on a scale of one to ten, I was a three minus and Barb was ten plus.

When rain confined us to our cabins, Barb and I devoured Nancy Drew mysteries. Because Nancy nicknamed her girlfriend George, Barb and I gave each other masculine nicknames: Herman and Melvin. For me, the lasting legacies of my first camping experience were a zeal for swimming, a dream of becoming

41

a detective just like Nancy Drew, and my secret nickname Herman.

On Saturday afternoons, in the fall of my fourth grade year, Dad bundled Mike and me up and took us to a football game at the high school stadium. Seated high up on the wooden bleachers filled with other Amherst fans, we could see our babysitter, Cindy the cheerleader, frolicking in her Amherst Tiger uniform. Her muscular legs were bare, and her feet were covered in white bobby socks under her shiny black and white saddle shoes. Her jumper's full black skirt flared out as she bounced, exposing its bright orange gores. In my eyes, Cindy was a star, but the faceless boys under their pads and helmets were not worthy of my attention. They just kept knocking each other down and stopping anyone from running toward the end goal line, which Dad said was the point of the game. I didn't get it. Cindy tried to teach me some cheerleading moves in our basement, but I always ended up falling flat on the floor. She said I'd get better at it when I grew older. I believed her because I wanted to. It was the first of many glorious dreams that, like the brightly fluttering cardinals that fed from Grandma's birdfeeder, were impossible to capture.

Dad, however, was seeing his dreams fulfilled. With Grandfather Schall as his mentor, he secured positions of power in clubs favored by Republican businessmen. Grandpa campaigned for Dad's election to the presidency of Greenfield Country Club. Grandpa was chairman of the Town Planning Board after Dad was elected councilman, which accrued to their mutual benefit, no questions asked. Dad directed the Buffalo Bowling Association and presided over the Buffalo Junior Chamber of Commerce. Because of their high profiles, pictures of my dad and grandfather began to appear regularly in the local newspaper, the *Amherst Bee.*

Dad organized and directed the Amherst Auxiliary Police, and the cops became his buddies. He was active in the Civil Defense Corps and the Amherst Fire Department. I remember that whenever the fire siren wailed in the middle of the night,

Dad threw on a big black helmet that looked like a steel cowboy hat, large rubber boots, and a shiny black waterproof coat and sped off in his car. Mom sat around smoking and drinking beer in the dark. I sat up with her, and she worried about him in my direction until I grew sick with worry too. Eventually she calmed down, but I didn't.

Although Mom went out with Dad to social and political gatherings, the only organization in which she played a role of her own was our church. My parents joined Snyder's Ascension Lutheran Church for the baptisms of their babies, because Mom had been baptized in a Lutheran church and Dad didn't care. As it turned out, many Lutherans were political or business associates of Dad. They convinced him to serve on church committees, and later he became Sunday School Superintendent. Mom took over the direction of the Altar Guild, a position traditionally held by a woman. When I grew older, I became a Sunday school teacher.

Our pastor was a mild mannered, serious young man. I liked him and his family. He was the last pastor we had before Pete's dad. I preferred Dr. French's sermons as soon as I heard one. I thought he was more attractive than the other pastor too. Both of them wore glasses, but Dr. French was taller, and his big blue gray eyes with their long lashes made him look like he couldn't possibly tell a lie. Pete's eyes looked similar to his dad's: big with long lashes, but greener, and they lacked sincerity. If they told me anything, it was that he was hiding something. They never let on that he was teasing me until I fell into some trap he laid to make me feel foolish. Whenever I tried to winkle out the truth about something, he changed the subject. Take that ring. He said it didn't mean anything special. Okay, so why was it shaped like a heart? He said it just happened to be shaped that way, and he thought I'd like it. Was that a white lie or a black one? Did he expect me to believe that all the rings in the store just happened to be heart shaped?

## Chapter 6
## YOUNG LOVE

*Six Schalls in 1953*

Dad took Mike and me to our first movie when I was about nine. We saw it downtown at Shea's Buffalo Theater. It was a second feature called *Smoky*, starring Fred McMurray. Dad probably chose it because it was about a horse, and he knew kids liked ponies. He hadn't read the book on which the movie was based, so he had no idea that it was actually quite a harrowing, grown-up tale. Seeing that film on the big screen threw me for a loop. The theater's grandeur, its sheer size, and its ornate design had my eyes reeling. The story made me want to cry, but I fought off tears, because I was determined not to break down in front of my younger brother and all those strangers.

On our ride home, Dad asked me if I had enjoyed it. "Was it a true story?" I asked, avoiding his question.

"It was just a movie, dumbbell," Mike said snidely.

"Be more polite to your sister, Mike. No, Sandy, I believe it was based on some novel."

"That poor horse went through so much," I sighed.

"Actually, it was just a bunch of actors and trained animals, but the story packed more punch than the ones on television because it was in Technicolor, just like real life," he said. Real life was always in Technicolor, as far as he was concerned.

Not long after that, Mom and Dad allowed me to go downtown on the green Kensington Avenue trolleys almost every weekend, as long as two or three girlfriends went along. As it turned out, we were among the last people to ride the old streetcars that ran on railway tracks set in the street, powered by electricity from overhead wires. We wore our Sunday coats, hats, and white gloves and carried pocketbooks full of babysitting money. The male conductors made sure that no downtown juvenile delinquent gang hoodlum, colored person, or any other undesirable annoyed us. Then suddenly the trolleys disappeared, and we had to learn the routes of the smelly oil-driven buses.

When we went downtown to see a newly released movie, my friends and I made a day of it. We window shopped and bought lunch and ice cream sodas before going into one of the three major venues: the Shea's Buffalo, the Century, or the Paramount, all luxurious old theaters converted from burlesque or vaudeville stages to accommodate the big screen. My heart pounded with excitement when the lights dimmed and the lion roared. I preferred romantic, happy movies, especially musical comedies, such as *Annie Get Your Gun* or *Singin' in the Rain*.

My passion for those movies served Mom well in her campaign to turn me into a lady. When I was a fifth grader, she enrolled me in a class where I'd learn ballroom dancing and social etiquette.

My earlier tap and ballet lessons had been such a klutzy disaster that I shuddered when Mom announced her plan. The prospect of dancing with boys made it especially worrisome. She told me to pretend I was Debbie Reynolds, Leslie Caron, or some other lady in gossamer gowns floating in the arms of handsome movie stars on the silver screen.

"I learned to dance from Hony when I was about your age," she said. "And my ability to dance helped me to win over your father."

"Oh, okay. I want to win over someone just like Daddy, someday."

"Of course you do. And you can take comfort in the fact that the boys in your dancing class are from the best families, sons of good Republicans like Daddy and me. They are clean-cut boys, smart too, and they plan to go to college when they get older so they can learn how to make lots of money."

"I wonder if Barb will be there."

"I doubt it. Irene isn't a member of our crowd," Mom said testily. "Now, how would you like it if I took you shopping for ballroom dancing dresses?" I was thrilled.

The first time I went to dancing class, which was held in a large room in a community church, I ended up with a hymnal on the top of my head. The teaching couple ordered us to walk with the heavy books on our heads and our backs held straight enough to keep the hymnals from falling off. They said it would improve our posture. To the tune of a march played on an old Victrola, we paraded around in a big circle, the books bobbing precariously. We looked like a long row of quails bobbing with those funny combs on their heads. I felt silly, and I giggled self-consciously and nodded sympathetically at my friends.

I became painfully aware that I was one of the tallest kids in the class. Since Mom and Dad were my models for the perfect couple, and Mom was shorter and a year younger than Dad, that was the way things were supposed to be. Someday I'd find a taller, older guy to marry too. For now, I'd try to be nice to these short boys who didn't look any happier about being there than I was. We counted off to form couples and faced our partners. Soon we were stepping back and forward together and from side to side like wooden dolls dancing stiffly on the lid of a wind-up music box. I wanted to laugh out loud. My wooden partner, a boy I recognized from school, looked miserable. I decided to cheer him up.

"Your name is Charlie, right? I'm Sandy."

For the first time, my little man looked up at my face. "Hi, Sandy. Did your mom make you come here too?"

"Yes, she did. But I must admit, it's not as bad as I feared it might be. I don't mind dancing with you at all, Charlie." I smiled encouragingly as if I was his babysitter.

"Well, you're a bit tall for me, but you're kind of nice, I guess. Do you like to go to football games?"

"My dad takes me sometimes. I like the bands and the cheerleaders, but I don't understand the game very well. Do you?"

Charlie gave me a shy smile. "Sometime I'll show you how it's played, Sandy."

"I'll hold you to that, Charlie," I said brightly.

The music ended, and he escorted me to my seat. As he walked away, I saw him signal to another boy. Was he telling him I was okay?

I tried the same approach on my next partner. He looked up at me in amazement. "I thought girls liked this sort of thing."

"Not me, Jimmy."

"Yeah. My mom says I have to learn how to dance with girls because someday I'll want to. I don't think so." He rolled his eyes.

"Don't you like me?" I smiled at him.

He answered me politely, quite unlike the way Pete talked to me when we danced together years later at another church. "Well, I guess if I have to dance with someone, you're easier to look at than most of the girls here."

"Thank you," I smiled. "What would you rather be doing now?"

"Watching TV, I guess."

"Me too." He smiled at me shyly. "Do you watch *Hopalong Cassidy*?"

"I love that show!"

Each week, we counted off in pairs, and the boys escorted us to our chairs and helped us get seated before returning to the center. Following the teachers' cues, they swooped out to find new partners, bowed to them, and asked for the honor of a dance. The girl was supposed to stand up gracefully, curtsy to the boy, and take his hand as he led her to the dance floor. I learned how to fox trot and waltz. Eventually we did more complicated dances, such as the samba and the tango. During each dance, the female teacher kept chirping, "Girls, hold your own weight in your arms. You want to seem as weightless as fluffy pink clouds." I pictured a boy with his arms around a gooey puff of cotton candy and had to stifle an unladylike guffaw.

Sometimes our male instructor asked me to be his partner. He probably chose me because I concentrated so hard, but I preferred to believe it was because I was one of the prettiest girls in the room. I was certainly one of the most cheerful. Dancing with boys wasn't as bad as I had feared; in fact, it was fun.

That February, as usual, the teachers at Amherst 18 decorated their classrooms with hearts and cupids and set out red and white mailboxes with slots for valentine cards. We had to bring cards for everyone, but some kids brought fancy ones to mail to their best friends. To my surprise, two of my biggest, laciest cards came from boys. When I showed them to my girlfriends, I feigned disgust, but in all honesty, I felt flattered.

Malcolm Campbell, a freckled, brown-haired boy who was the son of a respectable family in Amherst was taller at that time than most of the boys, and he was smart. When Cal, as he preferred to be called, asked me to dance with him, which he did quite frequently, I gladly accepted. We talked about school events, and I kidded him about his kilted ancestors. It came so naturally to me that it never dawned on me that he was developing a crush.

After school on the afternoon of Valentine's Day, the bell of our formal front door rang, an unusual occurrence in itself.

"Sandy, would you see who that is?" Mother called out.

When I opened the heavy, knotty pine door, to my surprise nobody was there, but as I closed it, I looked down and discovered a prettily wrapped rectangular present. A small card attached to it said, "To Sandy from Cal." I looked all around, but I didn't see him anywhere. So I took the present inside to show Mother. I expected her to be happy for me, but she scowled at me instead.

"What does this mean?" she asked sternly.

"I suppose it's a Valentine's Day present," I ventured.

"Well, you might as well unwrap it," she sighed. Inside the wrapped rectangular box was another box, heart-shaped and red. The color and shape of that gift was similar to the Christmas present I received from Pete several years later, but definitely more appropriate for a Valentine's Day gift than for Christmas. When I opened the box, I discovered delicious-looking chocolate-covered candies inside.

"Why did Cal give you this?" Mom asked me in a surprisingly accusatory tone.

"I don't know, Mom. I didn't give him anything. He's just a nice guy. These look good! Want to try one?"

"No, young lady. Don't you touch one either. You haven't been leading this boy on, have you?"

I didn't understand what she meant. The boys did the leading in dancing class. I was taught to follow.

"I'll speak to your father," she said, "but it's my opinion that you should return the candy, untouched, with a polite note. I'll help you write it. You'll thank Cal for his gift, but tell him that your parents feel that you are too young to accept presents from boys. His parents will respect you for doing this; trust me. I'll drive you to the Campbell house, and you can ring their front doorbell and leave the candy box and your note there."

My face red with chagrin, I dutifully jumped out of our car, ran to Cal's front door, rang the doorbell, and set the candy box on his stoop, making sure that the "thanks but no thanks" note that Mom made me write was still taped to it. Then I ran back to our car, hopped in, slammed the car door shut, and Mom drove me away. I felt badly about the whole thing. Poor Cal would be mortified. I would feel the same way, if our roles had been reversed.

Just as I expected, Cal didn't ask me to dance with him at dancing school for two weeks after the incident, and he ignored me at school. Cal and I had too much in common, however, to allow that to continue for long. Soon we began chatting amiably again. His puppy love had run its course.

My friends and I loved light, romantic movies. We brought movie magazines, such as *Silver Screen* and *Movie Magic*, read them from cover to cover, and compared notes. I taped a montage of pictures of Tony Curtis, Rick Nelson, Rock Hudson, Howard Keel, and other handsome screen idols to the inside of my bedroom closet door. My little sister seemed to consider this an intrusion on her privacy, but I forgave her. She was too young to appreciate the meaning of love.

I learned about sexual intercourse from my friend Claire Collins, a plump brunette who wore horn-rimmed glasses. Her round jovial face projected a lively sense of humor, and her features and demeanor reminded me slightly of Sergeant Bilko, a comical, likeable television character played by Phil Silvers. In the summer after sixth grade, Claire invited me to stay for a week at her family cabin on Lake Chautauqua, where the two of us went boating, played croquet, and swam off the pier. Claire's siblings, two older brothers whom I hardly knew, had enlightened her about the facts of life, and she was eager to share her wisdom, if only for the amusement of seeing its shock effect upon me. So one night before we were about to go to sleep in her cabin, she told me that boys' private parts did more than just pee. She described how a penis sometimes expanded and grew hard.

"Why would it do that?"

She had me hooked, and she knew it.

"It gets excited when it sees a girl."

"Claire, you have a filthy imagination."

"I'm not making this up. It's true. My brothers told me theirs do it."

"Dirty minds obviously run in your family."

"Don't you want to know the reason why penises work that way?"

"Penis is a dirty word. This *better* be true."

"You still believe babies are made by storks, don't you?"

Oh, oh, I thought. She's got me pegged. "Sure, Claire," I said, trying to appear cool. "Storks work in Santa's shop with the elves. And a penis is equipped with eyes."

"No. But the man attached to it is. When he sees a woman or even a picture of one that he finds sexy, his penis gets hard. It gets that way so, in theory, he can stick it into a woman's vagina; you know, the hole near where we go pee? His penis squirts seeds, baby-making seeds, into her vagina. It takes only one of them to unite with one of her eggs and make a baby. Each time he does it, the man gets a big thrill called an orgasm."

I must have stared at Claire in open-eyed disbelief.

"Oh, I know it sounds complicated," she assured me, "but it's really quite simple, once you understand all the technical bits."

"It expands to fit into the hole near where we go pee? I don't believe it. That would hurt."

"Yup. It does hurt at first, but my brothers told me women learn to like it as much as men do, if they're lucky. You know the hole I'm talking about? The place where the curse comes out? You do get the curse, don't you?"

"Of course I do. Boy, do I ever."

Mom had discovered some spotting in my panties months before my talk with Claire. That's when she told me about the curse. She described the painful cramps, lengthy and profuse bleeding, banishment from swimming pools and sports, the bulky Kotex pads, and the belt. She said it got its name because God cursed Eve with it for disobeying him. She passed the curse down to all women. Mom said its main purpose was to prepare women for the woes of motherhood. I concluded that Eve had caused God to be angrier with her than my Sunday school teachers had let on.

"The curse is part of the whole baby-making deal," Claire told me. "It has something to do with preparing the womb to receive the seed. I don't know all the details about that yet, but it makes sense, doesn't it? Women don't get the curse when they're pregnant."

"You're making all this up just to freak me out, Claire. I don't find it the least bit funny. It's sick! I'd rather hear a ghost story. At least they don't make me want to throw up."

"I'm sorry, kid. I thought I was doing you a favor. But if headless monsters and hatchet throwers are more to your taste, I know a good one."

"Go to sleep," I grumped.

I hoped she was making it all up, but Claire didn't usually tell such unpleasant jokes. I blamed it on her brothers. They put weird ideas into her head; now I was having a hard time putting them out of mine. After I returned home from Chautauqua, I went into Mom's bedroom during her naptime and nervously related to her what Claire had told me. I expected her to tell me Claire had just been fooling around. But Mom's eyes filled with tears, which I took as a worrisome sign. Then she sighed, which always signaled trouble.

"Go out to the refrigerator, will you, Sandy? Bring me back a can of beer. You interrupted my rest, so I need a drink to calm me back down. Then we'll talk."

Mom took several sips of the beer, sighed deeply, and said, "I guess now is as good a time as ever to have this talk. Claire has done much of the hard part for me anyway. What she told you is basically true."

"No!" I couldn't believe my ears.

"Don't argue, just listen," she said slowly. "Claire knows the facts, and intercourse usually hurts a little the first time, but after that, it doesn't hurt very much."

*Very much?* This was not going well at all.

"What I want to make perfectly clear to you, Sandy, is that intercourse is only for married people. People your age don't have to worry about it. There is no need for you to even think about it until after you're married. Good girls never think about such things."

"You and Daddy really do *that*? How often?"

"Oh," she sighed. "It's a private matter." She paused to get herself a Kleenex and to take another sip of her drink. "Maybe every two weeks or so, I don't know. I asked you not to think about it, Sandy. Now, leave me alone so I can rest." She turned over so that her back was facing me.

I left her room and wandered aimlessly around the unusually quiet house. Intercourse sounded terrible! I felt a knot in my stomach. The stork was another white lie. Why had I reacted so idiotically to Claire when she told me? She must have thought I was a fool.

Then I remembered that creep at the quarry. Had he planned to put his penis into me? No wonder Mom had been so upset when I told her about him. It would certainly explain why Dad had dashed home with a cop. The man wanted to make a baby in me? I was just eleven years old! I shivered all over. I felt dirty just thinking about him. He wasn't a freak; he was a rotten criminal. If he *had* tried to put his penis in me, I would have fought him like a wild animal. But he was a strong adult. Could he have killed me? Were there other creeps just like him out there waiting to hurt me?

Most men were good, weren't they? I needed to believe that. I left the house, took a long walk, and ended up at Barb's house.

Barb was a first child too, and she had been as clueless about the facts of life as I was. I told her everything Claire told me, not omitting a detail. As she sat in stunned silence, I shared my conclusions about the bad man who wanted to hurt me. Barb pouted and blamed me for scaring her. I felt guilty, yet it was oddly comforting to know that she reacted the same way that I did. Together we wondered how many bad men there were out there. Would we be able to tell a good man from a bad one? I said we were good enough detectives to be able to do that. The criminal who bothered me had really creepy eyes.

I couldn't imagine my parents having intercourse, let alone understand how they could have created such a diversity of kids. None of us looked alike. I had thick, brown wavy hair, green eyes, and olive skin. Mike had straight blond hair, narrow, slanted blue eyes, and fair skin. Pat had straight dark brown hair, slanted brown eyes and olive skin, and Jerry had round black eyes, thick, wavy blue black hair, and dark, ruddy skin. I was self-conscious and serious about my schoolwork, but I laughed at absurdities and comedians' capers. Mike hated school. He would find any excuse to skip out; a minor cold or a pretend headache would do. He seemed to like animals, but he sometimes displayed a mean streak toward people that frightened me. Even his sense of humor sometimes took a sadistic bent. Patty seemed to live in a world of her own most of the time. She had the uncanny ability to turn off her troubles and wander off into the woods to commune with nature or escape into a dream world. Jerry acted as if he resented being the youngest. A timid soul, he always checked behind the shower curtain to make sure some fiend wasn't lurking to attack him before he used the toilet, and he jumped onto his bed to avoid floor monsters.

Mom got a kick out of calling him Pancho Gonzales, the name of the Cisco Kid's partner. Jerry told me he hated being thought of as somebody's sidekick. Who wouldn't? Mom labeled all of us. She called me "the big-boned, brainy one;" Mike was "athletic nature boy." As my thin sister matured, Mom turned her into "the fashion model." My parents' most pejorative epithets were saved for people who weren't what they perceived themselves to be, namely white and right about everything. Naturally, we kids learned to think the same way. I had no time to question their ideas anyway; I was too busy with schoolwork to keep up with what was happening in the world. Occasionally, I picked up slivers of news. I was vaguely aware of some sort of movement going on against segregation in the South. My parents disapproved of it, so I did too. In the fall of 1954, Irene Dandridge, a famous black actress, became the first African American woman to appear on the cover of *Life* magazine. Dad cut out the face of a white model from a fashion magazine and pasted it over Irene's. I remember this, because it seemed like a strange way for an adult to behave, until he pointed out that a Negress had no business being on a magazine cover.

Dad was good to me, to all of us; he was generous to a fault. I remember how excited I was when he bought our first television. It had a small screen, maybe ten or twelve inches across, shaped flat on the top and bottom and arched on the sides. We gathered around him breathlessly when he turned it on for the first time, twelve eyes mesmerized by the geometric test pattern that glowed in black and white.

One of the few spoilers of my elementary school years, strangely enough, turned out to be a cartoon turtle called Bert. Bert was the star of a short movie called *Duck and Cover* sponsored by the national government. We were required to see it, in spite of the fact that it contained frightening, slowly moving pictures of killer mushroom clouds caused by atomic bombs dropped on Americans by "the dirty Commies." That film gave me a recurring nightmare that haunted me for decades. I dreamed that I was running, but never gaining ground, powerless to escape the mushroom or save the lives of those I loved. I even ran to save Mike. I always awoke from that dream shaking, drenched in my own sweat.

Mike was the other bane of my generally idyllic existence. He was able to be loveable when he wanted to, so Mom and Dad never detected his youthful sadism. Among his arsenal of secret weapons was a slingshot he devised to propel clothespins. Early one afternoon when I was around twelve, I walked calmly past the boys' room, where Mike was hiding behind the door. His clothespin bullet hit me directly in my right eye, and I let out a horrified yelp. When I forced the eye open, everything looked blurry. I ran, wailing blindly, to Mother. She panicked, told me to lie down, and called Dr. Irwin, who advised her to take me to an eye doctor. Mom and Dad assumed that since they both had perfect vision, their children did too, so I had never had my eyes examined. Mom said the doctor would just patch up my eye until it recovered. The doctor's prescription came as a shock to both of us. I needed reading classes.

My stomach reeled. Glasses would make me look ugly! Once Barb had showed me Dorothy Parker's book *Not So Deep As A Well* on her mother's bookshelf. It was a collection of bizarre poems. She said she didn't understand most of them. One couplet, however, drew her attention and caused her to worry. She read it to me. It was entitled "News Item."

Men seldom make passes
At girls who wear glasses.

I told Barb not to allow that silly poem to bother her, never letting on that I believed its sentiment to be true. Now it was my problem too.

"Why did this have to happen to you?" Mom whined on our drive home. "People have remarked to me lately about your ... nice ... appearance. Glasses will ruin your looks!"

I held on to the one positive thing I had heard the doctor say: "You won't need to wear your glasses all the time, Sandy. You'll want them for reading and perhaps to see television and movies more clearly, but that's all."

When the woman who measured me for the frames told Mom that glasses were a popular fashion accessory, she let me pick the color. I chose blue, and she selected frames shaped like a pair of butterfly wings. When I tried my new glasses on, I was surprised at how much clearer everything looked. But I hated the way I looked in them. I knew better than to complain to Mom, but I resolved to wear the ugly things as little as possible, fashion be darned.

## Chapter 7
## GREAT BALLS OF FIRE

*The Illustrious Potentate*

Dad plowed through thirty-two degrees of Masonry to become one of youngest members of the Ancient Arabic Nobles of the Mystic Shrine in Buffalo, also called the Ismailia Shrine Temple. In 1953, the nobles of Ismailia elected him Illustrious Potentate, and *Smile*, the temple's magazine, featured a photograph of Dad on its cover.

Dad's exalted position had everyone in our family literally flying higher than the clouds. In 1952, during Thanksgiving vacation, we flew in a propjet to New York City, courtesy of Ismailia Temple. Dad turned green and refused to look down, and Mom complained about the "teenage pilot." But, when he marched down Broadway, Dad became his jaunty, smiling, fez-capped self again, waving and smiling at the strangers in the crowd as he proudly marched at the head of Ismailia's contingent in Macy's Thanksgiving Parade. I felt uneasy walking along the sidewalks of New York City, surrounded by strangers, but I enjoyed the touristy stuff: peering into the windows of the *Today Show,* looking down from the Empire State Building at the dot far below that was Dad, and feeding the pigeons in Central Park. Dad reserved a table for us at a famous New York restaurant called the Tavern on the Green. Dressed in Sunday school outfits, my siblings and I paraded between our parents into the fancy courtyard, sat quietly, watched our manners, and enjoyed our meal. Even Mike was on his best behavior. Mom, however, wasn't. Suddenly she stopped eating and whined that her turkey dressing "tasted funny." Dad sighed and signaled the waiter. Mom haughtily ordered the man to take her plate away and bring her a hamburger instead, *"well cooked."*

"At least nobody can spoil a well-cooked hamburger," Mom said huffily. The stiff waiter obliged, eyeing her as if she were beneath his contempt. Poor Dad looked like a fez-capped balloon with a helium leak. He ordered himself another scotch and water, gulped it down, cheered up, and ordered us all a sumptuous apple pie with ice cream on top for dessert. Mom and Dad each drank one more tall glass of scotch and ate some apple pie and ice cream too. After a third glass of scotch, Mom seemed ready to laugh at anything.

That spring there was another Shrine convention in Miami, Florida, and Dad decided to drive us South in the Chevrolet station wagon when school got out for Easter vacation. I enjoyed the subtropical scenery along the way, playing on the sand-covered beaches of Miami, and swimming in our motel pool. On the drive home, Dad made an astounding announcement: "I've decided to build the first backyard swimming pool in the town of Amherst. What do you guys think about that?" Our deafening cheers must have startled people five cars behind us.

Because my dad's engineering skills were exceedingly fuzzy,

our swimming pool was a masterpiece of misbegotten design. Happy Harry commandeered a town bulldozer to dig a deep hole in the ground beside the hedge of forsythia bushes that separated our backyard from Harlem Road. The lumbering machine carved out an irregular cavity that was over twenty-five feet long and nine feet deep at one end, sloping upward to four feet at the shallow end. The sides of the hole slanted gradually outward from bottom to top. Workmen from Cleveland Tramrail lined the irregular hole with meshed steel, and a cement truck dumped its contents into the bottom. One day, while Dad and I were watching the construction work, our neighbor, the scientist Dr. Jeb Ryan, sidled over to the pool site.

"Hi, Harry, hi, Sandy," Jeb greeted us with a smile. "I've been curious to see how the work on your pool is coming."

"We're making great progress, Jeb. We'll be swimming before the end of the summer."

"I see. That's great, Harry. Looks like you have an interesting design here. How do you plan to handle drainage and filtration?"

"I don't plan to have a drainage system, as such," Dad said, his body rocking from heel to toe.

"Really? You're not worried about sanitation issues, Harry?" Jeb sounded amazed.

"Oh, sure, Jeb. I'll be dumping some chlorine and stuff in. If the water gets too dirty, I'll just drain it onto the grass and refill it. Piping the whole darn thing for drainage would be a complicated, expensive, time-consuming job. No need to involve plumbers if I don't have to, I always say."

"Uh huh." I looked up at Jeb. To my surprise, he was shaking his head doubtfully.

"Well, I don't want to interfere, Harry, but I sure hope you know what you're doing."

"There won't be any problems, Jeb. Now how about a drink?"

The two men went through the porch toward the kitchen. The

project continued for the next two weeks. After the bottom layer of cement dried, more cement was poured. Dad's men raked it farther up the sloping sides and let that dry before adding another layer. Eventually the cement lined the hole all the way upward and over the top, creating a wide edge for what appeared to be an oversized bathtub. After the concrete had dried, my father and one of his men brushed a vivid turquoise latex paint over the whole thing.

They installed a spring diving board that they bolted into a mound of cement on the edge of the deep end, and they made a patio along the side of the pool nearest the house by setting stepping stones into a flat bed of concrete poured over the grass. Soon the water poured into the gigantic tub through our garden hoses. In the opinion of my immediate family, that sparkling blue swimming pool was perfect. I don't remember when my grandfather first saw it, but I'm certain that he couldn't have shared our opinion. A concerned neighborhood delegation researched the town files for rules on pool construction, only to learn that what some of them called "Harry's hazardous cesspool" appeared to be legal; that is, no one had tried to build a swimming pool in Amherst before, so there had been no need to establish regulations. They did manage, however, to uncover a town law stating that any area of possible danger to public safety must be fenced off from public access. When confronted by them with this concern, my dad obligingly fenced in the pool area with a six-foot-tall wire fence attached to metal poles. The only entrance to the fenced pool area was through one locked gate, and my parents kept the keys. Dad assigned his friends on the police force to patrol our street regularly in order to discourage children and intruders from risking death to get into his inviting pool.

I loved that pool. Wearing Jantzen one-piece bathing suits, I pretended to be Esther Williams, mimicking her choreography in *Neptune's Daughter*. When I wasn't practicing water ballet, I laid for hours on a chaise lounge on the pool patio, my skin soaking in the rays of the hot summer sun. I had to rest a good deal anyway because of my oddly recurring sore throats. As per his plan, Dad occasionally dumped chlorine and something he called HCTH acid into the pool in his typical "by guess and by gosh" manner. He drained and cleaned the pool every few weeks or so, after the initially crystal clear, translucent water became an opaque brownish gray. A pump Dad borrowed from the town fire department drew the water out of the pool, and heavy hoses emptied it into our back lawn. That way, our grass was not only watered; it was well fertilized.

The pool usually became so grungy about a week before Dad drained it that we kids played a game we invented called "Hide the Puck." One of us would dive down to the bottom of the deep end and hide a jet-black hockey puck under water. Then the others would dive to the bottom and grope around until someone located it. The winner would pop up from her dive, the black puck in her hand, and shout victoriously, "I found the puck!" As I look back at that now, it amazes me that we all survived.

An extraordinary event topped off the summer of 1953. A child on our street spotted flying saucers darting back and forth overhead in the dimly lit evening sky. The shocking news spread quickly up and down the street. Everyone ran outside to gape skyward in fear and awe at the mysterious lights. Two of the neighbors who had been to war dashed back into their homes to locate the guns they kept stored away as souvenirs. Dad phoned a town policeman. The credulous crowd watched the darting disks flying through the blackening sky, expecting them to land at any moment, open their hatches, and disgorge invading alien monsters. Speculation rose as to what they could do to us. The scene reminded me of the movie previews I had recently seen for *Invaders from Mars*.

Sadly, the saucers never landed. As I laid in my bed that night, I tried to imagine what aliens would look like, not realizing that my little sister, so silent in the bed beside mine, was shaking with fear of getting snatched up any moment by a terrible monster. She didn't tell me that until she could laugh about it years later.

If I had known her state of mind back then, I probably would have tried to talk her out of it. The idea of aliens was exciting to me, yet when I had time to think about what we had seen, other explanations occurred to me.

The next morning at breakfast I gingerly tried to share my thoughts with Dad.

"Do you think that those flying saucers might have been some sort of optical illusion?"

"That question makes no sense, Sandy."

"Couldn't they have been the tips of beams, spotlights, you know, like the ones the new Thruway Mall has been shining up lately to attract people? The lights we saw may have been them reflecting off the clouds. They'd look like circles flying and darting about, if you couldn't see the whole beams, wouldn't they?"

"No, you're wrong, Sandy. Those saucers were real. We don't know if they were friendly Martians or not, but I can assure you that we're ready for them."

I shut my mouth. I had other things to think about anyway.

Hours of lying under rays from the hot sun left my hair highlighted and turned my skin a deep shade of tan. Hours spent in the smoky film of the movie theaters filled my head with love stories and spiked my curiosity about how Mom and Dad had gotten together. I found the courage to ask Mom about it one evening when she was alone, relaxing with a beer.

"I was fourteen when I saw your dad for the first time, Sandy, not much older than you are now. Harry was so handsome, strutting along on the sidewalk near my house, his cheeks red in the crisp autumn air. He was the best-looking boy I had ever seen. I asked around about him and learned that he was from a very respectable, well-off family, and he went to Bennet High, my own school. So one day, on my well-planned, roundabout walk to school, I 'just happened' to literally bump right into him." She actually winked at me, knowingly.

"You bumped into him on purpose?"

"A girl does what she has to do." She shrugged. "All's fair in love and war, Sandy. It turned out to be a smart move on my part. That very day, the chemistry began. I just knew that we would be married someday, and I ran after Harry until he caught me." She giggled.

"I can't wait until I'm fourteen and can bump into a tall, dark, and handsome boy."

Suddenly, Mom stiffened, and her countenance took on a grave expression. What had I done now?

"Not all boys are as respectful to girls as your father was. Your grandparents brought him up right, but there are some boys who will try to take advantage of you. A good girl must never let a boy know how much she likes him. Do you understand me, Sandy? A boy wants to believe he's the one doing the chasing. Only bad girls, floozies, flaunt themselves at boys. You're a good girl, and I want you to remain that way. You must *never* chase boys. Such behavior can only lead to trouble." I sensed that our discussion was over, and I was confused. From other things she had said, I had deduced that Mom and Dad had spent some pretty wild times together as teenagers.

Late one weekend evening, after they had had a couple of drinks, they told me more about their dates. They admitted that they drank when it was illegal to drink. Prohibition was on the law books from 1920 to 1933, so Mom, Dad, and their friends went to illegal saloons called speakeasies. I had seen a movie about those places, and I asked Mom if they actually said "Joe sent me," to get into them. She didn't respond. I could tell that her mood was changing. "It's illegal and wrong for teenagers to drink, Sandy. Your Dad and I were ... almost adults when we went to speakeasies. We did it only once or twice, just to please our older friends."

Dad backed her up. "We never really drank. We just went there to dance and have fun."

I did the math, and their stories didn't add up, but I pretended to accept his revision.

When she was alone in a reminiscent mood another night,

Mom talked about getting married in the middle of the Depression, in 1936, when she was twenty-one and Dad was twenty-two years old. It was a small wedding attended by their parents and a few close friends. Mom wore a white, ankle-length dress that hadn't been designed as a wedding dress and a wide-brimmed white hat, no bridal veil. She showed me a photograph of her and Dad on their wedding day, standing outdoors with their parents. Everyone was in a line, and Mom and Dad were beaming at the camera. Both sets of my grandparents, however, weren't even smiling. In fact, they didn't look the least bit happy. As I looked at that photo, I decided that, if I ever did get married, my parents would be happier. I'd have a big wedding with a proper bridal gown: train, veil, and lots of colorful bridesmaids. That never happened.

# Chapter 8
# HOUND DOG

*Amherst High School*

In the 1950s, Amherst Central High School served well over a thousand kids in grades seven through twelve. Its most distinctive architectural feature, a solitary tower, jutted skyward from the center of its roof. To some, it looked like a blatantly phallic symbol: a neon sign announcing this was the place for kids with hyperactive hormones to find each other. Perhaps that's why seventh grade homeroom teachers kept reminding us of Amherst's highly touted reputation for scholastic excellence, constantly reviewing the rules of acceptable behavior.

For my first day at Amherst, I dressed like my girlfriends. Our fashion-conscious mothers bought us full wardrobes of cotton blouses, cashmere sweaters, lightweight cotton skirts and petticoats for warm days, and woolen skirts for cooler days. Wide leather belts cinched tiny waists, and matching purses hung heavily from girls' shoulders. A neck scarf or a pearl necklace completed the typical outfit for girls. Boys wore cotton, corduroy, or khaki slacks topped by pale cotton shirts and v-neck woolen sweater vests or cardigans. Everyone I knew wore bobby socks and saddle shoes. Most of my girlfriends sported shoulder-length hairstyles, but my mom insisted that my hair had to be short and "manageable."

Upon entering Amherst, my mission was clear: learn the ropes or get strangled by them. Mrs. Sullivan, my homeroom teacher, told us we were privileged to be there. The school rules weren't hard: no running or shouting in the halls, no gum or candy in class, no walking in the halls during class hours without a pass, no unexcused absences, no rudeness or swearing. I slipped up on the last one only once, when I was a senior. I committed the crime in chemistry class when Mr. Long popped a quiz on us. Without thinking, I murmured, "Oh, darn!"

"What was that you said, Miss Schall? Would you like to repeat it so the rest of the class can hear you?"

"No, sir. I'm sorry, sir. I misspoke."

"Was there something I said that bothered you?"

"No, sir. I was just surprised."

"You were *surprised*? Isn't that what a pop quiz is for? Now surprise me with answers that are 100 percent correct. And will you wash your mouth out with soup when you get home?"

"Yes, sir, Mr. Long." The other kids giggled at my struggle to keep my face straight. Mr. Long's pretensions of strictness amused everyone, and he knew it. He was aware that we called him Long John Silver behind his back. I think he was proud of it.

I turned thirteen in the middle of my seventh grade year in 1954. Technically that made me one of the first teenagers; the term wasn't in general use before the fifties. In the town of Amherst, being a teenager wasn't as bad as it is in many places today. No teenager that I knew back then made a habit of breaking the law or taking people hostage, killing anyone, or engaging in sexually motivated crimes. I heard about a tenth grader that became pregnant, but she was a well-known airhead: a "dipstick." Today she'd be labeled mentally challenged. She skipped school and ran around with bad kids from the inner city. When her stomach got fat, she simply disappeared from the school. Nobody I knew ever saw her again.

Like all young teenagers, I suffered from hormonal stress. But when I got the curse it lasted longer than it did for most girls, and I suffered more pain and had more drastic moods swings than most of the girls I knew. On the positive side, I never had acne. When I felt bloated and ugly, my mother, who wore corsets under her housedresses, had me wear a girdle to school so my belly wouldn't stick out. On weekends I wore garter belts to hold up the silk stockings I wore to church, parties, and other formal occasions. Wherever I went, however, I sensed that I was sticking out somewhere I shouldn't be.

One day, Mom eyed my face disapprovingly. "Your skin is too yellow."

I knew that. It worried me.

"I think some lip-gloss might help."

"Really? Gee, thanks, Mom."

I surprised my girlfriends by being the first to wear any form of lipstick. Mom also suggested that I could add more color to my face by pinching my cheeks. I felt that my nose looked too large, so one night when I got in a pinching mood I pinched my nose hard between my fingers. Luckily, this was not before a school day. The following morning, Dad eyed me with concern.

"Your nose looks black and blue, Sandy. How did that happen?"

"Harry, you're right!" Mom chimed in. "Sandy, have you been in a fight?"

"No, Mother," I answered her weakly, covering my nose with my hand. "It's nothing." I escaped to my bedroom.

"Your nose is blue," my little sister helpfully remarked when I walked in.

When football season drew near, seventh graders rushed to the room where Student Council members sold Amherst's requisite outer wear: waist-length, black corduroy jackets piped with orange silk and lined with warm flannel. Seen coming or going, orange A's sewn on the jackets' fronts and backs indicated we belonged to Amherst.

On Friday or Saturday nights, my girlfriends and I donned our jackets and went to school-sponsored dances or private parties where the boys were. Like masters monitoring puppies, parents and chaperones watched every move we made. Mom or Dad drove me there, picked me up, and asked me about my dancing partners. At parties held in private cellar recreation rooms, parents lurked directly overhead. It wasn't that they were worried about us getting into their liquor cabinets; they were just there to make sure that we didn't. Other drugs were not even in our vocabulary; in fact, I am fairly certain that in the midfifties, teenagers weren't involved with drugs anywhere in Buffalo. Even teenage gangsters didn't deal in drugs, as far as I know.

The dresses I wore to parties accented my slim waist and flattered my new female curves, but they were no more alluring than the other girls' dresses. Before I went out, Mom checked me over to make sure everything was girdled in place and that my stocking seams were straight. Some of the boys, those I favored, the guys who were getting taller than me, told me I looked beautiful. We danced slow dances to popular 45 rpm records, such as Perry Como's "To Know You Is to Love You," or Teresa Brewer's "You'll Never Get Away," and jitterbugged to faster music like Bill Haley's new "Crazy, Man, Crazy." We drank Kool-Aid and soda pop and ate cake and cookies. At ten o'clock in the evening, sharp, parents arrived en mass to scoop us up and take us home.

Sundays were family and church days. At the age of thirteen, I was confirmed at Ascension Lutheran Church. The kids in my confirmation class were nice: nice and dull. I didn't find them anywhere near as sharp or socially acceptable as my school friends. Our teacher, the uninspiring minister who preceded Dr. French, tried to recruit us into the Luther League, the church group for teenagers. Most of the others joined, but I said I was too busy. Actually I didn't want to associate with those dorks. On Sunday evenings I was busy enough anyway, finishing up school assignments for Monday and gossiping with Barb on the phone.

Along with several other girls, I attended after-school sessions with the girls' coach to learn how to be a cheerleader. My friends told me I'd be a shoo-in, with my looks, my long list of activities, my good grades and all, but on the black spring day when the names of the girls chosen to be on the junior varsity cheerleading squad were posted in the gym, I couldn't find my name on the roster. After checking vainly for it several times, I blindly bumbled my way home, threw myself on my bed, and cried my eyes out. It was a colossal tragedy.

Until I got a crush on a guy, that is. He was one of the JV basketball players, Wayne MacDonald, a good-looking, tall, popular ninth grader. Following Mother's advice about never letting a boy know that I liked him, I didn't smile at Wayne when we passed each other at school. We passed each other often, since I purposefully walked by him in the halls, hoping that he would notice how cool and pretty I was. Wayne's younger brother Roy was in my English class, and I could see that he admired me. Since Mom had taught me that all was fair in love and war, I figured it would be okay for me to take advantage of Roy. My ingenious plan was that through him, I'd get closer to Wayne, somehow. I smiled at Roy a lot, and one afternoon after the closing bell had rung, he approached me in a crowded hallway and shyly asked me if I'd like to go to a movie with him a week from Saturday. I told him I'd ask my parents.

They had settled upon thirteen as an acceptable age for me to start dating, so they couldn't object. Besides, Roy's parents were solid, well-respected Republicans. With my parents' blessing, I told Roy yes, and Mom and Dad set a curfew of ten o'clock. Roy came to our front door promptly at 6:45, the exact time arranged between us on the phone. I was ready and waiting nervously in my dress, church coat, hat, and white gloves, carrying a purse that held my glasses, comb, a tissue, and some emergency change. He walked me out to his mother's car, opened the door for me, and stiffly introduced me to his mother as if reciting lines from a play script.

Mrs. MacDonald drove us downtown to the Paramount Theater that was showing *Elephant Walk*, starring Elizabeth Taylor, Dana Andrews, and Peter Finch. As we sat side by side in the smoke-filled theater, not touching each other, I kept my eyes glued to the movie, coveting Liz's fluffy, figure-fitting costumes and admiring her feisty character. When the movie ended, Roy escorted me to an ice cream parlor, where he bought me a Coke and an ice cream sundae. Shyly we talked about elephants, neither of us mentioning the movie's love triangle.

Through the corner of my eye, I could barely see a group of older teenagers in green and gold Kensington High School jackets sitting at a nearby booth. They were handsomer prototypes of Pete: long-haired city teenagers with surly mannerisms. I figured that they were from some poor section of Buffalo. One of them had a face that reminded me of a photo I had seen in *Silver Screen* of Marlon Brando playing a rebel in *The Wild One*. My friends referred to guys like that as rocks, a word originally taken from black culture meaning radicals who didn't follow the rules. He spotted me glancing his way, and the jerk whistled. I pointedly ignored him, and Roy's pink countenance turned red. The rocks made loud wisecracks at our expense and snickered at us. One smart aleck said, "Bet ya two sissies are on yer first date, ain't ya?"

I refused to respond. Roy looked terrified.

"Will ya look at them two kids, guys? Ain't they cute?"

Another greaser chuckled and let out a half-whistle. "Oooooeee baby! Yer Mommy drove yous guys here, ain't I right?" He blew some smoke at us. "How much ya wanna bet them two don't even hold hands?"

Roy and I blushed. In my case, it wasn't due to embarrassment; I was angry. Before I had a chance to do something dangerous, however, the parlor clerk ordered the hecklers to pipe down. The greasers rose from their booth and stalked out, one of them whistling softly at me as he passed. In a low voice so the clerk couldn't hear him, he murmured into my ear, "Le'me show ya a big time, baby."

At exactly nine thirty, Roy's mother drove up in her long maroon sedan. He opened the car door for me, and we sat quietly in the back seat, a foot apart. Mrs. MacDonald asked us about the movie, and we gave her short, polite responses. His mom waited in her car while he walked me to my door. I knew he wouldn't expect a kiss from me, even if she hadn't been out there. No decent girl would kiss a guy on a first date: it was a rule. He thanked me; I thanked him, and I bounded into the house. Mom and Dad were waiting in the living room.

"Well, how did it go?" Mom asked.

"It was okay," I said flatly.

"Sit down," she said. "Tell us all about it." I couldn't discern from her tone if she was merely curious or if she didn't trust me.

"We saw *Elephant Walk,* had Coke and ice cream sundaes at a parlor near the theater, and some older Kensington rocks made fun of us for being on our first date. I guess it was obvious." I shrugged. "Roy was shy."

"I'm sorry. Did things go okay otherwise? Do you like Roy? He didn't kiss you, did he?"

"Oh, Mother! No. Roy is a good boy. He's a bit boring, that's all. I'm tired, okay?"

Mother exhaled a white cloud of cigarette smoke and sipped her beer. "I hope you're not too disappointed. You're bound to get asked out again, and you can't expect all boys to be as cute as your dad was." She giggled girlishly and smiled at Dad, who winked at her as he took another sip from his mug.

"You're a regular little lady now," Dad said. "Go get some sleep."

The next time Roy asked me to go out with him, I told him I was busy; I always managed to be busy when he called. His handsome brother never knew I existed.

ACHS soon began to feel like a second home to me. I loved my teachers, my classes, my extracurricular activities, my girlfriends, and most of the smart boys. I was willing to date any of them; I just didn't want to get into a touchy-feely situation with anybody. I was waiting for "that certain feeling," whatever it was, that stirred the hearts of girls in the movies. I went out with lots of nice boys, hoping for it to happen. If it didn't happen in one date, the boy was out. I managed the situation, and I liked it that way. Once, however, when I was in ninth grade, things slipped out of my control. I accepted a date with a handsome, popular, smart athlete named Gary that I didn't know very well. His dad drove us to the home of one of his friends, another athlete that I didn't know.

The game was already well under way when Gary and I walked down the stairs into his friend's rec room. The kids were seated in a circle on the cement floor. I took one look at what was going on and wished that I had stayed home. They were playing spin the bottle! Everyone greeted Gary warmly; some of the kids looked surprised to see me there. I watched them as a guy set the Coke bottle spinning. When it stopped, he planted a loud smack on the lips of the girl the bottle's arrowlike neck pointed at. I gaped at their heads coming together, heard that smack, and imagined myself running back up the stairs.

What was I to do? I had no desire to kiss a boy on the mouth for the first time there with everyone watching. In the movies, a kiss was the climax of a long romance, accompanied by flowery music. No orchestra was playing in that cellar. I balked uncomfortably when they urged me to sit down in the circle. One boy shouted, "Fraidy cat." Finally, Gary ordered me to sit down next to him in such a commanding tone that reluctantly, I sat. Through sheer luck, I managed to avoid the arrow until Gary took his turn. He knew how to spin it so that no luck was involved. I screwed up my courage, closed my eyes, and steadied myself for the kiss. Gary's eager lips felt damp and sweaty on mine, and his breath smelled of spinach. I wanted to barf. I jumped up, excused myself from the circle, ran up the stairs, spotted a telephone on the kitchen counter, and dialed my home number.

When Dad answered, I said softly into the speaker, "Please come pick me up, quickly, Daddy. No, I'm okay, but I don't want to stay here. I'm at Terry Murphy's house, remember? I'll you tell about it when you get here. Please, hurry."

A deep voice behind me shouted, "Sandy Schall, you're not leaving so soon, are you? Are you okay?"

The father of our host, who had been drinking beer and playing cards at the kitchen table with his wife and another couple, sounded concerned.

"I'm sorry, but I don't feel very well, Mr. Murphy. I need to go home and get some rest. My father is driving here now to get me." I tried to appear pitiful.

Gary popped upstairs, pulled me out of the hearing range of the adults, and whispered, "You're being a big baby, Sandy. I'll tell everyone in school that you're a cold fish if you don't come back down with me and play the game."

"I could care less," I responded coldly. "Will you please get me my jacket?"

"If you insist. You'll regret this, Sandy."

Dad told me I had done the right thing. He said Gary's father was an egg-headed blowhard. "If you don't like the boy, don't kiss him, Sandy."

Comfortably tucked into my bed that night, I worried. Would everyone say I was a prude? Gary didn't have that much influence, did he? I needed to be more careful about accepting dates from guys I didn't know.

I buried myself in my schoolwork and continued to earn good grades. At the end of ninth grade, the principal awarded me a membership card to the National Junior Honor Society. It inspired my parents to compose a poem:

In the past, we have heard you make mention
that to your good marks we pay no attention.
The reason we never have made much of a fuss
is that we feel you can't miss with parents like us.

I thanked them for their doggerel, but I knew it had been my own effort, not theirs, that had earned the accolade. Kids called me "the brain," as if having brains were bad, but I didn't care. I cared about my future. My teachers confirmed what Grandma Chrystene once said: "Anyone who wants to go to college has to work hard." Counselors stressed the importance of taking an active part in extracurricular activities, so I joined the Hi-Y, the newspaper staff, and my homeroom basketball team. I practiced making foul shots alone at home when the boys weren't monopolizing the hoop Dad had hung up above the garage doors.

During summer vacation, I swam a lot, babysat, lounged in the sun, and went to movies with my friends. One of the films we saw was *The King and I,* starring Deborah Kerr and Yul Brenner. The main plot of the musical involved an unacknowledged romance between Deborah, a pretty English teacher, and Yul, the king of Siam, a bald, short man with squinty eyes and a funny accent. I wanted to see them get together, but they never uttered a word of love.

"What is it about *The King and I* that makes me feel so, I don't know, funny?" I asked my sex guru, Claire Collins.

She looked at me as if I had just said the dumbest thing in the world. "Yul's sexy, moron."

"But he's ... so strange looking."

"Sure, he doesn't look like Burt Lancaster or Tony Curtis, but ... don't you get it? He's a powerful guy: a king. He has a cute smile and very sexy moves. Most girls I know are crazy about that movie because of him. It's so beautifully tragic, isn't it? He can't express his love to Anna. She loves him, but she can't have him because they're from different cultures. It's a romantic tragedy, an exotic version of *Romeo and Juliet*."

"So, Yul has what they call sex appeal?" I asked idiotically. Claire just crossed her eyes at me.

I was nearly fifteen and a half, the magic age when teenagers in New York State could apply for a learner's permit and start learning how to drive, but only under the supervision of a licensed driver. The licensing law was complicated. At sixteen, most kids took drivers ed; they still had to take a written test and a driving test to get licensed to drive alone during the daytime. Kids had to be seventeen before the law allowed them to apply for a license to drive alone at night.

On a mild October day, I eagerly jumped into the driver's seat of Dad's blue Buick, and he solemnly lowered himself into the passenger seat. He was a man without a parachute in the cockpit of a plane with a fifteen-year-old greenhorn pilot. Swallowing heavily, my father reviewed the automatic transmission gears before I put the key in the ignition. I eased my foot onto the gas pedal, while he admonished me to press very, very gently. I shifted to the "R," and dutifully looking over my shoulder, slowly backed down the driveway, stopping the car with a jerk when Dad ordered me to. He made me wait until there were no cars anywhere in sight on Harlem Drive. Then I awkwardly backed out onto Harlem, shifted into "F," and put my foot gently on the accelerator.

"Go slower," Dad shouted, as we inched along at a crawl. "Look all around you. Watch out for that kid!"

"What kid?" I twisted my head around, but I couldn't see any child.

"Keep your eyes on the road, Sandy. He was over there in that yard." He pointed down a side street off Harlem. "Kids can run out at any time. Watch the road now. Stay on the right. You're going too fast."

Dad was an airsick shade of green by the time I jerkily applied the brake as I navigated the car back into our driveway.

"Watch out for the garage doors!" Dad bellowed. He made me stop the car when I was four yards away from the garage. "You can get out now. I'll pull her in." To my chagrin, Dad ordered me to stay out of the driver's seat until I had taken driving lessons at school. My class schedule was full; I'd have to wait until the following summer for that.

My summer school driving instructor turned out to be a bulldog: a boys' physical education teacher who barked at me every time I got behind the wheel. At the end of the six weeks, he gave me a B minus on the driving part of the test, but I aced the written exam.

After that, my parents allowed me intermittent use of their Buick sedan. When I sat behind the wheel of that Buick, I felt a sensation not far from being drunk. I felt totally in control, like a young tightrope walker too sure of her own footing to think she needs a net. Alone at the wheel of that car, I barreled the engine on the thruway, sometimes as fast as 120 miles per hour. I went on those rampages at a time when seat belts and air bags were a thing of the future. Caught in the reckless high of deep play, I counted on my father's political pull. He had gotten his friends excused from fines for speeding tickets, so if a cop ever caught me, surely he'd get me off.

Mike and I had been getting along better since his voice had changed. He had several friends older than himself, athletes whom I found mildly interesting: tall, good-looking, and polite, at least to me. Mike himself was beginning to evince early signs of his future status as a lady-killer. As soon as he walked out of the house, he combed his blond hair like James Dean's, and he slipped into a flirty banter that was difficult for me, or any girl, to resist. That summer, his silver tongue persuaded me to commit a federal crime.

Personal possession of fireworks in New York State was illegal, but people brought them in from Canada. Every year

Dad managed to collect some for a Fourth of July celebration at our house. Neighbors gathered inside our back porch or directly behind the house, and Mike and the bigger boys helped him shoot off fireworks from the far side of the yard. They burst into loud, spectacular, expanding chrysanthemums of sparkling bright colors to the delight of the children and most of the adults in the neighborhood. Dad's police buddies looked the other way; some of them even came over to watch the show, knowing that Dad kept the refrigerator stocked with beer and snacks for the occasion. All of us knew about Dad's deal with his pal, Police Chief Hainsworth: the "Three Calls and You're Out Pact." The police chief allowed Dad to shoot off fireworks until the department received three phone calls of complaint. When the third call buzzed angrily over the lines, Dad's show was over until next year.

That year Mike stashed away some firecrackers that he salvaged from Dad's display, and he and two of his friends sweet-talked me into driving them into the country where they planned to set them off. Their idiotic plan involved tossing powerful firecrackers called cherry bombs into roadside mailboxes. My job as getaway driver was to take them out there and stop in front of rural mailboxes, so one of them could reach out the car window, open a box, light the firecracker, and complete the dirty deed. I followed their instructions and slowly pulled the car away while we waited for the thunderous explosions. After two out of three boxes flipped over, I sped off, all of us laughing like crazed gangsters. Ignorance is not a valid excuse, but I had no idea at the time that tampering with the mail is a federal offense. I suspected, however, that it was not something a Sunday school teaching officer of the Hi-Y should have been doing.

That night, after we settled in our beds, I bragged to my little sister about my adventure with Mike and the boys that day.

"You blew up three mailboxes?" Patty sounded outraged.

"Yup. You should have heard the explosions. Mike, Ron, Johnnie, and I nearly died laughing."

"Were there letters in them?"

"I don't know." Her righteous tone was getting to me. "I was just the driver. I couldn't see what was in those boxes."

"What if some important letters got blown up? What if you destroyed a message that might have changed or even saved someone's life? You all could be killers, Sandy."

"Oh, for heaven's sake. What a party pooper you are. Go to sleep."

I had not considered the possible consequences of what we did. Yet my ten-year-old sister realized the gravity of our deeds in two seconds. I buried my face under my blankets, ashamed.

It may be a stretch to mention karma here, but not long after I abetted the cherry bomb crimes, I awoke one morning feeling terrible stomach pains, worse than any I had felt in my life. Since I often complained about aches and pains, my parents weren't concerned.

"This is nothing new, Sandy. You're always bellyaching about something. Get it? Bellyaching?" Dad laughed.

"Aren't you apt to get the curse soon?" Mom asked. "It's probably just cramps."

"I bet it's the result of eating her own cooking," Dad jibed. "Marie, didn't she help you make the spaghetti last night? Come to think of it, I feel a bit sick too." Dad doubled over in feigned distress.

I was unable to laugh at his teasing. I went to my room to lie down, but the pain kept getting worse, and my groans grew louder. I couldn't suppress them. I was scared! After a couple of hours of hearing me howling, everyone in the house was convinced that something was really wrong. I knew I was going to die.

Now thoroughly alarmed, my mother consulted Dr. Irwin on the telephone. His first question, which Mom relayed to me, was, "Where is she feeling most of the pain?" I said, "On the lower right side of my stomach. Way down. Ohhhhh. Owwww. Ohhhh." Dr. Irwin ordered her to get me into the car and take me to the nearest hospital that could attend to me right away.

After making a few phone calls, Mom and Dad discovered

that the nearest hospital that could admit me immediately was Meyer Memorial Children's Hospital. It was so painful for me to get myself properly dressed that I felt in no condition to protest the fact that the patients in the children's hospital ranged in age from under a day to twelve years old. When I arrived, two nurses were waiting for me. They led me into a white emergency room, stripped me down, and put me into an embarrassingly small hospital gown. A doctor that I had never met popped in and probed my stomach with his gloved fingers, which caused the pain to intensify. Then to my horror, he stuck a gloved finger up my rear end. That was pain from hell, and I screamed. *Loudly.*

"Um, humm," the doctor said. "I want her lower abdomen X-rayed *stat!*"

I was scared out of my mind. My whining embarrassed me, but it was impossible for me to control myself. I rolled around, occasionally getting a glimpse of the doctor studying the X-rays. He called for Mom and Dad, and his diagnosis managed to filter its way through my groans.

"Sandra has a ruptured appendix and acute peritonitis, or put simply, she is full of poison from an infected appendix." His voice sounded stern. "Her condition was allowed to fester for too long. Now it's a very dangerous situation. She must undergo an emergency appendectomy immediately to remove the infected organ and get all the poison out of her abdomen."

I was terrified.

They stuck needles into my arm and began the countdown. As my mind floated into the darkness, I prayed.

"Heavenly Father, I'm sorry. I'll never be bad again. Please let me live. If you do, I promise I'll become a member of Luther League and go to the meetings every Sunday night."

At that point, I lost consciousness.

The next thing I knew, I was in a bed, feeling an intense urge to get up and get myself a drink of Coke, but unable to move because of the pink and green elephant that was pressing down heavily on my stomach. Then a child's voice cried out from somewhere in the distance, and I opened my eyes. The handsome, benevolent face of a young man in white smiled down upon me through some tubes running from liquid-filled plastic bags hanging from somewhere over my head.

"Where am I?" I croaked. My throat felt dry; I didn't sound like myself. "You're not an angel, are you?"

"No," he laughed. "You didn't make it to heaven, but it was a close call." His intelligent-looking brown eyes examined me intently, and he scanned a paper on a clipboard. "You're a very lucky young lady, Sandra. You were well on your way to heaven before your operation got under way. That appendix was uncharacteristically low, the diagnosis wasn't easy, and the operation was extremely tricky." He adjusted a long tube pinned into the skin of my arm, and I felt a tinge of pain under some heavy wrapping somewhere near the base of my stomach.

"Did you get all the deadly poison out?"

"Don't I look like a pro?" He laughed pleasantly. "Actually, I'm an intern in pediatric surgery here. But as I said before, you're a lucky little gal. The doctor who saved your life is the most experienced surgeon in the city. Emergency appendectomies are one of his specialties. He had just finished supervising a delicate one on a three-year-old when they brought you in, so he suited himself up again and saved your life. I observed the operation: an outstanding piece of work. He sewed you back up with the skill of a queen's seamstress. Your scar will be so miniscule that no one will notice it when you're wearing your bikini." He winked at me.

"Good girls don't wear bikinis," I muttered, smiling and wincing at the same time.

The young doctor cocked one eyebrow at me. Then he shook his attractive head and smiled quizzically, more to himself than at me. After he left, I mulled over what he had just said. Had it really been luck? Or had God answered my prayer? I owed him one.

Other interns knocked on the door of my private room at odd hours, saying they needed to adjust my tubes and bandages or to take my temperature. "Well, young lady, you certainly have caused a stir in this facility," said a cheerful nurse who helped me with the embarrassing task of using a bedpan. "The word has spread that there's a beautiful young lady here in the recovery room. Suddenly all the interns seem to feel they need to check in to see how you're doing."

Soon I was sitting up without help and feeling like a celebrity. My parents visited me, fussed over me, and brought me sympathy cards from neighbors, people at church, and kids at school. Claire managed to find one with a sexual innuendo that I hid from my parents. Most of the cards boys sent me were funny. Cal said the operation confirmed his suspicion that I'd go to any length to get extra attention. Charlie quipped that the real reason for my hospitalization had to be that long overdue brain surgery. Grandma and Grandpa sent me flowers, and Tanta sent me a box of homemade candy.

Once Mom and Dad got me home, I recovered quickly, undoubtedly aided by the surprise bundle of joy that Dad brought home a couple of days later. He was a gift to Dad from his cop friends: a ball of furry energy that would become the monarch of Harwood. The six-month-old German shepherd puppy's pedigree listed his name as King Izen von Bearsden. The first time I saw his highness, he was wiggling impatiently in my father's arms, his tongue hanging out, waiting trustfully for me or anyone else to give him something to eat. It didn't take him long to figure out that he could control the household, and he roved wherever he pleased. No one was about to argue with King. He had the deep, scary bark of an instinctive guard dog. His deceptively threatening appearance gave me an idea: King could help me handle those awkward moments when boys escorted me to the side door after a date. With King on guard, no sensible boy would dare to wait around for a good-night kiss.

*Mom and Sandy Dressed for Church*

## Chapter 9
## MR. WONDERFUL

*My Birthday Suit*              *Dad in Miami*

Despite the fact that I wanted to, I couldn't forget the deal I had made with God in the hospital. Afraid to risk almighty wrath, I joined the Luther League. Their Sunday evening meetings bored me out of my mind: dull business agendas followed by kids reading Bible reports and the pastor following up with simple questions they couldn't answer. After sitting through just one of those exercises in futility, I took a sketchbook to the next one and used the time for drawing practice.

At school I continued to earn good grades and to remain active in several school-related activities. I considered joining a sorority, although it was not, strictly speaking, a school activity. Amherst condoned fraternal groups by not condemning them, and kids openly passed out membership bids in school to those they deemed equal to their standards of popularity, sports ability, expensive clothing, or whatever. When I received three bids, Claire, who didn't get any, threatened to wring my neck. My parents encouraged me to join, so I did. After a humiliating pledge period culminating in an initiation ordeal involving blindfolds, raw eggs, and personal humiliation, I swore the vows of sisterhood for life. My sisterly devotion to Sigma Kappa Sigma lasted less than three months. Disenchantment set in when I witnessed a blackball session from the inside. I nominated Barb and Claire, and no one blackballed them, but soon the session began to feel to me like a chick party run amok. Blackballs were thrown down simply out of jealousy or spite. This was so incongruous with the stated principles of the sisterhood that I felt hoodwinked. I never did quit the sorority; I invited guys to their dances and some of the social events, but I skipped a lot of the meetings.

By that time, my schedule was so overloaded that I thought I couldn't possibly agree to another thing. Then the school's top music teacher who directed the school's highly touted operettas summoned me to his office. He announced that I had been selected to design the sets for the annual musical, *The Desert Song*. I couldn't say no.

"Great," he said. "Now how do you want to do Byzantine mosaic designs on the arches of the Moroccan set?"

"Please allow me to think about that for a day or two." I neglected to mention that I had no idea what Byzantine meant; I had to look it up in our encyclopedia. Designing the scenery for the musical and subsequent stage design work meant that I got to work closely with the all-male stage crew. The stage manager, Glenn Ackart, hung around with another mechanical genius named Russ Meyer. Like Mutt and Jeff, Russ was stocky, and Glenn was slim and agile. Both boys were also in my Advanced English class in my junior year. Each was witty, innovative, and technically adept. As I look back upon their relationship now, I imagine they could have been gay. "Gay," however, was just an adjective meaning happy back then. Most people who were homosexually inclined succeeded in hiding it, perhaps even from themselves.

I turned seventeen when we were in Miami during Easter vacation, where Mom took me to a chic department store and told me to select a new bathing suit. I found a black latex one-piece, figure-clinging Janzen shape-maker with pink panels covered with black lace, accenting my bust line and the curve of my hips. Mom winced at the price and worried about its "daring design," but she bought it for me. Wherever I wore it, men eyed me appreciatively; some guys even whistled. Following Mom's orders, I ignored "those mashers," but she couldn't prevent me from enjoying it.

On the drive north, we visited the campus of Gettysburg College in the southern foothills of Pennsylvania, a liberal arts college affiliated at that time with the Lutheran Church. A student guide gave us a campus tour, and afterwards my parents and I agreed that it seemed like the perfect place for me. The campus was relatively small, and the students were well dressed, well spoken, polite, friendly, and dedicated to their studies and to Gettysburg College. I thought I could feel at home there, and a degree from Gettysburg would eventually land me a decent teaching job.

After I returned to school, I received a notice that I had been elected by the faculty to the Amherst chapter of the high school National Honor Society, the highest form of recognition of scholastic achievement, school service, character, and leadership at ACHS. Although I pasted my election notice into my high school scrapbook above the caption, "I was lucky enough to make Honor Society," I knew better. I couldn't remember how many times I had heard my parents say something like, "Sandy, are you reading again? How can you study so much? You'll become blind if you keep that up. You'll have to wear your glasses all the time."

"Did you or Dad just say something, Mother?" I'd say. "I'm sorry. I had my earplugs in. I have to finish this chapter before I can study my geometry and Latin, okay?"

Patty learned to fall asleep with the bright reading lamp on my desk fully lit and shining her way. She contends that after having shared a room with me, she could fall asleep with a flashlight directed at her face.

In the spring of '58, my family attended a dedication service for our newly renovated church building. Dad had been one of the leading advocates for reconstruction, but I got bored listening to the speeches. The feeling reminded me of the fact that I still had one more year of dreary Luther League meetings ahead. How could I make them less mind-numbing? Would it help if I were to make friends with someone in the group? I decided to approach a jolly-looking, heavyset girl named Susie Ogden.

When I first spoke to Susie, she looked as if she were about to pop a cork. "Did you speak *to me*, Sandy?"

"I'd like to get to know you better, Susie. What are you planning to do when you graduate from Amherst?"

"I'm not nearly as good at schoolwork as you are, but I can type real fast. Maybe I'll take some business courses."

I couldn't think of anything exciting to talk about there, so I brought up boys, a subject all girls had an opinion about. "Do you like the boys in the league, Susie?"

"Some of them, I guess. But, Sandy, you're too smart and pretty for the best of them, even Neal Adolf."

This astute observation made me realize that Susie was by no means totally stupid. As I had hoped, knowing her made the Luther League meetings slightly easier to tolerate, but I still had a hard time stomaching the Bible stuff. The visits to the old folks' home and the orphanage depressed me. When the league served at the church suppers or decorated the nave for holidays, however, I could talk to normal adults. One of them asked me if the league ever held social events, and that gave me an idea. At the next business meeting, I raised my hand for the first time.

"Why don't we set aside a period after the Sunday business is over to have refreshments and just talk and get to know each other?"

Susie raised her hand. "I move that we take turns bringing refreshments."

That set the ball rolling. From then on, I tried to be nice to almost everyone, except Neal Adolf, who had the nerve to flirt with me. He obviously had no idea how far beneath my crowd I considered him to be. One of the sweetest kids in the league turned out to be Sally Marsh, the shy and pretty dark-haired daughter of the church secretary. Joyce Heckcr, a girl my age, was totally unremarkable, but kind and gentle. Her little brother Mark seemed like a nice kid. When the businesslike president told me that she was going off to a technical college in New England, I had an inspiration. I had to be there anyway, so why not take on the presidency myself next year? It would look good on my resume, and maybe I could think of ways to liven things up. I hinted about this to Susie; she nominated me, and I got the job.

By the end of my junior year, I had accumulated an impressive list of accomplishments: Honor Society, influential posts on the school newspaper and on the staff of the creative writing annual; chairmanships of theatrical scenery crews and school decoration committees, vice presidency of Hi-Y, membership on the Girls' Sports Council and the Water Follies team, and the pending presidency of the Luther League. Best of all, I held in my pocket, metaphorically speaking, an early acceptance to Gettysburg College.

I was proud of myself. I had done everything right, except for finding Mr. Wonderful. I made a list and put all the boys I knew into one of three categories: losers, friends, and short-term escorts. Gary was a loser; Cal and Glenn were two of many good friends. Escorts were easy-come easy-go. That spring I landed a popular football player to take me to the junior prom, a highly anticipated formal dance traditionally planned by the junior class in honor of graduating seniors. The prom theme for 1958 was "Sayonara," and the Student Council chose me to supervise the decoration committee. Several girls worked with me in the gym to create a veritable riot of pink suggesting Japanese cherry blossoms. We covered low beams and exercise bars with pink Kleenex fluff balls, and we intertwined yards and yards of pink and white crepe paper and splayed it outward from the rotating mirrored ball suspended from the center beam of the ceiling. Most of the girls wore head bandanas to hide their pin curls while they worked. When they goaded me for not having to pin my hair up, I fluffed my hair out, pursed my lips, and posed ala Marilyn Monroe.

The senior who escorted me to the prom was an easygoing frat boy named Jack, famous for having completed a winning sixty-yard run against Amherst's archrival football team. When the word had gotten to me that this athletic Romeo had just split up with his latest girl, I asked one of his friends to let Jack know that I needed a prom date. I figured that if my looks alone could snare him, I could also outsmart him if he tried anything fresh. It would be an all-nighter, since it was traditional for couples to go to nightclubs after the prom. Most of the seniors had turned eighteen by then, the age for legal drinking. The junior prom always involved some drinking, so it was customary for everyone to sober up near dawn at breakfast parties in private homes. My mother and father were aware of the drill, and I sensed their uneasiness when they escorted Jack and me out the door.

"Take good care of our girl, Jack," Dad said. I thought he sounded too stern, but Jack didn't seem to notice.

"Don't worry, sir, she's in good hands." He grinned. That's a joke, I told myself.

We arrived at the gymnasium, checked my coat, and I slipped the flowers Jack gave me onto my wrist. He led me onto the floor for the first dance. Shortly after, to my surprise, Cal tapped his shoulder.

"May I take a whirl with her royal highness, Jack?"

"Huh? What royal highness?" Jack looked confused.

"She's wearing a crown, isn't she?" Cal pointed at my rhinestone tiara headband.

"Oh, I get it. Ha! Sure, Cal. Good to see you."

As we danced, Cal whispered softly, "I wanted to congratulate you, Sandy, on your razor jet brain lover boy."

"Yes, it was rude of you to steal me from Jack so soon. We're nuts about each other."

I had a fabulous time flirting with the boys in my crowd, and Jack made his way around the floor, dancing with socially popular girls. When the dance ended, he rounded up two of his buddies, and the six of us squished into his car to drive to the town casino. Jack and I danced a couple of dances, but most of the time we just watched the floorshow. I ordered some food and soda pop, and Jack downed several beers. Even when he was sober, Jack was out of it, so by the time we had breakfast, I was amazed that he was still standing. At around 5:00 am, he walked me unsteadily to my door, and King sent him home with one bark.

Sayonara, Jack, I said to myself as I stooped to pet my dog lovingly. The house heaved a sigh of relief when I walked in.

In New York State at that time, high school students had to pass regents exams in all of the academic subjects in order to earn diplomas. Although seniors took the majority of these tests, the comprehensive English regents was a junior year hurdle. I felt confident that I could pass it easily, but I needed superior scores in both the literature and the writing and grammar portions of the six-hour-long ordeal in order to ensure continued placement in the Advanced English program. I ended up with a grade of 92. To celebrate our grades and the onset of summer vacation, I invited my English class to a pool party. Dad roasted hotdogs on his outdoor grill, and Mom prepared gallons of slaw and baked beans. Mildred Meese, our teacher, sat comfortably on a padded lawn chair near my parents and consumed two helpings of store-bought cake and ice cream.

I basked in the glow of the sensation my new bathing suit created. I couldn't help but notice Paul Hartmann, the tallest boy in the class, eyeing me up and down appreciatively. Grinning charmingly, he told me pink and black were his favorite colors. I eyed him up and down, and told him his suit was lovely too. We talked about our summer plans, and as he talked, his athletic physique, handsome face, dark hair, bright dark eyes, and smooth, tanned skin rendered me spellbound. He was tall, dark, handsome, and smart! Why hadn't I paid any attention to him before? I scooped up some water and splashed him. He jumped into the pool and splashed me back. We flirted shamelessly until the party was over.

That night I felt too wound up to sleep. I wanted to jump up and skip around the room, but I knew Patty would report to Mom and Dad that I'd gone bananas. So I tossed and turned, reliving each sparkling moment of that wonderful party. I had finally found my man! I wished summer vacation were over so I could see him again. Luckily I landed a job teaching arts and crafts at the YMCA's day camp. The work was fun, and it caused the vacation to go by quickly. The pay wasn't much, but I proudly banked most of it away for college spending money.

Perhaps because I was at the verge of my last year at home, my parents awarded me unexpected privileges that summer. One warm evening when we were talking on the porch, Dad offered me a glass of beer. I drank it, and it made me feel good, but I wasn't crazy about its taste. Another night, when they were relaxing with their cigarettes and beer, Dad offered me a Lucky Strike. Many of my friends smoked, so I was curious to give it a try. Dad lit one up for me; I held it between my lips and drew in a cloud of smoke. I belched and sputtered it out in a juicy, smoky ball. Mom and Dad laughed at me.

"Take it in slowly, Sandy," Dad coached. "Breathe the smoke in normally and let it slip out your nostrils."

Soon it became easier for me to inhale, and I began to feel a pleasant buzz somewhere in the back of my head. With each puff, I felt more sophisticated: blasé and sultry, just like Ava Gardner.

"Will you buy me a pack of cigarettes, please, Dad?"

He shrugged. "Sure, as long as you promise not to smoke in front of your teachers or the pastor." I giggled.

Grandma and Grandpa celebrated their golden anniversary in August at Greenfield Country Club. I saw it as another sign that they were getting old, but everyone else in the family made a big deal about it. Uncle Jim drove up from South Carolina with most of his family to help Dad host the event. He, Aunt Bea, and their kids spoke with southern accents now, and they felt like strangers to me. Judy was on her break from nursing school; we seemed to have very little in common anymore. To me the party was bittersweet, like a fading butterfly with a dicey wing, holding itself tenuously aloft, sensing that its end was near.

When the evening before school reopened arrived, I felt so jittery that I ached. Alone in the kitchen, I paced the floor, watching white circles of smoke dancing like Hula-hoops, expanding as they rose in the air over my head toward the lights. I took another puff from my new pack of Kents and picked up the yellow Bakelite receiver. My fingers rotated in the familiar pattern, and Barb picked up.

"Hi, Melvin. You ready for the big day?"

"Almost, Herman. Just deciding which skirt to wear with my new, golden oblong sweater set that I bought at Grants to go with my white bunny fur collar. Wait until you see it. I think it's fetching, but I'm worried that it's too fancy for school."

"No sweat. Everyone dresses up a bit on the first day. Your contact lenses aren't still bothering you, are they?"

"Nah. I can wear them for hours now."

"I know they were terribly expensive, but they make you look fabulous, so they're worth every penny. Bob will go crazy when he sees you."

"Oh, don't be stupid. I could go naked and he still wouldn't notice me."

"*Barb*, what a thing to say. You must be nervous too. Why are we still like this after all these years?"

"You know, ninny. It's them: my Bob and your Paul. Sandy, this year is our last chance!"

"I know. I know." I sighed and blew out another white hula-hoop. "Maybe we're doomed to be old maids. Mom and Dad were nearly married at our age. Grandma and Grandpa were high school sweethearts."

"My parents didn't meet when they were teenagers. But," she lowered her voice, "I don't think they're as happy together as your parents are. I hope they don't get divorced."

"Don't say that, Barb. It's unthinkable. We have enough to worry about now. I won't sleep a wink tonight, will you?"

"Nope. And thanks for cheering me up."

"I'm sorry. I need to make sure my outfit is okay. Can I call you back later?"

"Spare me. See you later, alligator."

"After while, croc—" Barb had hung up.

I went back to the closet, where my clothes took up three-quarters of the space I was supposed to share equally with Patty. Mom finally gave me free rein to tell Vinnie how long I wanted my hair to be and to select my own wardrobe. My first step was to toss my saddle shoes and bobby socks into the bottom of the Goodwill bag that I eventually filled up with last year's outfits before tackling the serious business of shopping. Tan was out. I chose brightly colored clothing, including several sets of knee socks, and I sewed elastic strips to wide ribbons to make hair bands in various shades to match my ensembles. They looked groovy over my shoulder-length pageboy.

I had absolutely no doubt that Paul was the guy for me: six foot three inches in height, athletic, and brilliant. He had traveled all over the world with his dad, a United States Air Force officer, and he was a quarterback on the varsity football team, a position that went to the smartest players because they called all the plays. I'd have to keep that in mind, I thought. Paul wasn't just manly either: he was sensitive. Mrs. Meese had praised his poetry. One of his poems, entitled "I Am the Captain," was tucked in the back of the drawer by my bed. When I read it to Barb, however, she didn't sound impressed.

"'The deep dread sea of passing life'? Give me a break!"

But what did she know? She wasn't in Advanced English class.

Paul moved with ease in popular crowds, as well as among the most intelligent kids at Amherst. He was more popular with the opposite sex than Barb was. Was that what Barb held against him? He served on several committees, and he was president of the Varsity Club, vice president of the Student Council, on the Executive Staff of the senior yearbook, and a fellow member of the Honor Society.

Why hadn't he ever asked me out? I often walked past the door of Paul's homeroom, where he stood in the hallway with his friends, watching the girls go by. The fact that I had ignored him should have made me unique. Now how could I catch him?

## Chapter 10
## DANGER! HEARTBREAK AHEAD

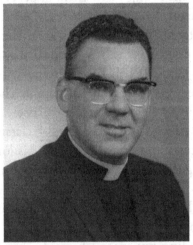

*Pastor French*

A thin shaft of pink light poked its way through our bedroom curtains, heralding the first day of my senior year. I got up as early as I dared, dressed myself carefully, pecked at my breakfast, and urged Mike to finish his, so Dad could drive us to Amherst as soon as possible. Dad's brown eyes looked away from the article he was reading in the sports section of the *Buffalo Courier Express*. He shook his head at me.

"Calm down, will you, Sandy? You're acting like a kindergartener going to school for the first time."

"I'm perfectly calm, Dad." I checked myself over one more

time. "Where's my purse?" I shouted. "I just had it. Have you seen my purse, Patty? Oh, it's hanging on that chair. Did I put it there?"

"I repeat. Calm down, girl. We'll leave when I'm ready and no sooner."

"You're nuts," Mike said, looking at me as if he thought I needed another whack with a clothespin. "What's the big deal about school? I think I'll stay home today."

"No you won't, Mike," Dad said sternly. "It's obvious that you kids won't allow me to enjoy a moment of peace," he sighed. "We might as well be off."

When I entered the girls' locker area, the girls I ran into seemed to be as excited as I was. We squealed as if we hadn't seen one another for years. When I went upstairs, the only person I pointedly ignored was Paul, who was happily checking out every female in the hallway. After my first two classes, I walked through the door of Mrs. Meese's Advanced English classroom, where Paul had already seated himself near the back, his long legs stretched out, surrounding the empty desk in front of him. I hopped down into it.

"Hi, Paul," I said to him brightly, congratulating myself on my clever maneuver.

"You're invading my space," he said, "but better you than melancholy Malcolm." He winked at me. I turned my face away, pretending not to swoon.

Suddenly, two boys walked into the classroom that I had never seen before. One was tall, dark-haired, and looked lost. The second was also tall, but extremely well dressed in a nifty v-neck green sweater over a yellow shirt. The colors of his outfit complemented his most outstanding feature, his well-groomed carrot red hair. Mrs. Meese welcomed both newcomers warmly. "Archibalt, Ken, I'm happy to see you. Sit down anywhere. I'll introduce you both after the bell rings."

She presented the dark-haired boy first. He was the foreign exchange student from Germany. "Archibalt Konig has come all the way from the province of Saar," Mrs. Meese proudly announced. "He has studied English for almost four years, and you will find that he speaks it very well. Probably better than most of you do." We laughed. Archibalt studied his hands. "During his stay in America, he will be living with the Montgomery family. Archibalt, do you want your classmates to call you Archibalt, or do you prefer to be called something else?"

Archibalt's handsome face reddened, and he said with a slight accent, "Please call me Archie. That is what I am always to be called in Saarbrucken."

"Fine," Mrs. Meese replied with a smile. "Archie you shall be. Archie is interested in sports, music, and literature. He is remarkably well read, which is one of the reasons he was placed in Advanced English. He has traveled to France, Spain, Italy, and Austria. He has an older sister in Germany with whom he attends concerts and the theater. You will find him to be a valuable addition to our class. Let's all give Archie a welcoming hand."

We clapped, and Archie, still looking uncomfortable, put on a pair of dark-rimmed glasses and studied the cover of a book on his desk. We had something in common, I thought. Both of us use reading glasses. He might be a very interesting, safe date if I can't get Paul to ask me out right away.

Mrs. Meese introduced the redhead. "You are lucky to have another very accomplished new classmate this year. Kenneth Skiller moved to Amherst from Connecticut. He's an only child, and his father is a professor who has just joined the faculty at the University of Buffalo. Ken enjoys soccer and swimming, and he was a member of the Student Council at his previous high school. He tells me that literature and creative writing are his favorite subjects. Let's show Ken we're pleased to have him here."

We clapped and Ken smiled, his blue eyes darting around the classroom curiously. When those stunning eyes lit on mine for a brief moment, I could see that they radiated intelligence and sensitivity. Humm, I thought, Skiller. I'll probably be seated next to him in chemistry; Mr. Long seats his kids alphabetically. Then my thoughts returned to the boy behind me, whose legs were still stretched out so that I felt as if he were holding me between them. Could he have been more distracting?

On the phone that night, Barb and I babbled breathlessly. I described the new boys in English, and then I talked about Paul until she told me to shut up. I let her rattle on about Bob, muttering "Um" or "Oh?" intermittently, while I enjoyed a Lucky Strike, so she would think I was interested. Finally, both of us ran out of steam. We let the line go silent for a few seconds, and then she said, "Well, one thing's for sure, Herman, we'll be out of there before we know it."

"Yeah," I sighed. "Now I'm not so anxious to leave. This could be a big year. The only thing I'm dreading is that darn Luther League. They elected me president."

"Why did you let them get away with that?"

"Oh, those dorks need me, Barb. Besides, it looks good on my resumé."

Barb wasn't interested in my church affairs, so I had never bothered to tell her about the changes that had taken place. We had a new minister, for one thing. Dad had been attending meetings of the church council all summer long, and near the end of August, he told us that a new pastor was on his way. The news shook me up.

"What about our old pastor? Where will he go?"

"He has a new position at a church someplace way out west, like Minnesota."

"Okay. So who's the new pastor?"

"Well, thanks to the shrewdness of your clever dad," he pursed his lips and rolled his eyes in his distinctive, pseudo-modest fashion, "you're getting the very best minister in Buffalo."

"What's his name?"

"Dr. Ernest C. French. For over ten years he's been pastor at Resurrection Lutheran Church downtown. They love him there. They couldn't bear to give him up. He's the reason they have a congregation that is so much larger than ours. But yours truly won him over by getting the council to provide him with a house of his very own, not very far from here. He's moving in as I speak, and he'll start at the church in September."

"Is he old?"

"Nah, Ernie is not too much older than I am. Two of his kids are around your age, I believe."

"Why is he called Doctor French?"

"He was a minister in a New Jersey city that was full of criminals. He chased them away and earned an honorary doctorate for preaching against crime and promoting religion in an area where there wasn't any. It was in the newspapers—a pretty big deal there, from what I understand."

"So *he's* why you went to so many church council meetings this summer. I see. But, if this Dr. French has such impressive credentials, what took so long? Why wasn't he offered the job right away? What was the problem?"

"Well," Dad winced, "there were … troublesome … rumors going around about Dr. French's personal life."

"What rumors?"

"You'll probably get wind of them soon enough, so you might as well hear the truth from me, I guess."

"Yes, please, tell me, Dad. I'll be working with the pastor too, you know."

"It's a complicated story. Let me pour myself a beer." He got his drink and sat on the living room couch. I sat in the chair across from him. "Now where was I?"

"You were about to tell me the rumors about the new pastor."

"Oh, yeah. Well, Dr. French lost his first wife, the mother of his two older children, to stomach cancer."

"That's awful!"

"There's more. Now his second wife, the mother of his youngest son, is dying of cancer too. She has a brain tumor. She's almost a vegetable, so she's in a health institution somewhere."

"A human vegetable?"

Dad looked uneasy. "Her brain has shut down. She doesn't know where she is or what's going on around her or anything. She's been that way for a long time. But she's not the worst part."

"Oh, no! There's more?"

"The problem is that Dr. French ... well, he has a girlfriend."

"*What*? He has a girlfriend? While his sick wife is still alive?"

"That's just the sort of stupid knee-jerk reaction the council was worried about, Sandy. People need to see things from Ernie's point of view. Try to imagine what his life has been like. If you're as smart as you think you are, you should be able to understand that the man needed someone to help him get through this ordeal. He's been very discreet about the woman who has helped him. She's the director of the choir at Resurrection. I'm sure he felt it was wise to make this move for that reason too."

"You're right, Dad. It's a complicated situation."

"Yes. And you must keep quiet about it. Don't make me sorry that I told you. Do you understand me? If you hear people whispering about it, report what you hear back to me. Can I trust you to do that?"

"I appreciate what you've been saying, Dad. You can trust my discretion. I just didn't expect to hear such a ... sad story."

"Yes, it is sad, Sandy, but it seems to have turned Ernie into an incredibly good minister. Wait until you hear him speak from the pulpit. He's a fabulous preacher, and our church needs him. He's highly respected in the whole Lutheran Synod. In fact, he's president of the Western Conference of the Synod of New York and New England. They wouldn't elect him to such a prestigious office if they thought he was anything but respectable and top notch at his job."

"What about his kids? Who takes care of them?"

"Dr. French's mother, a widow, lives with the family. She's a nice little old lady. I've met her. The family has been through some hard times, but they're doing as well as can be expected.

Now don't fret about it this, okay? Just be very nice to Ernie's kids when you meet them."

"How old are they?"

"Why are you asking so many questions? You know I don't like it when you ask me too many questions."

"I'm sorry. I'm interested, that's all. I suppose, after all he's been through, Dr. French's sermons will be a bit depressing."

"No! Didn't you hear what I just said? Pay attention, will you? You'll like his sermons. Trust me. He's a fabulous minister who's managed to survive bad luck better than most of us could. You should welcome him and his family warmly, okay? Now go do your homework or something."

Although the changeover in pastors at our church grabbed my attention, it was far less stimulating to me than what was going on in my English class. On that front, I was in for a huge shock. Weeks later, when I looked back on the incident, I could only guess why it happened. For whatever reason, as I gathered up my books after class on Friday, I sensed his presence beside me.

"Sandy, can we talk a minute? Out in the hall?"

"Sure," I said, my heart jitterbugging.

We walked side by side in the hall. Suddenly, he stopped me, and his soft, dark eyes looked intently into mine. "Sandy, have you heard about the Football Frolic? The big dance after Homecoming game next weekend?"

"Yes. Why?"

"Well, I wondered. If you haven't made a date to it with anyone yet, would you mind going with me?"

Would I mind? Would I mind having my prayers answered?

"I'd be delighted to be your date, Paul." I fluttered. "Of course, I'll have to make sure it's okay with my folks." I said that out of habit. Mom and Dad would be more than happy to send me off with the quarterback.

"Sure. See you." He darted off, looking as if he had just intercepted a pass, skillfully zigzagging through the throng, holding his books close to his chest like a football. Stunned, I floated to my next class.

By the following Sunday, I had forgotten about the new pastor, so Dr. French's sermon was an unexpected pleasure. It moved me like no sermon had ever done before. The tall man hunched over the pulpit as he spoke, which made him look as earnest as his name suggested. He preached as if he was teaching me instead of preaching at me, and his message was uplifting. He almost glowed with an aura of strength and hope. In my imagination, that put him somewhere between Job and the angel Gabriel.

I fell for the man himself the moment our eyes met. One look into the big blue gray eyes behind his glasses, and I was in love. He spoke with a charming New England accent that made words like "large" sound like "lodge" and "idea" sound like "idear." At his official installation in late September, he wore the most intricately embroidered, white surplice over his long, black cassock that I had ever seen on a Lutheran pastor. He almost looked like a Catholic priest. I supposed his outfit signified his high rank in the synod. Our whole family sat in a row in a pew near the front of the church, where we could easily hear his rich baritone as his sang unfamiliar rituals and recognizable hymns.

After the service, he and his family lined up to greet the congregation as everyone filed out. When it was our family's turn, Dr. French greeted Dad like an old friend. He addressed Mom warmly too. I was next in line. He smiled down at me and said, "Sandy, how good it was to see you sitting with your family right up front today. I hope I'll see you often." His beautiful eyes radiated sincerity. He also spoke kindly to Mike, Pat, and Jerry; then he introduced his family.

"This is my mother, Mrs. Frieda French." I felt it would be proper to remove my right glove before I reached down to take the old woman's bare, wrinkled hand. Her skin felt like paper, dry and fragile. She was about half the height of her son, slight and white-haired, and she wore thick glasses that magnified her penetrating, intelligent-looking blue eyes. As she peered up at me curiously, I thought I detected a mischievous twinkle in them.

"This is my son Thomas," Dr. French said. Then, sternly, "Thomas, shake hands with Miss Sandra Schall." Thomas was a frail boy of about seven or eight. He looked lost and uncomfortable in his suit and tie. He shook my hand weakly.

"Hi, Thomas," I said, tightening our grip. "I'm Sandy."

"Hi," he replied in a barely audible voice.

"And this is Judith, or Judy."

The girl, who looked about fourteen, gave me a toothy shy grin.

"And this is my elder son Peter."

"Pete," he said to the back of the boy's head, "shake hands with Mr. and Mrs. Schall and their children."

Pete was looking down the reception line extending beyond us, as if counting how many people he still had to greet. He was tall, thin, and totally unappealing. His suit didn't go well with his tie, and his excessively long, light brown hair was loaded with Vaseline and greased into a DA. His father nudged his shoulder, and he extended his hand out and turned his head in our direction. He gave generic, polite responses to the greetings of my parents and shook their hands. When it was my turn to shake his hand, I found myself looking up into a pair of thick, horn-rimmed glasses. I had one brief glance into the large, greenish gray eyes looking intently into mine. Did I detect a glimmer of ... what? Curiosity or disapproval? His hand felt strong and dry, and his shake was firm.

"Welcome to Ascension, Pete," I said as graciously I could, given the revolting way he looked at me.

"Sandy is the president of the Luther League," his father told him.

"That figures," Pete mumbled, dropping my hand abruptly, steering his face away from me.

"Happy to meet you too, Pete," I said to Mike, rolling my eyes.

Pete shook hands with Mike. "Nice ta meet ya," he said halfheartedly.

"See you around sometime," Mike responded, heading past me toward the church door.

As I started out behind him, Dr. French called me back. I reversed my steps. "Yes, Dr. French?"

"Sandy, I'd like to talk to you about something when I have more time."

"Of course. I'm here at the church a good deal, Pastor."

As we drove home, I told my parents that I really liked Pastor French, and I thought that his mother and daughter seemed nice, but I thought the boys were weird.

Dad said, "Give them a chance, Sandy. It's hard for kids to get used to new neighborhoods and leave old friends behind."

"I bet I wouldn't like Pete's friends," I replied knowingly.

Mom nodded. I could tell that she didn't like the looks of Pete either.

## Chapter 11
## POOR LITTLE FOOL

Mr. Long was explaining a complicated chemical reaction, but I wasn't paying attention. My mind was trying to solve a different chemistry problem. How had I discovered the right formula for catching Paul on my very first try? Was it luck or fate? Maybe, finally, things were going my way in romance. The Football Frolic was the first big school dance of the year. I had been to past Frolics, but never with a superstar like Paul, the most attractive quarterback in the world.

In preparing the gym for the Frolics, the cheerleaders traditionally printed varsity team players' names on small, orange construction paper footballs and taped the paper footballs to the gym walls. When the dance was over, each player took down his football and gave it to his date. It was a romantic custom, I thought: a girl could take home a personal memento of the dance. If my magic formula held true, it would only be a matter of time before I would be wearing a more precious memento of Paul's devotion: his solid gold varsity football charm hanging on a chain around my neck, signifying to the world that we were going steady.

When I excitedly jabbered my news to Barb, she wasn't as happy for me as I had expected. In fact, she tolerated my Paul prattle for less than five minutes before she told me to shut up and get my feet back down on the ground. "Don't be so sure things will work out the way you think they will," she warned. "Maybe he asked someone else first, like one of the cheerleaders, but she already had a date. It was a bit late for you to be asked. Wasn't it just last Friday? That's only a week before the dance."

"He was in plenty of time, Barb. You're just jealous because you don't have a date."

"Yeah. Maybe I am. But I'm more clear-eyed than you are right now. Remember Paul's reputation, Herman. He likes loose girls. You've been out with other football players, right? Guys talk to each other about girls. Maybe Jack told Paul about your sexy prom date with him. Everyone is aware of your reputation for being a prude. Why would Paul want to ask you to the Frolic, unless someone else had turned him down?"

"Thanks for your support, Barb."

"Oh, I'm sorry, Sandy. I hope you have a good time."

"That's convincing," I said sarcastically. "I'll call you later." I hung up, miffed.

In spite of the fact that our team lost the homecoming game, Paul was in surprisingly good spirits when he arrived at my house to escort me to the dance. He didn't have access to a car, so we walked along the sidewalks through the neighborhood, from my house to the school gym. Paul was chatty, giving me a virtual play-by-play recount of the game.

"Coach Werner should have given me more time on the field. Old Tony made a couple of dumb calls that I wouldn't have made. Probably cost us the game."

"Coach Werner doesn't appreciate you as he should," I said sweetly. "I think you're undoubtedly one of the best athletes at Amherst." Then, worried that I was going a bit overboard, I told myself to shut up, listen to him, and appreciate how fabulous he looked in the fading glow of dusk, his white cardigan letter sweater accenting his perfect complexion. Tone-deaf to his football babble, I never took my adoring eyes off him.

When we stepped unto the dance floor at the gym, Paul apologized for his lack of dancing skills. I understood. He was an athlete, not a dancer. His poem about being a ship captain popped into my mind. As far as I was concerned, he was my captain, no matter how he chose to steer me. All too soon, however, I realized that I was in for a bumpy ride. His slack dancing position made it easy for him to stop without causing me to trip over our feet, and he stopped often, introducing me to everyone he knew. Apparently he had forgotten that I already knew almost everyone. What made me seasick was that he introduced me to every girl in the gym too.

In subsequent weeks, I reviewed every moment of our date, trying to discover what went so terribly wrong and concluded that it was on our walk home that I made my critical error. Hoping to get Paul to talk about something more vital to our future than a football game, I asked him what his plans were.

"Huh? You mean for the Orchard Park game?"

"No, I mean when you graduate from Amherst. What college are you going to?"

"Oh. The new Air Force Academy in Colorado. I'm getting a scholarship."

"Oh? Won't you have to go to war then?"

"Sure. I'll be commissioned a second lieutenant. I'm looking forward to fighting for our country. My dad was in the air force, you know. It's a good life."

"You mean you actually *want* a military career?"

"Why not?" He shrugged. "It's as good as any. Early retirement, if I ever get that old. You agree, don't you, that military service is important?" He smiled devilishly down at me. When we had discussed *The Red Badge of Courage* in English, I had asserted that most wars are unnecessary. Paul had politely contradicted me by pointing out that the last war had saved the world from tyranny.

"But with your intelligence and your way with people, wouldn't you want to, say, go into national politics and find peaceful solutions to world problems?"

"Look up there!" He pointed toward the starry black sky. "Did you see that bat?"

"What? Where?" I looked up, but I couldn't see anything.

"Bats scare me, Paul. Ugh!" I shivered, hoping that might make him put his arm around me, but he didn't take the hint.

"If you do become an officer, Paul, wouldn't it be an advantage for you to have an attractive, intelligent partner?"

"Sure. But that's too far off for me to worry about. Did you know bats have radar? Like the air force planes?"

"Paul, bats are blind flying rodents. They've been known to attack people or try to nest in their hair. The very idea of them revolts me. If you don't mind, let's talk about something else. Isn't it exciting to be a senior now?"

"It's cool. Except for all the work they throw at us. Do you remember Mrs. Meese's last assignment?"

"The fourth chapter of *American Essays?*"

"Yeah. I thought so. But I forgot to write it down. Do you understand all that stuff?"

"Would you like to discuss it with me now?"

The rest of the way home, Paul and I talked about the ins and outs of writing essays and the subjects we liked to write about most. I was happy because we were so comfortable together discussing intellectual matters. It proved that we belonged together. When we reached my house, I led him around to the back, away from King's guard post. I leaned back on the outer wall of the garage, and Paul jumped up and chinned himself on the edge of the roof. I giggled, perhaps a bit too loudly.

"Shhh," he said, his face expressing mock alarm. "If your parents hear us, I'll be in deep trouble. Your dad's a big wheel in this town. I don't want him getting mad at me."

"Paul," I blinked up at him and smiled, "we've had such a wonderful evening. I'm so glad that you asked me out."

"Thank you for going with me, Sandy," he said with a disarming smile. "I'd better be getting home now though. Your dad's going to sic that dog of yours on me if I keep you out here too long, or even call out his buddies, the cops." With that, he pecked me on the forehead and walked me around to the front side door, where he hastily wished me good night.

"Are you okay with walking home? It's awfully dark tonight."

"No sweat. I'm used to it. See you, Sandy." He took off at a swift trot down Harlem Road, and I floated inside.

Mom and Dad were waiting up for me in the living room. "Well, how was it? You certainly look happy. Did he kiss you?" Mom asked with a knowing smile.

"Maybe." I smiled secretively.

"Look at her, Harry; she's blushing. She reminds me of myself after our first kiss."

All day Sunday, I waited in vain for Paul's call. I was almost glad to have the dumb Luther League meeting to go to that evening. It would take my mind off the wait. He would call me while me I was out, and I would return his call when I got home.

Dr. French, dressed in his clerical black, tab-collared shirt and a dark suit coat, accompanied Judy to Luther League. He gave the opening prayer and listened attentively to me as I outlined my goals for the year. He suggested possible speakers; I thanked him profusely, and he picked up a Bible to read a startling passage from Samuel that ignited the most interesting Bible discussion I'd ever witnessed. I even joined in on the debate. Afterwards, while I was chomping down a cookie, Dr. French asked me to come with him to the back of the room, out of earshot of the others.

"Sandy," he said, "I need you to do me a favor."

"I'll be glad to help you any way that I can, Pastor."

"Thank you. It's about my older son Pete. He told me that he had a prior obligation tonight, but I insisted that if he expected to leave the household tonight, he had to promise to come to Luther League next Sunday evening."

"Oh, please don't force him to come."

"I know what I'm doing, Sandy." His tone reminded me of my father.

"Of course you do, Pastor. I'm sorry."

"That's all right. You meant well. But you don't know Pete.

He refuses to face the fact that he needs to make new friends here. I'd like you to assign him something to do at the league meetings. Make him feel like a contributing member. Do you understand?"

"I understand, but—please forgive me for saying this—but when I met him at your installation, he didn't look too keen about, well, about being there. I'm afraid that he wasn't very congenial, at least to me."

"I know." He sighed. "He's a difficult kid. But he *should* be here."

"Could you give suggestions? What might he be interested in doing?"

"Well ..." The pastor appeared stymied. Suddenly his magnificent eyes lit up. "Pete enjoys music. He has amassed a significant collection of popular 45s, some of them with special labels, I believe. You kids will understand. Maybe you could put him in charge of bringing them to the social periods at the end of your meetings. The kids could dance to his records, as long as they behave themselves, of course." He winked at me.

I said I'd do what I could; he told me he was very grateful. I left, eager to get home and find out when Paul had called. He hadn't.

Paul was just busy, I told myself. My disappointment was compounded by the fact that I had a new plan. My Hi-Y was going to sponsor a hayride next Friday, and I intended to ask Paul to be my date. The next day after English, I cornered him on our way into the hall and invited him. He looked down at me sadly before politely declining. He was already going to the hayride with Joyce, one of the varsity cheerleaders.

"But I'll see you there, okay?" For once, his winning smile failed to score, but I responded as nonchalantly as I could fake it.

I told myself not to be discouraged. I needed to be more like Mom. She had planned one step ahead of Dad. I had fallen behind. Meanwhile, I'd ask someone else to the hayride. Surely I could rekindle Paul's interest just by being there. So I asked Dick, a mild-mannered fellow I had been out with before.

That Friday evening was nothing but misery for me. Dick was a perfect gentleman, but our date was horrible. Paul's undivided attention to Joyce broke my heart. I sniveled with hay fever and depression throughout the entire hayride, sneezing and watching Paul making out in the hay with Joyce.

I slept in the next morning, and when I finally got up, I was useless. I was mad at myself and unable to concentrate on anything but self-pity. Patty was sleeping over at a friend's house that night, Mike had a date, and Mom and Dad were going downtown to a Shrine function. Since I had no plans, they asked me to stay home with Jerry. I invited Barb over. Jerry disappeared into the living room to watch TV and then put himself to bed. Barb and I munched listlessly on potato chips and cottage cheese dip at the kitchen table, and I lit up several Kents and groused in Barb's direction. I could tell she was annoyed with me for resisting every effort she made to conquer my determination to be miserable. But I didn't care. While I sulked, I happened to look up at the high cabinet where Dad kept his scotch.

"I know what I need. Whiskey will cheer me up." I pulled up the step stool, grabbed a bottle, and unscrewed the cap. "Care to join me?"

"That's an idiotic idea, Herman," Barb said.

"Why? In the movies people drink whiskey when they feel the way I do."

"This is no movie, Hermie, and you're not only underage, you're nuts. I know you well enough to know that I can't stop you, but I refuse to join you."

I poured myself a glassful of scotch and took a few sips. The bittersweet, golden liquid burned my throat, and I sputtered. But I continued to sip it defiantly. Each sip that I swallowed felt better going down. Soon I had downed the entire glassful.

"Ya sure you don't want some? It really, truuuly is good. My head feels a nice sort of buzzy. Buzz, buzz. You don't know what you're missing, Melvin."

I poured myself a second glassful.

"Haven't you had enough?" my spoilsport friend said, frowning at me and sipping her Coke.

"Sure. I'll just take a few more swigs, and then we'll take a wee little walkie, okay? Get it? Wee walk? That's the way they talk in Scotland." Barb didn't appear amused. "They always walk it off in the movies, right, ol' buddie? Remember Grace Kelly in *High Society?*"

"We're not in a movie, Herman. Why can't you get that straight?"

"Cut it out. You're depressing me. I want another glass. Might as well empty up, or is it down?, this whole darn bot ... tle. Won't you have 'nother glass too? Oops. It's getting em-py. Oooh kay, com'mon, le's go 'round the block. I'll tell you my troubles, ol' bud. I need to tell you 'bout what Paul and Joyce did that made me so sad."

"Geez. This is a bad idea. But you shouldn't be out there alone, that's for sure."

The only thing I remember about that walk was that I told Barb I feared that I was committing a terrible sin by loving Paul more than I loved God.

My next recollection is of my parents coming in the door. Then I remember being slapped in the face and shaken hard by my furious father. That was just before I threw up all over.

Dad's booming voice echoed around in my whirling head. "You two walked around the block?" he roared at Barb. "Sandy can't walk a straight line. She's blind drunk. If a car had hit her, she wouldn't feel anything. She'd go to her maker stinking drunk. The liquor might still kill her. Look at that nearly empty bottle, Barb! I know Sandy drank it all. You're dense, Barb, but you're sober. Shame on you both!"

He picked up the phone and shouted angrily into it at Irene, ordering her to come for her stupid daughter. My frightened, frustrated friend escaped out the side door, while Dad continued to holler at me. He just yelled, while Mother fumbled through the slime to get my putrid clothes off. After she had me stripped half naked, Mike came in the door. Although I was stone drunk, I still remember the shocked expression on my brother's face, something between empathy, incredulity, and sheer amusement.

"I see big sister is blotto."

"Shut up, Mike. We don't need your snide remarks. Get to bed," Dad roared.

He yelled upward toward heaven that he was too embarrassed by me to call the doctor.

"If you die, Sandy, it's God's punishment. Remember that when you're in hell."

The next morning I awoke naked in my bed with a splitting headache. I couldn't remember everything that had happened the night before, but I recalled enough to know God would send me to hell. I prayed fervently for his forgiveness, promising him that I'd attend the next communion service, gratefully receive the body and blood of Christ, and pray for forgiveness. For the first time, I wished I were Catholic. Then I could go see a priest, confess my sins, and begin doing proper penance at once. I ached all over, and my stomach kept turning over on itself, but that wasn't sufficient punishment. I had narrowly escaped death by alcohol. Was that attempted suicide? Suicide was a sin too. I had shamed myself in front of my best friend and my parents, and my younger brother had witnessed me naked and disgraced. How could I face any of them again?

Although I didn't feel like moving, let alone drinking anything, and the thought of eating gagged me, Mom made me put on my pajamas, sit up in bed, and swallow some water. Then she served me a cup of black coffee, which tasted horrible and made my stomach hurt more. She tried to get me to nibble on some dry toast, but my stomach resisted. All day long, my parents kept popping in and out of my room, telling me how disgusted with me they were. They enumerated my wrongdoings until my head pounded with the rhythm of my sins.

"You drank hard liquor, which is a crime at your age, you got blind drunk, nearly committed suicide, indecently exposed yourself, caused your family both shame and unnecessary concern, and you may have been seen by the neighbors in that scandalous state."

Dad fumed furiously all day long. I don't remember everything he called me, but I remember the shame. It will haunt me forever. Perhaps that's my atonement.

I made no excuses. How could I? Dad was right. Ashamed and unwell, I moped miserably in my bed. Dad dragged me up long enough to call the pastor and tell him I was sick and couldn't make the Luther League meeting. Even Mike knew I was beyond teasing and avoided me. The little kids tiptoed around me. On Monday, I still wasn't strong enough to go to school, but I began to eat again. I apologized over and over to my parents. I told them I wouldn't touch another drop of scotch or beer or any strong alcohol until I turned at least twenty-one.

Barb and her family remained silent about the incident. Thanks to them, my reputation at school remained untarnished.

# Chapter 12
## WITCHCRAFT

Once during the following week, when I was moving with the flow of students in a hall between classes, I recognized Pete silently passing near me, seemingly oblivious to everyone. I was surprised that the PK blatantly dared to skulk the halls of Amherst with his shirt collar turned up, flaunting his DA by tucking a cigarette in the grease behind his ear. Surely, a hall monitor would give him demerits. I realized how embarrassed I would be if one of my friends ever saw me speaking to the jerk and decided that if he ever did try to speak to me, I'd pretend not to hear him. If poor Dr. French wanted Pete to make friends at Amherst, why didn't he force his son to fix up his appearance? Looking the way he did, the only place Pete could possibly find friends at Amherst would be the detention room.

In English class, in order to escape from Paul's influence, I told a white lie: I said I needed to move closer up front to see the blackboard better. Mrs. Meese balked at first, but she liked me, so she asked Vivian to change places with me. That put me beside the German exchange student. Archie and I sparked up friendly conversations, and one afternoon he followed me out of school and invited me to a party. I accepted on the spot, knowing that my parents would approve of him and that Paul never went to beer parties. I usually avoided them too, but I figured Archie, being German, was used to beer. Besides, I both liked and respected the party host.

When Archie arrived at the front door to pick me up, I lead him into the living room where Mom and Dad were waiting with King on a leash, curious to size up Archie. They wanted to like the German boy, and Archie didn't let them down. He was polite and deferential. Dad embarrassed me by rattling on and on about our German heritage, but Archie didn't seem to mind. After he helped me into my coat, our German shepherd allowed him to take me away with a fraction of his usual fuss.

We walked the few blocks to Joe's house. Downstairs in the recreational room, a bucket of iced drinks was waiting. Archie offered me a can of beer, but I declined cheerfully and pulled a Coke out of the bucket. While Archie was in another part of the room, chatting with some friends, Vivian and Nancy told me they envied me for being Archie's date. That boosted my morale, as did the fact that Archie was good looking, popular with the right kids, and intelligent. Most of the time we stood next to each other in the crowded room and talked. He said that school in America was much easier than school in Germany.

"What do you Americans say? It's as easy as duck pudding?"

"Duck soup," I corrected him.

"What is easy about duck soup? It is not easy to prepare a duck for making him into a soup. Do you not think so? He has many feathers."

I laughed. "It does sound funny, come to think of it. I can't make duck soup, that's for sure. I don't think I ever had, that is, *have eaten* duck soup. I don't know why we use that idiom anyway. Come to think of it, why do we say 'as easy as pie?' Making pie is a complicated process. Of course, it's easy enough to eat pie." I rolled my eyes, and he laughed at me. "English has evolved from many languages," I observed, "so it's full of odd expressions that most Americans just take for granted. I take Latin, and ..." He looked confused. "Oops, maybe I should say that in English. I'm *studying* Latin, and I'm amazed at how many English words are based on Latin ones."

"Ach, I can speak four languages, at least a little. All are different, but they have many words that are almost the same. And each language has its own odd sayings. What did you call them, idioms? It is very funny, no?"

"Is Latin one of your languages?"

"Oh, yes. I will be a lawyer. I know some Greek, too. I study English, of course, and French."

"So, counting your native tongue, you know five languages? I'm impressed, Archie. I wish I had taken at least one living language, that is, a language people still speak today. I intend to do so in college."

"You are planning already your college studies? *Das ist gut.*"

Obviously this boy understood the importance of planning for the future. If he weren't returning home to Germany at the end of the semester, it's possible that the two of us could have a future together, I thought. We continued to chat comfortably on our walk home. He asked me if I would go with him to a Halloween party at another friend's house. Although I was barely acquainted with the host, I felt I could trust Archie's judgment now, so I gladly told him I'd be happy to go out with him again. When we reached my door, he stooped to kiss my hand, a charming old world gesture that I had only seen done in the movies. I wished him a good night, and he walked off into the dark whistling. He seemed to be very sure of where he was going, exhibiting that uncanny surety of direction that most males have, even if they are as far from their actual home as he was from his in Germany. For once my parents were not up waiting for me. I patted King's head and walked back to my room, giggling at the thought that it probably wouldn't have worked if I had tried to scare Archie off with him. They shared an ethnic bond.

That Sunday evening, the Luther League meeting took place as usual in an area blocked off by tables from the rest of the church basement. Rows of chairs sat in front of my small lectern; the other officers sat at a table beside me. The pastor wasn't there, so Neal delivered the opening prayer. As the secretary read the minutes, I heard a chair squeaking into place in the back and looked up from my notes to see Pete slumping his lanky body into it. He was all in black: his black long-sleeved shirt had its collar turned up, and he wore dark denim jeans. He looked like someone I'd be afraid to run into if I were alone. He slouched down, stretched out his legs, crossed his arms, and bowed his head down gloomily. Then he slowly cocked one leg over the other, so that one of his black penny loafers rested on his other knee. He studied the shoe intently, as if it were the most interesting object in the room.

His disgruntled demeanor reminded me of how I had felt when I started going to Luther League meetings. But whereas I had come to fulfill a promise to God, he belonged there; he was the pastor's son. If he had been friendly, the other simpletons would have responded kindly toward him. But he didn't look like he felt an ounce of good will toward anybody. He studied his shoe while I presided over the business agenda, and since I had no other program planned, I invited the kids to gather around a back table for refreshments. Pete leapt up and strode quickly toward the back door.

"Hey, Pete," I called out to the hastily retreating figure.

He stopped and turned toward me. "Yeah?"

"Please stay a while longer. The kids want to get to know you better."

"Did my dad tell ya to say that?"

"Uh, no." Now I was telling white lies in church. Well, the pastor made me do it. Determined to be polite, I countered Pete's irritated expression with a smile. "Susie brought her lemon cake tonight. She's a good cook. Join us, please. I need to ask for your help on something."

His upper lip curled into a sneer. "Yeah, I bet. What d' ya want? I gotta get goin'."

He didn't move toward me, so I walked over to him.

"We could use better 45s to play every Sunday; songs the kids might enjoy dancing to, you know? The records we've got are out of date. Your dad says you have an excellent collection of popular records. Would you share them with us? We have a brand-new player with a good needle. You could take them back home at the end of each session, and nobody but you need touch them, if that's what you want. I'd really appreciate your cooperation here." I pleaded with him as sweetly as I could, given the way he was looking at me. He stared at me as if I were asking him to jump over Niagara Falls.

"Wha? Yer crazy. Yous kids ain't gonna like my music. It ain't no Perry Como or other white bread."

"White bread?"

"Fergit it. Ya wouldn't understand. Yer crowd don't listen to Chuck Berry, Fats Domino, or Little Richard."

"I've heard them on the radio, I believe. They're Negroes, aren't they?"

"So? What's important is they make great music."

"Of course. That's why I'm asking you to share your music with us." I was trying to sound sincere. Why was Pete staring at me in such a disconcerting way?

"You're somethin' else, ain't ya? Maybe I'll consider bringin' in a few of my records sometime. *Maybe.* But now, Madam Prez, I gotta take off." He abruptly turned his back on me and moved toward the exit like a black panther with long, smooth strides.

What a rude beast he is, I thought, and his grammar is horrible. Why would a son of Pastor French speak that way? Surely Pete knows better, unless he's an idiot, which is probably the case. I hated to think that Dr. French had a retarded son to add to his other woes.

When Archie phoned me about the time of the Halloween party, I warned him that I would be in costume, and I suggested that he might want to pick up a facemask. He laughed, saying, "I will make a surprise with you."

At Grant's, I bought a long, red wig and a black, pointed hat, and I got some green facial cream at the corner five-and-dime. I scrounged up the rest of my costume from my own wardrobe: anything I could find that looked witchy. I wasn't trying to be an ugly Hansel and Gretel type witch; I saw myself as an enchantress. I practiced doing my makeup by smearing the green cream all over my face and using a dark eyebrow pencil to slant my brows upward into what I hoped would be seen as a charming, mysterious expression. The green goo looked ghastly on me until I applied pink rouge on top of it over my cheeks and painted my lips with a bright red lipstick. Once I did that, the cream merely accented my eyes.

Friday evening Archie arrived wearing a black half-mask and a long, black cape. He said Mrs. Montgomery had lent him her cape. She bought the mask for him so he could be Zorro. I told him he made a handsome Mexican, but he needed a big sombrero. He laughed heartily at my misconception. "Do you not know the story? I am Don Diego de la Vega, a noble adventurer, not a peasant. I should be carrying a sword, but Mrs. Montgomery expressed the objections."

He took my hand in his. We must have looked like a dangerous pair: the green-skinned witch walking hand in hand with a tall, dark, masked guy in a black cape. When we got there, male monsters congratulated me for my improved complexion, and an evil pirate, a fuzzy bear, and a cigarette box asked me to dance. Archie didn't seem too happy about that. When I wasn't dancing with him, he drank more beers than he had done on our first date, and he held me too tightly when we danced. My attempts to get him to talk to me were met with silence. Archie just smiled dreamily down at me as if he were not on the same planet. Was he drunk? I grew concerned. Unwilling to take any chances, I reluctantly told him I needed to leave because my parents wanted me home early.

Archie looked wounded. Then his face lit up. He whispered into my ear conspiratorially, "I know what you want, little *hubsche Hexe*," and winked at me. The look in his glazed eyes made me feel queasy. It reminded me of something I wanted to forget.

Archie grabbed my hand, and we left the party. As we walked on the sidewalk leading to my house, we slipped in and out of the darkness between the streetlights. I realized that, in the darker areas, we were nearly invisible. In a dark area near the woods, he suddenly halted, grabbed my waist tightly, and pulled me to his chest. He repeated the German expression he had used before, and I pushed him away from me with all my might, stood up straight, and eyed him straight on.

"What do you think you're doing? What are you saying to me?" I demanded coldly.

"I called you a pretty witch. You are my pretty witch." He forced me against him again and pressed his lips to my mouth. His lips parted, and before I knew what he was up to, he ran his tongue over my lips, then used the soggy organ to try to pry my lips apart. It felt disgusting. I kicked him hard and screamed, "Stop that!"

He groaned, "Sandy, why do you tempt me if you don't want me?"

"Tempt you? I wasn't trying to tempt you. Archie, you're drunk. I said I had to leave the party for your sake. How would you have enjoyed getting sick there, or behaving more idiotically than you were? And this is how you thank me? What in the world are you trying to do? Is that the way friends treat friends in Germany?"

"*Friends?*" Archie appeared dumbfounded. "I don't understand you."

"I don't love you, Archie, if that's what you think. What would be the sense in that? You'll be going back to Germany, for heaven's sake."

"You can't really mean that, Sandy. *Ich liebe dich.* I love you! I'll take you with me back to Germany."

"No! *Nein!* Never! If you won't take no for an answer, I'm going to run home alone, Archie. I want you to go home too. Do you know the way?"

"I know where I am. But, please, don't leave me."

I broke free of his grip and ran off as fast as I could in what I hoped was the direction of my house. I never looked back. I slammed the door shut, ran into the living room, and plopped down breathlessly on a big chair. The house was quiet. Patty was already asleep, her Daniel Boone hat on her nightstand. I undressed, showered off my makeup, and got into my pajamas and robe. Then I heard my parents arriving home noisily.

I walked down the hall to greet them as they passed through the dining room area. They were dressed in elaborate George and Martha Washington costumes, looking slightly silly in curly, powdered wigs.

Mother Martha gaped at me. "Sandy? You're home before curfew. We said you could stay out until twelve thirty tonight."

"Can we go in the living room a minute? I need to tell you what happened."

"Harry, get me a little nightcap, will you?"

The father of my country, dressed in a bright blue satin faux colonial outfit with frilly white lace, sat beside his neon pink lady and listened to my confession in disapproving silence.

"Then Archie tried to get his tongue inside my mouth. Can you imagine that?" My parents looked at each other knowingly. "*What?*" I demanded. "Don't you think that was grody?"

Mom and Dad seemed embarrassed, and they giggled. "He really likes you, Sandy," Mom insisted. "Come on. Admit it. You were flirting with him, weren't you?"

"*No.* Well, I certainly didn't mean to if I did. I was worried about him, that's for sure. He had had too much to drink. He's big and strong. And tonight he was icky and gross. My only recourse was to run away."

"Sandy! You didn't leave him alone somewhere, did you?" Dad was angry, *at me.*

"It sounds to me like you were way too harsh on the poor boy. I hope the Montgomerys won't be upset," Mom said.

"The Montgomerys? What have they got to do with this?"

"For a supposedly bright girl, you can be amazingly naïve,"

Dad said, shaking his head. "Remember, Archie is a foreign exchange student, a guest of the Montgomerys. If he's unhappy, it won't reflect well on them."

"Does that mean he can do anything he wants while he's here?"

"No. Don't be so idiotic. But customs are different in Europe. You should have allowed for that. The kiss he gave you is the way some people kiss, especially in Europe. Didn't you read up on teenage courting customs in Germany? Or France? Don't you know anything?"

"No German girl would have behaved like you did," Mom said, shaking her head at me. "Instead of pushing him away and running off like some silly little child, you could have explained to him that you aren't used to being kissed that way. Would that have been so hard to do?"

"He just grabbed me, Mother! I was disgusted by what he was doing to me. Is that my fault? If you knew he was liable to do this, why didn't you warn me?"

"We're sick of your stupid questions," Dad said. "Why can't you figure anything out for yourself? The best thing you can do now, Sandy, is to go off to bed. You'll need your sleep. Tomorrow you'll probably have to face the consequences for your thoughtless treatment of that poor, lovesick German boy. I wonder if I should call the Montgomerys and tell them he's on his way."

"No. Please just call one of the policemen in the area now, okay? He'll make sure Archie gets back to the Montgomerys' home. Please?"

"All right. I'll do that. But you certainly can cause trouble, young lady. Now get to bed."

I started crying. "I just can't figure out what I did wrong," I sobbed. "I thought you'd understand why I had to treat Archie the way I did."

"We understand a heck of a lot more than you do, Sandy. Go to bed."

The next day I called Barb. I could always count on her sympathy.

"You don't know about French kisses?" She asked me incredulously. "I can't imagine you haven't read about them. You read romances, don't you? On second thought, I suppose that classic lit you read leaves out all the juicy parts."

"Okay, okay. No, I didn't know about that sort of kiss. I can't believe that other people don't find it repulsive too. Have you ever done it?"

"In my dreams!"

"In your nightmares, more likely. As for me, I was grossed out."

"I bet it's not over, Herman."

"What do you mean? Believe me, I won't go out with Archie again."

"That's the problem. The Montgomerys will try to change your mind."

"Some consolation you are, Melvin."

Soon after I hung up, the phone rang again. "Mom, can you get that?" I pleaded.

Mom was standing next to the phone. "Okay, but I don't think it's for me. It's for you, Sandy," she said with a smirk, extending the receiver out on its cord so I would take it.

I winced. "Who is it?" I asked. "Please ask who it is."

"May I ask who is calling, please?" She spoke formally into the talking end of the Bakelite receiver like a secretary.

"It's Archibalt Konig," she said loudly, and then she whispered to me, "He sounds contrite."

"Tell him I don't want to speak to him. I'm sorry. But I have nothing to say, and I don't want to listen to him either."

"Sandy, you're in the wrong," she whispered loudly. "You *must* be more courteous!"

"He wasn't courteous to me. Please tell him I don't wish to talk to him."

"I'm sorry, Archibalt," Mom said into the phone, "but Sandra is not available." After hanging up, she turned to me and said testily, "You know perfectly well that he probably heard you. How do you think he feels?"

"I don't care."

## Chapter 13
## DO YOU WANT TO DANCE?

Sunday evening Pete showed up at Luther League carrying about a dozen of his records in a small case. He set the case down gingerly next to the player and mumbled grumpily, "I want 'em back *tonight.* No one but me better touch 'em." He strode gloomily to the back of the room, where he slumped his long body deep into a chair. Before I adjourned the business meeting, I thanked Pete for bringing the records.

"Let's all give Peter French, the pastor's son, a hand for bringing some 45s from his valuable collection." They clapped, and Pete glowered at me. "Oh and remember, no one can set a finger on any of them, okay?" Most of them nodded. A few spun around to see if Pete was going to say anything. He wasn't. He was staring at the floor.

"Pete, will you provide the music for future league socials?" No response from the dark figure in the back. "You will help us out, won't you, Pete?"

"Whatever ya say, Madam President," he muttered disdainfully from his slouch.

"Thank you for your enthusiastic cooperation," I said dryly.

After Pete gingerly loaded his records on the player, the music began. To my surprise, Neal asked me to jitterbug with him to a strange rendition of "Tutti-Fritti." Several other kids began to dance too. Neal asked me for a second dance, this time to a slow song I didn't know. Suddenly, Pete appeared and tapped Neal on his shoulder. "I'm cuttin' in," he announced. Neal looked annoyed, but he stepped aside.

"Well, what'd ya think of Little Richard? Don't he beat Pat Boone?"

"Are you referring to 'Tutti-Frutti?'"

"Yeah. Sharp, ain't ya? Can't put nothin' over on *ya*, Prez." He smiled at me, which caused dimples to form in his cheeks. For the first time, I noticed that, except for the cleft in his chin and his thicker glasses, his resemblance to his father was remarkable.

"I bet ya don't have one record with the labels I got. Ever heard of the Chess label?"

"No. I'm afraid that I don't notice labels. Sorry."

"Ya never heard of Imperial?"

"Sorry."

"Atlantic? Specialty? How about Decca, Dot, or RCA?"

"Yes. I recognize those."

"Figures." He eyed me scornfully. I returned his look.

His unorthodox dancing position bothered me. He held his hand too firmly against my waist, pulling me close to his chest, uncomfortably reminding me of how Archie had held me. I tried to wiggle myself into a looser position, looking down at his feet to get the hang of his technique and prevent them from stepping on mine.

"Relax, will ya? I ain't gonna bite ya."

"You bet you're not. So how do you like Amherst High?"

"It stinks," he said flatly.

"You're kidding me, aren't you? Amherst is the best high school in western New York."

"Huh? Where'd ya git that idea? Boy, have they got yous kids hoodwinked. Compared to Kensington, this school's nothin' but a bore. The teachers are dumb as sh … They're stupid. They think they're hot shots, but they can't teach nothin'."

"Oh, I can tell by the way you talk that the teachers at Kensington have done a great job teaching you."

"I talk the way I wanna talk. Somethin' botherin' ya about it? Yous ain't understandin' what I'm sayin'?"

"Oh, I understand *yous* all right." The music stopped. "Excuse me," I said coolly. "I need to talk to Susie."

I was fuming when I reached her. "If I look annoyed, Susie, I am. I've had enough of that PK. I wish Pastor French hadn't asked me to be nice to him. He's horrid. No manners at all."

"Oh, he's not all that bad, Sandy, He's just not the sort of guy you're used to. Sally thinks he's cute. Her mother invites him over to their house for dinner."

"It takes all kinds," I shrugged.

"Sandy," she laughed, "you hardly know him. He's really quite smart." I didn't say what I was thinking, that Sue couldn't tell a smart person from a dumb one to save her soul. Instead, I asked her to tell me where she got that impression.

"He's writing poetry. I don't know any other boy who can do that. He asked me to type out his poems for him. He's also writing a book about his old friends at Kensington."

"Well, Susie, I'd appreciate it if you would tell me what you think of Pete's poetry when you're done typing it," I said, doubting that she would detect my sarcasm. Later as I was picking up my jacket in the church cloakroom, I asked Sally to make sure that Pete got his precious record collection back in perfect condition.

The next day in English class, Archie nearly drove me nuts. Why did he have to stare at me with his big, pitiful, contrite eyes? I lingered until everyone else had dribbled out of class and then virtually begged Mrs. Meese to change my seat again. I told her that the glare from the window bothered my eyes.

"Miss Schall, I shall not have enough seats to satisfy your sensitive eyes. I don't believe it's the glare from the window or proximity to the blackboard that's been bothering you. The only way to solve your problem is to sit you with the windows on one side of you and three girls surrounding you." I nodded gratefully.

"This is the last alteration of the seating arrangement that I intend to make on your behalf. I'm only doing it to avoid a Trojan War. Do you understand?"

"I can't thank you enough. Your literary allusion is a bit hyperbolic, however. I may have a knack for stirring up a little boy trouble, but not for launching a thousand ships."

"Just get out of here now, and behave yourself," she chuckled.

"Yes, ma'am," I said, smiling brightly.

Mrs. Meese was my favorite teacher. That irritating PK would change his tune and revise his unjust criticisms of Amherst teachers if he had heard how sympathetic Mrs. Meese had just been to me. On second thought, he probably wouldn't be able to grasp anything that Mrs. Meese and I had just said to each other. The idiot had probably never heard of *The Iliad*.

Mother was waiting for me when I walked in the door.

"Mrs. Montgomery and I just talked on the phone," she announced solemnly. "She's worried about Archibalt."

"Why? I saw him in English today. He looked a bit sad, but he'll get over it."

"She tells me that he's very depressed about how you've been treating him, and he really wants to apologize to you. As your father and I suspected, he didn't understand the rules of proper … dating in America, that is. He's sorry that he upset you, Sandy, and he's asking for another chance. Mrs. Montgomery will call back this evening. She wants to speak to you directly."

"Oh, no! I don't want to talk to her. Do I have to? Why is she interfering with my life? Why doesn't she mind her own business?"

"This *is* her business. How many times do we have to tell you that? She feels responsible for Archie's happiness while he's under her care. She's only thinking of the poor boy. Your father and I agree with her. You're being stubborn, selfish, and overly harsh on Archie. This self-centered behavior of yours has to change."

"What good would it do for me to pretend to like him, Mother? He's going back to Germany, isn't he? Please try to see things from my point of view. Archie should be dating other American girls, shouldn't he? Maybe I taught him how to behave correctly, or at least what not to do. With me anyway. Oh, I don't know. Now I feel awful! I don't want to talk about what Archie did to me, not to a lady I don't even know. It would be so embarrassing. Didn't you explain it all to her?"

"She's a very influential woman in town, Sandy. I didn't want to offend her."

"I wouldn't know how to tell her why Archie offended me without risking offending her either. Please understand me, Mother. I can't do this."

"You're being willful and self-centered. I'm disappointed in you. So is your father."

I began to tear up. I hated disappointing my parents. I turned away and walked toward my bedroom.

"Where are you going, young lady?"

"Mother, I know I mustn't fight with you. I'm sorry that this whole mess ever got started. Leave me alone for awhile now, please?"

"Well, you're going to have to talk to Mrs. Montgomery. I promised her that I'd persuade you to listen to Archie's side of this matter."

I wanted to say to her that it might have been considerate if she had consulted me first. But I knew that she would never see things from my point of view. She was my mother, and mothers were always right, even if mine was willing to sacrifice her first-born daughter's self-respect to maintain her own social status.

That evening, Mrs. Montgomery telephoned. I was polite and respectful, but resolute.

"I promise you, Mrs. Montgomery, that I shall be nice to Archibalt and talk to him in school. But I feel that it would be best for his happiness if he were to date other girls. An exchange student should become acquainted with several kids, boys and girls."

Although I was tempted to do so, I didn't tell her that I suspected that one of Archie's problems was that he drank too much beer. I didn't want to get him into trouble. Anyway, who was I to preach about the evils of drinking too much? I just wanted to get Archie out of my hair. Before she hung up, I told Mrs. Montgomery that I was sorry that Archie and I had a falling out, and that maybe I'd date him again before he went back to Germany. She told me she would convey this to Archibalt, but she hung up on me with an abruptness that indicated displeasure and made me feel dissatisfied with how I had handled the situation. I went over our conversation in my mind and concluded that I had not been disrespectful, but I hadn't been tactful either. I should have thought of some white lie that would compliment her and Archie and make me seem more contrite. But I couldn't even tell a white lie without worrying about it.

I wanted to whack my brain with a hammer, straighten my life out, and think about my future. I had already laid down most of the groundwork by deciding between an art career and teaching. My parents argued strongly against going into an art-related profession, because they feared I'd end up "working with a bunch of faggots," as Dad put it. They warned me I'd end up living like a beatnik in a bohemian loft, doing abstract paintings like those in the Albright. My art teacher at Amherst told me that to establish a decent art career in advertising or design I'd need to go to art school in New York City, and I'd probably end up working there too. I knew I'd never be happy there. So I ended up facing the three options open to most career-orientated young women before the sexual revolution: secretary, teacher, or nurse. Teaching clearly was my best choice, elementary school teaching in particular. Hadn't I been teaching children all my life: younger siblings, YMCA campers, the kids in Sunday school?

I decided to major in English literature at Gettysburg.

Reading and writing were what I did best. I liked to analyze why the characters in books acted the way they did, and I wanted to achieve a deeper understanding of psychological motivation, so I planned to pursue two minors: psychology and elementary school education. Yes, that's what I wanted to do; I felt ready for college. All I had left to do at ACHS was maintain good grades and wrap up all my extracurricular obligations. At church, I'd complete my tenure as president of the Luther League with as little annoyance as possible. I would put my personal affairs in order, mind my parents, and date only occasionally and wisely.

Ken Skiller seemed like a guy who would be safe for me to date. I had become acquainted with him during our discussions while working together in chemistry lab. He missed his literary crowd back in Connecticut. He said they were into the beat movement. I told him, quite frankly, that everything I had heard about beatniks sounded weird. He conceded that many people didn't consider beatniks respectable, because they were unconventional and critical of middle-class life and values.

"It sounds like a literary version of abstract art to me, Ken. I don't like abstract art."

"Now don't judge too hastily, Sandy. Have you ever been to a beat poetry reading?"

"You've got to be kidding."

"Would you let me take you to one?"

"I'll have to think about it."

I put him off because I wanted to further vet his qualifications. He gave me the impression that his parents were Democrats, which was slightly worrisome. But Barb's mom was a Democrat, and I hadn't caught anything scary from her. I told Mom and Dad that I had made friends with a new boy in my English class, a polite redhead who was just a nice guy. Mom said she didn't like red hair, but Dad didn't seem to care. I don't think he saw Ken as a threat.

On Sunday evenings, I never felt up to facing the Luther League, and I certainly wasn't keen about having to organize plans for visiting the orphanage in November. When I asked the group for ideas, I got nothing but blank stares until, surprisingly, Neal Adolf raised his hand.

"We could host a dance for them, sort of like our socials here."

"What a good idea. Maybe we could provide entertainment for them too."

"Joyce and I could lip sync to a record," Susie suggested. "'Sisters' from *White Christmas* is a good song for two girls. Joyce and I have been doing it just for fun."

When Neal asked me to do a number with him, I suggested "Anything You Can Do, I Can Do Better" from the old movie *Annie Get Your Gun*. I could do the Betty Hutton part, and he'd be Howard Keel. It could be fun, and the costumes would be easy. I'd dig up some stuff we had around the house from the days when we played cowboys and Indians.

The PK sat in the dark in the back of the room, hunched over in his chair with his arms folded as usual, observing what was going on with his now all too familiar frown. I ignored him as long as I could, until my pledge to the pastor moved me to ask him to help choose the dance music for the party. He unfolded his body out of his chair, stood up, and walked forward. I stepped back surprised.

"Yer big show needs an emcee, Prez. I s'pose I could do that."

Caught off guard, I didn't know how to respond. "Sure, I guess that would be fine. Uh, do you think you … uh—"

"If ya don't want my help, fergit it." He shrugged, plopping heavily into a seat in the front row, arms folded.

"No, no. It's a good idea. We'll need an emcee. You just took me by surprise."

"Heh. That ain't hard."

"Well, thanks for volunteering anyway. I welcome good ideas."

"Ya need 'em, that's fer sure."

I said nothing. I just shot the look at him that Mike called my "evil eye." Soberly, I adjourned the meeting and reminded everyone to stick around. Pete was ready with more of his prized records. I danced a couple of dances with Neal and Mark, and then one of the girls suggested a lady's choice. I asked a younger boy named John to dance with me, and Sally Marsh pulled Pete up out of his chair. Neal and I danced another dance, but Pete cut in. This was the second time he had done that to Neal. I found it obnoxious.

He grabbed one of my hands and arranged us into his unorthodox dancing position.

"How's ol' lady Meese's pet?"

"Must you always be so abrasive? We've been sharing book reviews. Does that interest you?"

"What books ya talkin' about?"

"Do you care? *The Scarlet Letter*, Homer's *Iliad* and *Odyssey*, some Shakespeare plays, *Jane Eyre*, and other classics. She gave us a list of twenty books and plays to read last summer. We had to read five; I read seven. Sharing summaries helps us know where to look for literary allusions to write in essays."

I knew he had no idea what I was talking about.

"Sounds like cheatin' to me. Why don't ya just make the allusions up? Fer Christ's sake, ol' ... Why ya frownin'? I say somethin' wrong?"

"What would make you ask that? I always take the Lord's name in vain too."

"The lady does sarcasm. As I was sayin', ol' lady Meese won't be able to understand yer literary allusions, not without lookin' stuff up. She's such a phony. Did ya like the *Iliad*?"

"Mrs. Meese knows a good deal, and she's a dedicated teacher. What, if anything, do you know about the *Iliad* anyway? You probably read a comic book version of it, right?"

"Ya think I'm dumb er somethin'?"

"I think you're crude and rude, if you must know. What, pray tell, if you can, is your opinion of the *Iliad*?"

"It's okay." He seemed amused, although I didn't have the faintest idea why. "War epics have their place. Wars are dumb; Homer got that right. Paris is a real prick. He stirs up a big mess over some broad and then gits saved by a goddess because he's a pretty boy and the ladies and goddesses dig him. Achilles goes off to his tent and pouts like a spoiled brat. His buddy Patroclus gits killed 'stead of him because he puts on Achilles' armor. Achilles then kills Hector an' drags him around in his chariot. All the time the gods keep gittin' their two cents in. Lots a good fights, but a sad ending. Do girls like that sort a book?"

"Well, I didn't, but I needed to know about it. If you did manage to wade your way though it all, maybe you liked it better than I did. I liked *Jane Eyre*, but my favorite of the all books that I've read so far is *Pride and Prejudice*."

"Yeah. Austen's a good writer. She wasn't prolific; poor gal died too soon. Jus' six books. What'd ya think of *Northanger Abbey*?"

"Uh, I haven't read that one yet."

"Oh? Ain't ya in the hot shots' English class?"

I didn't want to give him the satisfaction of knowing he was confusing me. Had I just heard him use the word "prolific"? I was glad when the record stopped. When I asked him to excuse me, he laughed and said, "My pleasure, Meese's Pet." As I walked over to the refreshment table, I tried to recall the whole convoluted plot of Homer's war epic. Pete had certainly oversimplified it. Had he gotten it right? I wanted to check. His superior attitude was as repulsive as his sneering, slumping posture, poor grammar, and greasy mannerisms.

Sue, who appeared to have been trying to hear us from across the room, pulled me aside.

"Remember when I told you I was doing some typing for Pete?"

I had forgotten, but I didn't say so. "What have you learned?"

"Sandy, I'm shocked by the stories and poems he writes. Either he has a very good imagination, or he knows a lot more about life than someone his age ought to."

"What do you mean?"

"I think he drinks. And he runs around with nasty kids."

"Nasty kids? Are you talking about other greasers like him?"

"Oh, I'm probably just worrying about nothing. His stories could be make-believe, couldn't they? I don't want to start rumors about something I don't understand. You could figure it out better than I can. Tell you what. I'll keep the carbon copies and show them to you, okay?"

I agreed just to please Susie.

## Chapter 14
## You Don't Owe Me a Thing

Ken Skiller picked me up at eight in his mom's car and drove me to The Hideaway, a small, dimly lit coffee shop at the end of an obscure alley off Main Street. We sat at a small table in the back, and Ken asked me if I trusted him to place a dessert order.

"No marijuana in the fudge?"

"Cross my heart." His blue eyes laughed. While waiting for the entertainment, we had ice cream sundaes and hot herbal tea. Many of the people filling up the tiny tables in front of us looked like the bohemians I had seen in a magazine article: men in black berets and rumpled dark turtlenecks with tiny goatees on their chins, long-haired women in short skirts and black leotards. Finally, two guys casually sidled over to the empty stools on a raised platform, sat down, and began reciting verses. The audience listened in rapt silence, apparently engrossed in every word. When the poets concluded their performance, the people around us began to discuss the work. Ken asked me what I thought, and I plied him with questions.

"Those poems were ... strange. What's the origin of the term 'beat movement'?"

"Originally it had something to do with circus carnies; you know, nomadic types, gypsies, people who feel beaten down by the world? Of course, it had a connection to the drug world too. Feeling beat meant something like feeling cheated or robbed by drug dealers or maybe by the drugs themselves. Jack Kerouac and other members of the movement seem to feel that life just keeps beating them down until they reach a level of mystical truth."

"Um, truth encompasses a good deal, I guess. Obviously I know nothing about this. The drug world is not somewhere I'd want to visit. But I'm interested in this literary movement. I must admit that I'm having difficulty interpreting a lot of this poetry; the poetry of, who was it? Cosco? For instance."

"Gregory Corso." He corrected me gently.

"Thanks. It's difficult for me to interpret what Corso means by 'leopard apples,' 'cypress skeins,' and such. Cypress trees are symbols of death, I know that much. Some of these poems are rather morbid, I guess?"

"All serious writers think about the fleeting nature of life, don't they, Sandy?"

"My English teachers have pointed that out. My father, however, says it's better to think about the cheerful side of life."

"Do you agree with him?"

"Well, I certainly would prefer to. But, unfortunately, death is a part of life. My church teaches me that I need to accept the truth of death in order to grow in spirit."

"Fair enough. Death is difficult for anyone to think about. Beat poetry has other themes, however. Surely you share the concern about all living things that runs through much of beat poetry?"

"Oh, I agree with that. I'm ashamed to admit that I haven't been good to Mother Nature. I've killed too many butterflies and whatever they call the snail-like things that create seashells. Now I pick up only empty shells and leave butterflies alone."

"I'm afraid the world will miss many natural treasures before long. It's not your fault, Sandy. Everyone has committed crimes against Mother Nature. But sooner or later, we'll have to stop doing it or we'll destroy the whole planet."

Ken sounded wise beyond his years. I found him comfortable to talk to, and as we left the coffeehouse, I caught myself hoping that he'd ask me out again.

I had to shout at him when he took me to my door. King was exceptionally loud that night. "Thank you, Ken. You've been a good teacher tonight. I'm sorry I missed the marijuana fudge though."

He laughed. "I hope you'll go out with me again, Sandy. And soon."

The following Friday afternoon, while I was at my locker exchanging some school supplies, I sensed that someone was watching me. I spun around; it was Pete French. Checking anxiously to make sure that no one I knew noticed him there, I said coolly, "Pete, I'm surprised to see you around here."

"Ain't no sin ta walk the halls here, right? Like me ta carry yer books 'n stuff?"

"What?"

"Wha'sa matter? Don't guys carry books for gals in this dump? Com'mon, gimme me yer stuff. Where's yer next class?"

My mind went blank. I didn't want to be seen with him, especially if he were carrying my things. "Uh, to my art class. Up a flight." At least it was away from the regular flow of my classmates.

I gave him my sketchpad, notebook, a set of pastels, and a heavy history book. "Did you want to talk to me about the party at the orphanage?"

"Nope."

"Excuse me! If you have nothing to say, I've got a question. Are you ready for the orphans' party?"

"Ain't nothin' fer me ta do. You and Nealsie boy got yer act together?"

"We're practicing our number on Saturday night at my house. Whatever we come up with will be good enough."

"Ya think orphans are that hard up, huh? Maybe some a 'em got real taste. They may be a hellava lot more perceptive than ya give 'em credit fer. I s'pose ya think you're so much better'n them?"

"Don't swear. Why do you always say such revolting things? Here. This is my art room. Please give me back my book and supplies."

He shrugged and disappeared down the hall.

Pete arrived late for the next Luther League meeting. He sidled in during the social period. I was dancing with Mark Hecker, and he cut in on the poor kid, startling me as well as Mark. I hadn't noticed him come in.

"Did you forget what time Luther League starts?" I asked him archly.

"Nope. I wouldn't a showed up all, if I didn't need the dough. Can't let the ol' man cut off my allowance."

"If I tell him how late you came in, will he dock your pay?"

"That'd be sweet, sweetie."

"Don't call me that."

"Right. Yer no sweetie, that's fer sure. Anyways, not that it's any of yer business, but I just got off work at the A&P."

"You work on Sunday nights?"

"My job is to stock the shelves," he shrugged. "They need ta git ready fer Monday. Trucks come in on weekends, and somebody has ta unload the junk, take it into the stockrooms, and put the older crap out on the shelves. That's business, baby."

"Don't call me baby again, or I'll stop dancing with you."

"Bloodcurdlin' threat, baby."

"Well, it's a good thing we had extra records stored here. Obviously, I can't count on you."

"Ya want me ta call ya when I gotta be late?" Luckily, the song ended, and I escaped into the arms of Neal. Pete danced with Sally. It puzzled me to see them laughing. I didn't think Pete ever laughed. Later, somehow, I ended up dancing with him again; this time to Elvis's "Hard Headed Woman."

"You're going to be sorry that you missed the meeting tonight," I said smugly.

"Yeah? Why?" He looked worried. "I told ya I don't need ta prepare for the orphan gig."

"We made plans for December. The league is going to take part in a Christmas play for the spiritual gratification of the whole congregation."

"Spiritual gratification? Ooee! Wha's that got to do wit me?"

"I assigned you a role."

"Shit! Ya can't do that without askin' me first."

"I'll pretend I didn't hear you. Don't *ever* use that word here again. I forbid you to use it."

"Oooooh, sorry, baby."

"Please try to be more civil and careful about what you say here, okay? There are impressionable younger kids around. You're the pastor's son. You have to participate in our projects and do it nicely, like it or not."

"Heh. It's his reputation he's worried about, not me. How would it look if the pastor's kid wasn't showin' up? So what's this puke about a play?"

"Puke is an ugly word. No decent person would use it to describe a church event," I said, feeling like a third grade teacher scolding a naughty boy. "Choose your vocabulary more carefully, Pete. I mean it."

"Like I said before, yer somethin' else," he said, grinning obnoxiously.

I sighed. "I suppose I'll have to reiterate to you what I told the others at the meeting." He looked around the room: the panther was seeking a pathway for escape.

"Listen to me now, will you?" He scowled at me reproachfully. "We're doing a play with the choir, a musical pageant. It's called *No Room at the Inn,* and it's the story of Mary, Joseph, and the baby Jesus. The choir sings Christmas carols, and—"

"Yeah, yeah. I know all this crap. Git to the point, will ya? What'd ya hook me inta?"

"You will be the last of the three magi to come down the

aisle, because you're the tallest. You'll carry a gift of myrrh for the baby Jesus."

"Fuck!" He snapped his fingers and appeared genuinely chagrined. "I have to work then. Sorry. Guess you'll have to find another wise guy."

"Will you *please* keep your voice down?" The music had stopped, but I needed to finish chastising him. "You mustn't say that despicable word here. Never again! I mean it, Pete. Your language is atrocious. I ought to submit an official request to your father on behalf of the whole league to teach you to talk decently."

"What's buggin' ya now?" he shrugged and raised his hands, palms up. "I didn't say shi … the forbidden word. What'd I say that I shouldn't a?"

He wasn't going to trick me into repeating it. I just snarled at him. "We never, ever use the 'F' word here, or anywhere, for that matter. And another thing; I didn't tell you when the play is going to be held. So how do you know you'll be busy then?"

"Whenever it is, I'm busy."

"You're lying. That's a sin."

"Good call, baby."

"I'm holding all the cards now, big shot. I bet you'll agree to play the role in the pageant if I threaten to tell your father how you've been upsetting the other kids in the league. He'll take away your allowance if I do, won't he?"

"Ya would do that, wouldn't ya? That's extortion, Goody Two-Shoes."

I didn't understand what he said; I imagine my face showed it.

"It's a term attributed to Oliver Goldsmith. Ya know? The Irish playwright? Ring any bells, sweetie? It means too good to be true or somethin' like that. Extortion is—"

"Don't change the subject," I growled, cutting him off. "You'll be one of the wise men, like it or not, and you'll be at the rehearsal at your house on the first Saturday in December. Your sister invited us there."

"Saturday? Yer goin' ta ruin my Saturday? Judy would do that to me."

"Judy's an angel. In fact, she'll be an angel in our pageant."

"Geez. That's perfect." He shook his head. "I'm a wise guy, and she's an angel. I bet ya gave yerself the Mary gig, didn't ya?"

I reddened, and he proclaimed triumphantly, "I knew it! An' I suppose sissy Nealsie boy is Joseph? The two a ya make a perfect pair."

The others were all listening to us, so I moved away from Pete and announced that it was time to go. But I couldn't resist taking one parting jab. "We have a policy of mutual respect here like good Christians. You should try it."

"Right, baby," he laughed. He turned to Neal as he strode out of the parish hall, and I heard him say, "Women. They make ya say the damndest things. No offense, okay, man?"

On the following Saturday, Neal and I briefly rehearsed our number in my basement. I made some excuse about needing to go somewhere else, so he wouldn't linger. On Sunday evening, everyone gathered at the church. Chaperones and kids old enough to drive at night parked in the lot to wait for passengers to take to the orphanage. The stars poked through the darkening scrim overhead, and beams from car lights lit up the rendezvous area. Neal drove his sedan into the lot and parked it parallel to mine. Kids getting dropped off by parents carried refreshments, props, and costumes into waiting cars.

A loud squeal of brakes interrupted my attempt to take a headcount. I looked around for the source of the racket and spotted Pete in a black leather jacket behind the wheel of the most outlandish car I had ever seen. It was a blue Ford convertible with its top down. Undulating waves of yellow flames outlined in orange red were painted on its sides. Sally and Joyce, wearing headscarves tied under their necks, sat in the front next to Pete. Judy and Mark were in the back, scrunched down into their coats.

He aimed his car at mine and stopped it with another chalkboard nail screech, just as I was about to scream at him to put on his brakes before he hit us.

"What is *that?*" I asked incredulously, pointing to his garish vehicle.

"A '53 Ford. Don't ya know yer cars?"

"It doesn't look like any automobile I've ever seen. Why is it painted that way?"

"She's cool, ain't she? Her hood's got flames too. Come on, admit she's cool."

'It certainly is ... different."

"Yeah. Different is cool, right, girls?"

Sally and Joyce giggled.

"How many more ya got comin'?" he asked. "Ya need me ta take anyone else?"

I wondered if I would be responsible for anyone's death if he cracked up that flaming automobile, but I said nothing. I counted heads again. Two kids were still missing, but another car pulled up and dropped Tommy and Johnny off. I told the only kid in my back seat to open up a back door for them before Pete could scoop one of them up. With me at the wheel, they'd be safe.

When we arrived at the main building of the orphanage, leaguers began unloading their paraphernalia and carrying it into a small gymnasium. Two low bleachers were set up along one side of the gym floor. We piled our coats on a back table and set bottles of pop and plates of cookies and cupcakes on a long table beside the open area set aside for entertainment and dancing. Soon the orphans filed in, herded by two solemn, hatchet-faced women.

The orphans looked pitiful, dressed in old cast-off clothing that somebody had donated to them. Most of them had blank faces and dull eyes; a few walked with slow, uncoordinated movements. Some of the older boys greased their hair back, attempting to make DAs, I supposed. The older boys didn't acknowledge us, but a few of the younger children greeted us with shy smiles.

Pete strode onto the floor dressed all in black, the collar of his long-sleeve shirt turned up, his hair greased back into a DA, as usual. "Ready, Prez?"

"Ready as I'll ever be," I said uncertainly, mumbling a prayer to myself.

Pete glided confidently out to the center, in front of the stands full of seated orphans. In a loud, clear voice, he said, "Hi, kids! Ready for some fun?"

The younger orphans gave a resounding, "Yes!" The older ones sat silently, looking defiant. Pete introduced the first act, flinging out his atrocious grammar with gusto. It was a lip sync by Joyce and Susie, dressed in ruffled pink party dresses. The pantomime was overly sugary, I thought. When they finished, Pete took each girl by a hand and said, "Well done, girls. How about a big hand for the ladies in pink?" The younger orphans clapped; the older ones sat sullenly, still unresponsive.

"Com'mon. Ya can do better'an that," Pete bellowed. "Give the girls a hand, guys!" This time everyone clapped, and the two girls curtsied.

Neal and I donned our cowboy hats and did our number. We were a handsome couple, I thought, even if our style lacked polish. Responding to the enthusiasm of the forceful emcee, everyone clapped for us. The next performer was Mark, who surprised me with an amazing display of dexterity with two Hula-hoops. Pete turned and winked at me during the act and whispered, "I discovered a talent ya didn't know about, right, Prez?"

I mumbled, "Chalk one up for you."

When the show was over, Pete urged the orphans to climb down from the bleachers and enjoy the "delicious refreshments," insisting they had to earn them by dancing. As I watched them descending awkwardly from the bleachers I wished this part was over too. It didn't look like anyone wanted to dance, but Pete didn't seem to notice. "Okay, everybody take hands and make a circle," he commanded. The older orphan boys groaned.

"Whatsa matter, boys? Com'mon! Help me keep the littler kiddies happy. Find yerself a pretty little lady and take her hand.

We're gonna do some Hokey Pokey. Whatsa matter? Ya ain't scared, are ya? Just follow my lead." He grabbed the hand of one of the girls from the orphanage.

The boys stepped up to Pete's challenge, and each of them grabbed a girl's hand. Soon all the leaguers and orphans had formed a big circle. Pete said, "Ya know the drill, right, everybody? Ya put yer right foot in and take it out, like this." He demonstrated with jerky movements. "Just follow me. Sally, help me show 'em how, okay?"

Sally smiled up at him. She looked pretty with her curly, dark hair held back by a red hair band and her cheeks blushed by her shyness. She began to sing along with Pete. Although he seemed amazingly gung-ho, he needed her sweet voice to cover his uncertain notes. Soon every kid in the orphanage moved herself or himself around with little concern for what anyone else chose to do. The younger orphans laughed and wiggled; the older boys attempted to outdo each other with outlandish movements. By the time the dance had ended, everyone was active, and most kids were laughing.

After a short time-out for refreshments, Pete announced a mixer: no one could dance with anyone he or she knew. It was a fast tune, Little Richard's "Long Tall Sally," which sustained the excitement generated by the Hokey Pokey. I danced with an orphan boy who smiled shyly at me. I returned his smile weakly, making a valiant effort not to wrinkle my nose. He had a sour odor. Once when the floor became almost deserted, I saw Pete huddle with Tommy and Sally. They organized a Bunny Hop line, which drew everyone back onto the floor. Next Pete announced a lady's choice. Uncertainly, girls from the orphanage asked boys from the league to dance. Feeling obliged to compliment him on his job as emcee, I invited Pete to dance with me.

He frowned and shook his head. "You don't owe me a thing. We're here for the orphans, ain't we? Go ask one a them fer a dance."

It felt like a slap in my face. He had deftly managed to be rude and right at the same time, and I couldn't think of a comeback. I turned my back on him and went over to ask an orphan boy to dance.

Pete announced the last dance at the exact time that I had told him the director of the orphanage wanted the party to end. I was looking around for a partner when he said, "How about it, Prez? Wanna dance?"

"Go ask an orphan girl," I snapped.

"Don't be stupid," he growled and grabbed my wrist tightly to lead me into the crowd of dancers.

We danced to Sinatra's "Learnin' the Blues" in silence. I pulled as far away from his body as his tight grip on me would allow. "Don't be so dumb, Sandy," he said, softly. "You know I was right, don't ya?"

"Well, you did a good job tonight. On behalf of the Luther League, I wish to thank you."

"Sure," he grunted. "Thanks fer the dance." He released me before the music was over and walked toward the table, where he began to pile up the empty serving platters belonging to members of the league. I supervised the loading of the cars.

## Chapter 15
## SMOKE GETS IN YOUR EYES

*Young Aunt Tanta*

"Did the orphans enjoy their party?" Dad asked me when I walked into the living room, exhausted. I plopped onto the couch and lit up a cigarette.

"I think so. They're such a sad bunch of ragamuffins that we cheered them up. Our show wasn't great, but they seemed to like it." I shrugged. "They ate up all the food, and Pete did a good job of getting them to dance. He turned out to be a lively emcee, but I found him personally offensive—discourteous and uncivil toward me like he always is."

"He wasn't rude to the orphans?" Mom sounded surprised.

"Oh no, he was nice to them. I think he likes *them*. He just hates me. I don't think he likes many of the leaguers either, except the sweetest girls like Sally Marsh, who doesn't go to Amherst. He was dressed all in black again. Why is he always in black? He's such a greaser. He can't seem to open his mouth without offending me with his outrageously ignorant way of speaking. Is he really that dumb? How did a man as kind and well-spoken as Pastor French end up with such a jerk for a son?"

"Most people start out good, but when life tosses them a few hard blows, they can turn mean." Dad took a sip of his beer. "Boys who get involved in sports vent their steam under the rules of the games. Maybe Ernie's not interested in sports himself, so he doesn't realize how they build a boy's character. Ernie has a lot to cope with anyway: the work involved in starting at a new position, as well as his synod duties and other stuff. I imagine it's hard for him to find time to be with his kids."

"I don't see how that explains Pete's generally antisocial behavior or his bad grammar," I sighed, blowing out soothing rings of smoke. "If Pastor French is too busy, why doesn't his mother give Pete more guidance? She's his grandmother, but I suppose Pete's too unruly for her to handle. Why did Judy and Pete's mother have to die anyway? Kids need their own mothers. It doesn't make any sense to me. Why does God let people die so young?"

"Maybe she didn't want to live any longer," Dad said, savoring an ample sip of beer.

"What? Dad, do you really believe a young mother would want to get cancer?"

My father pursed his lips and looked at me in that paternalistic way that caused me to brace myself. "There are many mysteries in life, Sandy," he said. "Who knows what was going on in that woman's head? Just remember that everything always works out for the best. When you've lived as long as I have, you'll understand that there is a good reason for everything. Now you look tired; it's time you turned in." I scurried off to my bedroom.

But I couldn't sleep. Did Dad actually believe what he had just said about Pastor's first wife *wanting* to get cancer and die? It never occurred to me that it might have been his beer talking. As far as I knew, all adults drank as much as Mom and Dad did. Every adult in our neighborhood drank beer, even Dr. Irwin did; but none of them acted crazy like the alcoholics did in the movies, so I had no reason to suspect that my parents had the disease. In fact, it was not until decades later, after Mother had nearly died from a terrible bout with what may have been alcoholic hepatitis, that a doctor finally diagnosed both my parents as alcoholics.

They were senior citizens living in Florida then, and a battery of medical tests revealed that if they didn't give up smoking and liquor, they'd die before their friends did. That diagnosis did the trick; they both went cold turkey on booze and cigarettes. I didn't witness what the pair of them went through to accomplish that daunting feat, but they had professional help. The fact that they valued their lives must have been their main motivation. They had always valued life. That's why I attributed Dad's mind-boggling suggestion that the pastor's late wife wanted to get cancer to his lack of education. He had never analyzed the life-and-death conflicts, the "to be or not to be's" that classical authors wrote about. He and Mom had survived the Great Depression and the war years, and they wanted to believe that everyone was able to do the same. Who wouldn't prefer life to be that way? But, through no fault of her own, Pete's mother had died, and I couldn't accept Dad's explanation.

The next week we had only three days of school due to Thanksgiving holiday. It was up to Mother and me to prepare the turkey feast for the six of us, along with my grandparents and Tanta. The process involved defrosting the big bird, cooking the giblets and chopping up stuffing ingredients. We mixed the stuffing, stuffed the bird's cold cavities, and basted and baked the thing until a rich aroma permeated the house and caused every stomach to growl.

On Thanksgiving Day, Tanta sat down beside me when I took a break from meal preparations to have a smoke. I told her what was going on at school. She wanted to hear about my boyfriends, so I described Ken and our date at the coffeehouse. It intrigued her; she pumped me for details. As I talked, I studied the red garnet ring on my left hand that she had given to me for my sixteenth birthday. She noticed me doing this and told me that she had another ring stowed in a safe that had two matching perfect diamonds. She said one of the diamonds was for me, and the other was for Pat. "You're so popular with the boys, Sandy," she said. "Some boy may need one of my diamonds to have an engagement ring made for you before you know it."

"Thanks for the thought, Tanta. But your garnet is more than sufficient for the ring finger of my left hand, at least for a long time to come."

"We'll see about that, young beauty," she laughed heartily.

"Tanta, I mean it!"

That weekend I made my Christmas shopping list, leaving blanks for people I wasn't sure about, mainly Dad, Mike, and Jerry. It was never easy for me to come up with ideas for presents for males. I arranged the decorations for the living room and drew a crèche scene in ink on tinfoil to hang over the mantel. I felt relieved to have those chores done early, because December was shaping up to be extraordinarily busy. I still had two long-term class assignments to finish, and I needed to set up committees and get started on the scenery for *Show Boat*. My social calendar was filling up too. Ken Skiller invited me to the senior ball, scheduled for a Saturday evening in mid-December. Mom drove me to a small formal dress shop where we found a green taffeta gown with a puffed hemline that would be perfect for a holiday ball. Its clear, rhinestone spaghetti straps matched my rhinestone tiara and my clip-on earrings.

Although I would have preferred it to be otherwise, Luther

League events were on my mind too. As church membership grew, the league grew, and to my chagrin, some highly motivated new members wanted to plan more social events. A motion was offered in favor of a New Year's Eve dance party in the basement parish hall with a fifty-cent-per-person admission fee that would add to the treasury funds. I had hoped for a more exciting New Year's Eve invitation, perhaps from Ken, so I argued against the dance party, but the motion passed. I assigned the planning of the affair to Pete, who didn't appear any more thrilled about the dance than I was, not that he ever appeared to be thrilled about anything. He accepted the assignment with his now all too familiar shrug of resignation.

Thankfully I had only a couple of lines to learn for the pageant. My main job was just to lean on Joseph while we walked together down the aisle of the nave, acting like a pregnant Mary searching for somewhere to give birth to the baby Jesus. One of my lines was to ask the innkeeper if he had a place for me, the other was to repeat "thank you" three times to each of the wise men. To prepare my costume, I bought a few yards of shiny, light blue satin and then utilized the skill I learned in home economics class at Amherst to sew a simple T-shaped, floor-length dress on Mom's Singer and hem the edges of a matching head drape.

The rehearsal at the parsonage started out badly. All but one of the cast members gathered in the pastor's unfinished basement, which was sparsely furnished and had enough room to partly replicate the chancel and nave of the church. Although they had read the script, many kids seemed confused. They asked me what to do and where to stand. I wasn't sure; I had never directed a pageant before. Thoroughly flummoxed, I botched up the initial reading, trying unsuccessfully to get the kids to say their lines correctly and pose believably. I couldn't figure out exactly how or where they were supposed to pose. I was engrossed in this overwhelming task when the missing cast member's loafers clinked down the top of the cellar steps. I heard him coming, but I was so annoyed that he was late again that I didn't urge him to come down any faster. He stopped in place, apparently listening in. Finally, he bounced down the rest of the stairs with a cynical grin on his annoying face.

"Yous guys sure are makin' a mess a this thing," he chided with a snicker, interrupting my attempt to get a young angel with an unruly disposition to look angelic.

"I suppose the late wise man can do better?" I snapped.

"It wouldn't take much. Ya don't get it, do ya? It's not Shakespeare fer Christ's sake. This is the same damn dumb story I've had to do hundreds a times in my ol' man's churches. The lines are easy. Ya just have to work on yer positioning. Susie, yer the angel that does the announcement, ain't ya? Yer mommy's making ya wings, right?"

"I'm making them myself."

"Whatever. This Mickey Mouse church crowd'll git it when ya git yer wings on. Just stand over here, raise your arms, and say yer two lines as if you mean 'em. Sandy, kneel over here and looked blessedly humble. For you it'll be hard, but just do it."

I glowered at him. But under his ruthless direction, the pageant came together quickly. After we had done it once with only a few mistakes, Pete ordered everyone to take a fifteen-minute break. "Refuel yerselves upstairs. Grammy baked cookies, and there's cans a pop on ice in a bucket. Then we'll do it again. After that, all a ya can take a split."

Resenting his success at giving the cast, including me, direction, I darted upstairs, grabbed my coat and snuck outside to have a cigarette. I sat on the cold cement steps of the door to the backyard and enjoyed my smoke. But my peace was soon unpleasantly interrupted.

"Ladies don't smoke," he said gruffly, sitting down beside me.

"Oh, right. What am I then?"

"Ya ain't no lady."

"A lot of boys disagree with you there, Pete." I blinked, forcing myself to offer a halfhearted smile. His face remained stony; he seemed disgusted. "Go away," I said, irritably. "Leave me alone. You're no gentleman anyway. You wouldn't be able to tell a lady from a barmaid."

"It's my house," he pronounced, mumbling, "even if I did have ta find it the hard way." Then his tone changed. "Go somewhere else if ya need ta have one a them coffin nails."

"What a morbid thing to say. And I don't *need* this. I enjoy it. You have no right to preach to me anyway. I've seen you with cigarettes, Mr. High and Mighty. And in school too, where they're forbidden. I suppose you don't believe in equality for women?"

"Heh! Well, I ain't no punk idiot. I carry them nails for guys in my gang."

"Oh, that's rich. You're in a gang?" I snuffed my cigarette out on the cement and tried to bury the butt in the frozen dirt at the foot of the steps.

"Sure. Wha'd ya think? That I'm one a yer square Amherst wimps?"

I knew very little about city street gangs. Curiosity tempered my distaste, and I graciously inquired, "How does one become a gang member?"

He looked at me suspiciously. Then he picked up the cigarette butt I had unsuccessfully attempted to hide and held it at arm's length, as if it were a poisonous worm.

"It ain't no big deal, if ya really want to know. We just hang out together in my old neighborhood. We're the Bachelor Boys; mostly Polacks, Micks, 'n Krauts. They're a lot like me, except their dads're big tough guys. Black is the gang color. We all dress in black."

"So that's why you wear so much black? I surmised you chose it because it suits your disposition."

"Thanks, sweetie."

"You say their dads are tough? Your father doesn't shy away from danger. I heard he was a crime fighter."

He winced. "I had to apologize hard about my ol' man so they'd quit razzin' me 'bout bein' a PK."

"Tell me, what do you gang members do when they're together, besides razz each other?"

"We shoot people."

"Please, I asked an honest question."

"When it's not rainin' or snowin' we play baseball on the turf of the hospital fields near where I lived, if ya must know. In the fall, we collect chestnuts from the trees there, so's we c'n play kingers. Ya know where I mean? Na, you wouldn't. It's by the grounds of the part of the hospital that's for the criminally insane. Course we ain't allowed to be there."

"Oh, of course," I said sarcastically.

"Sometimes the guards unleash their German shepherds on us. Hah. Them dogs ain't nothin' but bark, but we'll jump away from 'em up onto the tower if we have to."

"Tower?"

"The big cement water tower near there. It's part of the gang initiation to walk around its narrow, I don't know, three- or four-inch ridge, several feet up from the ground. Guys break bones if they fall off, but most a 'em ain't dumb enough to. Back when I was a kid, in junior high, before I had my car, one a the guys busted an air filter in his car. He got me ta find him a new one so's he could play chicken. I stole it from my ol' man's car. He never knew it. Heh. He don't know jack shit about engines."

"Is this all true? Or have you been making it up?"

"Believe what ya want." He shrugged. "Ya asked me. I told ya. I don't give a damn what ya believe."

Dumbfounded, I looked at him intently for the first time since he had joined me outside and noticed that he wasn't wearing a jacket, his glasses had steamed over, and his hands were red. "We probably need to get back inside," I said. As I followed him through the door, my head teemed with questions. Why was he so bitter toward his father? Had he not known where his own house was? Was he drunk when his family moved? And why had he been allowed to run around, unsupervised, with gang members, no less? Did he really play chicken?

155

We passed though the kitchen, and Pete said, "Hi, Grammy," respectfully, as I nearly bumped into the elfin woman who seemingly appeared from nowhere carrying a thick book. Her ancient eyes, magnified by her spectacles, lit up pleasantly when she recognized me. "How are you? Sandy, is it?"

I smiled down at her and replied, "Yes, thank you for remembering my name, Mrs. French. I'm fine. How are you?" Then I noticed the title of her book: *Peyton Place*. This innocent-looking little old lady was reading a notoriously dirty, sexy book! Out of the corner of my eye, I saw Pete toss my cigarette butt into a trash can while his grandmother and I talked. As I started to go downstairs, I saw her signal to him that she had something private she wanted to say.

"Such a pretty girl," I heard her whisper. He grunted something unintelligible and then said aloud, "We gotta get back downstairs, Grammy. See ya later, okay?"

After I got home, I sat down for a smoke with my parents and complained about Pete again. "He's a street gang kid! Can you believe that? He doesn't belong in Amherst." Mom agreed with me, and Dad repeated his theory about boys needing to play sports. He told me to go easy on "the poor kid."

A few days later, Ken was escorting me to English class, enthusiastically carrying on about a Kerouac novel, when I happened to look around and catch a glimpse of Pete skirting us in the hall, glaring sullenly in our direction. Typical of that jerk, I thought. A day or so later, as I was on my way to my locker, he appeared out of nowhere. Without so much as a hi, he announced, "I gotta work on Saturday, the thirteenth."

"So?" I asked him absentmindedly. "Oh! You'll miss the rehearsal then?"

"Big deal," he mumbled. Then he took off.

Our phone rang around ten that evening, and Mom answered it. "Sandy, it's for you. It's Peter. Don't stay on long. It's late."

"Peter who?" I shouted from the dining room, where my

books were laid out so that I could memorize the underlined passages for an English test.

"French," Mom answered, looking at me quizzically. Reluctantly, I accepted the receiver from her.

"Hello?" I said, warily.

"Look, I was in a shi … bad mood today. Soo sorry I didn't explain. I really do have to work on Thursday. At the A&P. Some fuc … stupid checker is sick."

"Oh, okay. I can manage without you. I think everything's under control now; except, maybe, for the costumes. Do you have yours?"

"I got Betty Marsh fixin' one up for me. So, how'sss … ss … things?"

His voice sounded strange; he was slurring his words.

"Fine. How are you?" I answered coolly.

"Jus' great. Couldn't be bitter. Ah, better."

"Your manner of speaking sounds worse than usual. I didn't think that was possible."

"Sorry, ma'am, but I always soun' dis way."

"Why do you work so much? You get an allowance, don't you?"

"'S not enough. Fer my car. She needs lots a care. I wouldn't want her to let me down in chick … en."

"You actually participate in that illegal activity? You must be crazy. You're risking your life."

"Ya *would* think that way. It figures. Ya always do what yer mommy wants, right? Wadda ya know about shicken anyway? 'S jus' a game the guys play 'gainst other gangs. Promise ya won't tell if I tell ya 'bout it?"

"I promise." He couldn't see that I had my fingers crossed.

"Wellll, see … we do it out on country roads. Near Cheek … towa … ga and places like 'at. Roads where cops don't go, ya git me?"

"Sure, it's illegal."

"That don't matter. A guy from one gang challenges a guy

157

from another gang, and they drive straight at each other. The first guy who veers off loses. 'S a blast."

"That's incredible. Someone could get killed."

"Heh, heh. Ya got that right, sweetie. Knew one who did 'sa matter a fact."

"Are you telling me that *you* have played this ... game is not the word for it. It's no game when lives are at stake."

"Lots a games're dangerous. People get killed huntin' for Christ's sake. 'S what makes 'em fun. A bullet at a damn shooting range at camp hit me once. Shit happens. So I got another scar. 'S not no big deal. Some o' the guys in the gang ask me to drive their cars fer 'em 'cause I know how to win."

"I knew it! You're bragging. That's why you do it. And just how do you imagine you've escaped getting killed, at least up until now?"

"No imaginin's involved. 'S logic. I figure out how far it's possible fer me ta drive on the road fore I gotta veer off, and the other gang's guy chickens out fore I get there. Sim ... ple."

"You are out of your mind."

"Nope. Just feelin' good, baby. I been to Our Place."

"Stop calling me baby. I have to study, Pete, and I don't have time to listen to more of your inane bragging and your foul language. You sound drunk or tired or both. I'm sorry you'll have to go to work, but that's all. In my opinion, you should finish up your obviously long overdue homework."

"Wha for? Amhers's boring. The teachers do bullshit teaching."

"If you swear again, I'll hang up on you."

"Sorrry, ma'am. The stupid earth science teacher at yer school, if ya can call 'im that, said 'der-bis' instead of 'da-bree.' When I laughed out loud at that, he gave be a B 'stead of the A I shoulda got on the test, just for 'bad deportment,' fer Chris' sake."

I didn't reply.

"Okay, I know. Ya want me to shut up. Sorrreee. Tha's wa I git for tryin' ta be nice ta ya."

"Apparently you don't have any idea how to be nice. I really can't understand why you behave so outrageously. Maybe you're crazy. I do believe you're drunk. Have you been drinking? Don't answer that. I have to finish my homework."

"Okay, okay. I git the picture. Sooo long, sweetie."

"Don't call me that. Good-bye."

I slammed down the phone just as my mother and father entered the room. "Anything wrong?" Mom asked.

"Not with me. That Pete French is impossible. Just now, on the phone, he sounded drunk."

"You didn't make a date with him, did you?" Mom looked concerned.

"Are you kidding?" She frowned. "Sorry, Mom. Please don't worry. He wouldn't ask me out for anything in the world, and if that idiot ever did ask me out, I would refuse him."

"Why did he call you then?"

I sighed. "I can't tell what's going on in his head. He never says anything that's even remotely sensible, or civil either for that matter."

"Forget Pete, Sandy," Dad said. "Just finish up your work and get to bed. It's a school night."

It wasn't easy for me to concentrate on finishing up my studies. I thought about Pete and his friends foolishly risking their lives out on some country road. Was he telling me the truth? Why would he do such a dangerous thing? Did he have a death wish? I hated him for diverting my concentration away from my work, and I was angry with myself for letting him get away with it. My stomach hurt.

## Chapter 16
## THE GREAT PRETENDER

Where is he? I wondered anxiously. The Christmas pageant was the first item on the agenda. The performance was just two weeks away; everyone in the cast needed to be present in order for me to set the date for the dress rehearsal. The choir director told me I could choose one of three afternoons next week, and everyone had to be at the rehearsal. That included the least reliable of the wise men, whose availability apparently depended on the whims of the A&P. Since he was missing, I decided to present the three options to the rest of the kids, take a vote, and somehow get Pete to come at that time, even if I had to seek help from the pastor. We narrowed it down to two choices. Then I had to eliminate one more when one of the shepherds insisted he had to do something else that afternoon. I called for a motion to confirm Tuesday, when Pete swaggered in and flopped down on a chair in the back. I glared at him.

Responding to my fierce look, he shrugged nonchalantly. "Sorry, Prez, I couldn't git here any sooner."

Ignoring this halfhearted apology, I repeated the motion on the floor. Everyone except Pete raised a hand in favor of Tuesday. "Those against?" Pete's hand went up.

I sighed out loud. Keeping my voice as level as possible, I said, "You're not able to be there at four o'clock next Tuesday?"

"Nope. Gotta work. It's okay. Someone else can take over the wise guy gig."

"Don't be absurd. You're the only one tall enough for the part." I turned to the younger boy who was playing a shepherd. "Bill, is there any way you can change the date of your plans for next Friday?"

Bill was only thirteen. He asked if he could call his mom on the phone in the church office. I assumed that door was locked, but Pete stood up and motioned to Bill.

"Come wit' me. I got a key."

The two of them went out of the room together, while the rest of us waited. I was too anxious to get this matter settled to get on with the other business. Soon Bill and Pete returned, smiling and chatting amiably.

"Billy boy worked things out fer ya, Prez. Turns out he didn't want ta go shopping wit his sister anyway. Friday afternoon's okay now fer him, as long as ya understand ol' Bill has to git home by six."

Happy to have that issue resolved, I reminded everyone to be at the church Friday afternoon, no later than four, dressed in costume. I repeated the word "*everyone,*" looking pointedly at Pete. Then I asked him for a report on the progress of his plans for the New Year's dance. Pete shook his head, as if he deeply regretted what he was about to say.

"It turns out that I've been terribly ... in demand lately. Guess I'll have ta choose the committee right now. Any volunteers?" He flashed a dimpled smile that he probably kept filed away for charming church matrons. He gazed encouragingly around the room. "Help me out here, kids, okay? Raise yer hands if ya can help me."

Mark, Joyce, Sally, and Susie raised their hands.

"Good." He grinned. "I truly thank the bunch a ya." They smiled back at him. "Mark and I will handle the music, and the girls'll arrange for the food. Can you do anythin', Prez?"

"She's an artist," Susie volunteered. If I had thought to bring

Mike's slingshot, I probably would have aimed something more powerful than a clothespin at her. Why couldn't she keep her mouth shut?

"Okay, Prez, you're in charge of the decorations. Ya probably need a theme, right? I'll make it easy. Call it 'Imagination.' It's a doo-wop number by the Quotations. Can ya handle it?"

"Of course I can handle it," I responded through gritted teeth. I glowered at him. I hated him for trapping me into this and making me look foolish in the process. I couldn't care less about this silly dance, but with the sole exception of Pete, everyone else in the room seemed thrilled. I felt sorry for them. Most of them probably had never been to a semiformal dance in their lives. I quickly ran through the rest of the agenda, and everyone rose to gather around Pete as he set up his music.

When Pete asked me to dance, I nodded despondently. It was a slow dance to "Earth Angel." I was in no mood to talk, especially to him. "What's th' matter, Prez? In a shi ... bad mood?"

"I wasn't until you got everyone worked up about the stupid New Year's dance."

"Aww, come on. Don't be a bitch ... er ... a grouch."

"Look who's calling whom a grouch. Since you seem so silver tongued tonight, I dare you to answer a question. Was there some reason why there was a day when you couldn't find your own house?"

"That's personal." He frowned. "I fergit."

"No one *forgets* where they live. Except maybe if they're stone drunk. Were you drunk at the time?"

"Which time?"

"I can't tell if you're joking or not. How long have you worked at the A&P?"

"Jus' since I got moved to Amherst. I've had lots a jobs. My ol' man is always tryin' ta git me outta his hair. He doesn't like me nosin' into his affairs, ya might say. Heh!" I guessed that he was referring to Pastor's lady friend. "He hired me hisself to do my first summer job, when I was thirteen."

"Your father *hired* you to do a real job at thirteen?"

"Sorta. Some guy connected with Resurrection Church set up a deal wit him ta git ninety-nine acres of land out near Cattaraugus. A town in the country, ya followin' me?"

I nodded, shooting daggers at him with my eyes.

"He had this big scheme ta make money growin' Christmas trees out there. He gave me a few bucks fer livin' supplies and told me ta plant two hundred pine saplings he got somewhere cheap. It got me outta the house and made us both happy. I git a kick outta livin' in the country. There's rollin' hills, animals, 'n things."

"I agree with you, for once. I like open countryside too. My great aunt once had a country farm that I had fun visiting. "

"Yeah? So ya git what I'm sayin' then. My ol' man dropped me off for almost two months at a hunter's cabin on his land. The place had no electricity or runnin' water. It was great."

"I don't believe it. How did you survive without water?"

"There was a water pump outside and a small pile of wood. I chopped more wood for the stove, so's I could cook. It kept me warm at nights. I walked and hitched rides into Gowanda or Cattaraugus when supplies ran low."

The music stopped. The next record was a jitterbug that I danced with Neal. Then Pete asked me to dance with him to Teresa Brewer's "You Send Me."

"Tell me more about your summer in the cabin. Weren't you lonely there? Or scared?"

"Naw. Well, maybe at a little at first. Not after a couple a nights though, after I got used to animal noises. I met a few people in town, and there was one or two workin' farms not far away."

"How large was this cabin of yours?"

"One big room and a couple a little ones." His face lit up as he remembered. For a moment he looked almost human. "It had a fascinatin' wind-up Victrola, wit some old 78s from the twenties and thirties, Glen Miller and Caruso and stuff like that. Someone left some books on a shelf too: Robert Louis Stevenson and Alexander Dumas. Good stuff. Had to read at night with a flashlight or the old kerosene lamp. After I finished them books, I used some of my food money to buy *Classic Comics* at the drug store in Cattaraugus. They set the new ones aside just fer me. I planted trees by day and read by flashlight at night."

"Ah hah! I guessed that you read *Classic Comics*."

"Wha's wrong wit that?"

"Nothing, if you don't enjoy reading an author's actual words. I relish the beauty of good writing, but I'm sure you're satisfied with summaries."

"Think ya got me pegged, don't ya, Prez?" He grinned.

"I have no doubt. So you lived all those weeks with no electricity? Did you have an icebox?"

"Yeah, sure. Once a week an ice trucker came by ta deliver ta the farms a couple a miles up the road. He honked for me ta come down to the road so's I'd go out ta git a block of ice from him on his way back."

"How did you get the ice to the cabin? Those blocks are heavy, aren't they?"

"There was a pair a big ice tongs in the cabin." He shrugged. "I dropped one a couple a times and had ta wipe some junk off."

"You cooked for yourself? I didn't think that boys could cook."

"Lotsa guys cook. Chefs are guys fer Christ's sake."

"Not at age thirteen," I argued.

The song ended, I danced with other boys, and Pete and I danced once to "Rock Around the Clock," a number not conducive to conversation. I managed, however, to ask him what he ate in his cabin. He shouted that he warmed up canned food on the stove and had crackers and pop that he bought in the town store.

"It was better 'an spendin' summer at home, better 'an the crap job the ol' man had me doin' fer a couple a summers after that: diggin' graves."

"Now that sounds like a job you'd be well suited for."

"Scares ya, don't it?"

Pete left before I could probe for more details. Later I wondered why I wanted to know anyway. Maybe I had become Nancy Drew again, bent on solving *The Mystery of the Ghoulish PK.*

Once between classes at school the next week, Pete materialized out of the throng of students in the hall. This time he actually said hi to me. Looking around to see if anyone I knew had heard him, I gave him an indifferent hi. I saw him eyeing a book I was carrying. I told him he didn't have to carry it for me.

"Yer an odd dame, ain't ya? Readin' *A Tale of Two Cities*? It's one of Dickens's worst. Over-the-top, if ya ask me. Characters not well drawn."

"That's your opinion. It's romantic. I happen to like it."

"All a Dickens's novels have some romance in 'em, but *Bleak House* is his best, no arguin' wit that."

"You like *Bleak House*? Oh, of course *you* would. I haven't read it, but I understand that it's long, complicated, and, well, bleak. Did you actually read the whole book? Or some *Classic Comic Book* précis?"

He grunted and took off down the hall. I congratulated myself for calling his bluff.

Ken Skiller was not so easy to shake off. His blue eyes often sought me in the halls, and soon I resigned myself to walking beside him between classes. It wasn't that hard: he always had something kind to say. One afternoon, he sensed that I was feeling low.

"Want to tell me why you're unhappy, Sandy?"

"You're perceptive, Ken. I've been regretting the fact that our last year at Amherst is going by so quickly."

Ken responded, "Oh time, arrest your flight! / And you, propitious hours, arrest your course. / Let us savor the fleeting delights of our most beautiful days."

"Now, that's exactly how I would have put it," I laughed.

Ken laughed too. "That was Lamartine, an obscure romantic poet of the nineteenth century."

Who but Ken would know that? Did any of the other seniors feel the passing of time as keenly as Ken and I did?

Tall, Dark, and Handsome didn't seem to. Paul always behaved the same: flirty and fun. Enough time had passed since I had nearly died from loving the idea of him too much that I found myself once again able to counter his banter with more of the same. The only feeling he aroused in me now was undying admiration for his looks. I would miss seeing him next year; I would miss all my old boyfriends, the stage crew guys, and even Archie, who had finally begun to smile at me again. I would miss my girlfriends, especially Barb and Claire. And I'd certainly miss Ken.

King got locked in the boys' room when Ken came to our door to take me to the senior ball. He looked stunning. His ginger hair appeared to be newly trimmed, and I couldn't spot one teensy wrinkle anywhere on his immaculate, blue dress suit. He even gave off a whiff of musky cologne. He told me I looked beautiful, and his blue eyes sought my approval; I pronounced that he looked terrific. Smiling broadly, he handed me a boxed corsage. I opened it to discover two delicate mauve and white orchids, tied together with a tiny silver bow.

"They'll look sensational with this dress!" I exclaimed. "Thank you, Ken. I'll wait to pin them on when we get to the dance."

Wishing that I had ordered him a rose instead, I pinned a white carnation unto the lapel of Ken's suit before he helped me into my coat. It was a mild December evening; the sparse snowfalls spared me the need for overshoes. Before the dance, we dropped in at a mutual friend's home, where we drank unlaced holiday party punch and joined Cal and Cindy, with whom we double-dated during most of the evening.

The theme of the dance was Moonlight Mist, and metallic, silver, crepe paper moonbeams flared out from the multifaceted mirrored ball that hung from the center of the ceiling like a glowing silver moon. Ken was a superb dancer, but we switched partners often. At one point, I caught myself looking around to see if Pete was there, but I saw no sign of him. I was relieved. What if he had tried to break into my crowd to ask me to dance?

I felt so comfortable with Ken that I didn't shy away from kidding him about his hair. "Maybe you should have worn a green suit, Ken." He pretended to be hurt by that remark. "Not that you don't look great in that blue, but everyone seems quite taken with your hair tonight, probably because of my complementary dress color."

"Want to see what I'd look like next to your dress? Suppose I put my head down against it." He nodded toward my bosom.

"Nice, but naughty, Santa."

"You suggested it."

"Not exactly."

After the formal dance was over, the serious partying began. The four of us went to Ken's house for canapés and then drove on to the Italian Village, a nightclub restaurant, where we danced and ate spaghetti and meatballs, and some of the kids had more than a few glasses of wine. Ken and I had one glass each, a safe exception to my vow of sobriety, I felt. The last event of the evening was a delicious brunch at Vivian's house. When we finally returned home at four in the morning, I was almost too tired to say good night. King barked loudly as we neared the door. I thanked Ken and planted a quick kiss on his lips before ducking inside. Ken smiled appreciatively, his blue eyes glowing. Dad coughed loudly as I passed their bedroom door.

"Don't worry, Dad," I called out. "I'm perfectly sober, my stomach is full, and I had a *good* evening." I ducked into my bedroom, where I quickly undressed and plopped onto my bed, exhausted, taking care not to wake Patty.

They had to blast me out of bed the next morning in time for Sunday school and church, and I felt as if I were sleepwalking all day. My very bones ached. I had set aside an hour or two for getting some rest that afternoon, having had the foresight to finish most of my homework early Saturday, but worries prevented me from relaxing. It was two weeks before Christmas, and I still had so much to do. Homework assignments were more demanding than I had expected them to be, Operetta Scenery Crew chores seemed overwhelming, and I still had more presents to buy. Sometime next week Dad would bring in our Christmas tree, and I really wanted to help decorate it. Luther League commitments had gotten ridiculously complicated, especially with the pageant about to take place on the following Sunday. Would everyone be at the dress rehearsal? If all that wasn't enough to worry about, I had foolishly agreed to help decorate the nave for the Christmas Eve Candlelight Service. Our neighbor George Becker, Shirley's dad, who was head of the church decorating committee, talked me into it and asked me to nominate more volunteers from the league, older kids, tall enough and reliable enough to help with the hard work.

After a hearty Sunday roast beef dinner, I arrived at Luther League, tired and anxious to make the meeting as short as possible. For once Pete was on time, and I went through the agenda expeditiously. I asked Neal, Pete, Susie, and Joyce for their help on the Christmas Eve decoration project on the twenty-third. Three out of the four seemed eager to help, so I could count on them. If Pete didn't show up, we'd make do. I couldn't tell if he understood what I had asked him to do. When I requested him to give us a New Year's Eve party report, he came to attention long enough to say that plans for the music and food had been set.

"Ya got plans for the decorations, don't ya?" he asked me.

I improvised a vague notion about doing a mural, probably of musical notes and instruments outlined in shades of pink.

"Why pink? Ya sure ya want pink?"

"It's festive."

"Yellow ain't?" he said to himself, and then he shrugged and slumped down.

During the social hour, I could barely hold my head up when Pete asked me to dance to the Platters' rendition of "The Great Pretender."

I groped around my foggy brain for what we had talked about

the last time. "Oh. Did you say last week that you once were a grave digger, or were you, umm, just being a pretender?"

He seemed annoyed. "Yer pretendin' not to be tired. Big date last night?"

"Not that it's any of your business. I guess you didn't go to the senior ball?"

"Ya goin' steady with that carrot-topped cube?"

"No, I'm not going steady with anyone, not that it's any of your business. But, yes, Ken and I were out very late last night. What were you doing? Haunting a graveyard?"

"Ya don't believe I dug graves, do ya?"

"Did you get that job because you passed the personality test?"

His gray green glare sawed through me.

"Yer cute, Sandy. Naw, my ol' man got me that work ta git me out of the way, like I said. And he has connections to cemeteries, in more ways than one, ya might say."

"A church cemetery?"

"Nah, the big Polack cemetery in southeastern Buffalo, where he sometimes buries people. I worked wit a guy 'bout my age. We was supervised by this older guy who gave us chores when we weren't diggin' like mowin' the lawn or paintin' the wrought iron fence."

"You really dug graves?"

"Ya been listenin' to me? When there was a funeral, the older guy staked out a place fer the grave. After we done our job, he checked out the size and depth to make sure we done it right. On our breaks, we played mumbley peg."

"Mumbley peg?"

"Geez, either ya don't know nothin' or yer asleep. Everyone's got a knife, right?"

"Who doesn't?"

He either ignored or failed to comprehend my sarcasm. "There are different rules, but basically ya flip yer knife off some part a yer body, say yer knee, in a jazzy way. If it lands and sticks, the other guy has ta match yer move. Fer points. Git it? We had ta hang around in the background durin' the funeral. Then we had ta fill in the grave wit dirt. Sometimes we got paid a couple a bucks by the undertaker ta stand around with our heads down, lookin' sad."

"How depressing." I yawned.

"Naw. It was a job, that's all."

"Someone had just died, and no one cared enough to come? You'd understand how sad that is if you had normal feelings. Surely you must have been unhappy when your mother passed away. Weren't you only about five then?"

He shrugged. "I didn't remember her. They always kept me away from her because she was so sick. Only thing I remember 'bout her burial is that when we drove ta the cemetery, some dumb old folks in the car kept pattin' my head. They said they were sorry she had 'gone away,' so I told 'em, 'No, she died.' That shut 'em up."

"You never cried?"

"Why should I?"

"You're not human."

The next day a hall monitor at school knocked on the door of our English classroom with a note to Mrs. Meese. She read it and looked up, directly at me, a puzzled expression on her face.

"Sandy, it seems that you have been summoned to see the school counselor at once. You are excused from class." There was a low murmur of sarcastic "ooohs" and "ahhhhhs." A male voice murmured, "Is Sandy in trouble, *again*?" I left my books on my desk and hurried out of the room.

My friends seemed to think it was a joke, but I didn't. Never in my whole school career had a counselor summoned me out of class. What had I done? Had they discovered errors in my SAT scores? The counselor usually dealt with cases of bad behavior. Had someone accused me of doing something wrong? Was I going to have to defend myself?

I almost ran down the hall to the counselor's office.

## Chapter 17
## You Don't Know Me

When her receptionist announced my arrival, Miss Maxmillian called me into her office. The counselor was a thin, prim-faced woman who wore unfashionable rimless glasses on her nose. She smiled at me warmly and invited me to sit in the chair opposite her desk. As I sat down, I blurted out, "Is anything wrong?"

"Oh, no. I'm sorry to have worried you. Relax, please, Sandy." I heaved a deep sigh of relief. "Please forgive me for taking you out of your English classroom so abruptly. I thought that, with your excellent record, a few moments away wouldn't hurt. You see, I've been racking my brain trying to come up with some way to help a perpetually delinquent student whom you appear to know, and I came up with a plan that involves you. I wanted to tell you about it before the Christmas break. What I am about to say is confidential. It must remain a secret between us. May I rely on your silence?"

"I believe I know who this is about. Is it Pete French?"

"Before I answer that question, I need your solemn oath that what I am about to tell you will not go outside the walls of this office."

Relieved of any personal concerns, I was curious to hear what the counselor had to say.

"I promise not to tell anyone what you tell me unless you give me permission."

"Good. As you already guessed, we saw you talking to Pete French one day. Is he just an acquaintance, or do you consider him a friend?"

"I can't call him a friend. I know him because I'm the leader of our church youth group, and our minister, his father, forces Pete to come to the Luther League meetings. That's what the group is called. Pete is a reluctant participant, in spite of the fact that I've tried to make him feel welcome. At the pastor's request, I assigned him to bring in his 45 records for the Sunday socials, when we dance and have refreshments. I even dance with him occasionally, but we always end up arguing. He complains about Amherst, but I love it here."

"This doesn't surprise me. Peter resents the fact that his father relocated his family without consulting him. It's my understanding that Peter's younger siblings moved into their new home with their grandmother, but Peter learned about the move only after the fact. It's a shame, but some parents don't communicate well with their children. I'm certain that's not true in your family, Sandy, but you're smart enough to comprehend what I'm telling you. Sadly," she continued, "Peter's family history has been quite tragic. That's often the case with delinquents."

"He doesn't seem to feel sorry for himself; not from what I can tell."

"Peter hides his feelings. Many supposedly tough delinquents do. What I want you to understand, however, is that Peter is no ordinary delinquent. When he first arrived at Amherst High, we didn't have his records from his previous school yet, so we gave him the usual battery of tests: intelligence quotient tests, aptitude tests, and achievement tests. I'm sure you know what I'm talking about."

"Yes, we all had to take them."

"Well, this young man's initial scores surprised us so much that we retested him."

"He did that poorly?"

"On the contrary, my dear. His IQ is so high that it is, to put it bluntly, off the charts. Your own IQ is a good deal above average, but his is one of the highest that I have ever seen. He has an unusually vast knowledge in many areas, quite unexpected in one of his years. His aptitude test results, however, were … shocking. I suspect that he's so clever that he purposefully chose all the answers that would lead us to conclude that the only occupation he's suited for is that of a truck driver." She laughed. "Oh, he's a rebel, and he has very little respect for authority. I don't want you to get the wrong impression, however. The boy is by no means evil at heart. In fact, he has a good deal of compassion for the downtrodden."

I was not sure I had understood her correctly. "Pete's IQ is so high that it is *superior to mine?*" I asked, dumbfounded.

"Yes. That's what the tests reveal. He could do very well in almost any profession, but he dislikes school, and he's not interested in attending college." She sighed.

"If you know all of this, you must also know how stubborn he is. His speech is laced with atrocious grammar, and he swears, even at church. That's one of the reasons I thought he was an idiot."

"Yes. He speaks that way because he wants to appear, how shall I put it? This is difficult to explain to someone of your more conventional background. Perhaps the best way to convey this is to say that he tries to come off as a tough guy. Surprisingly, his earlier school records indicate that he started out doing well in school: he received outstanding grades in elementary school and junior high. In high school, however, he began to behave disrespectfully to his teachers, and his grades dropped, frequently due to bad deportment. This sort of behavioral change has been frequently observed in exceptionally gifted students, especially when they realize that they're actually more intelligent than their teachers. Such students are walking a tightrope. One misstep could lead them to a lifetime of despair. This young man has already become a member of a gang of boys who negatively influence his behavior, leading him to do things that place his very life at risk."

I nodded. "He told me about his gang. I think I understand what you're saying. But he has been this way for quite a long time, hasn't he? Obviously, the counselor at his last school couldn't help him. I know Amherst is better than any other school. But, please forgive me for saying this; you're his counselor, not me. How can I help him when we two don't even get along?"

"What do you dislike about him?"

"Everything. He's rude and ill mannered. He looks like a greaser. He thinks he knows all the answers. Well, okay, now I understand that he knows more than I thought he did. Still, he staunchly refuses to make any effort to be nice ... except, maybe to orphans."

"Orphans?"

"Our Luther League gave a party for the orphans at St. John's. I appointed Pete to run the party. He did a great job of that. He was nice to *those* kids."

"That figures. He cares about people who are needy or oppressed. Don't you admire that trait?"

"I suppose so."

"But he isn't nice to you?"

"No. Quite the contrary."

"Would it be possible for you to overlook his ... impoliteness? I understand that you are very busy, but—"

"Miss Maxmillian, I'm sorry, but I fear that I may have already taken on too much this year."

"I know, I know. Everyone admires how much you do for Amherst High. I'm sorry to have to ask one more thing of you. But you're the only person, the *only one* who takes school seriously to whom Peter will give the time of day, so to speak. That's more of a breakthrough than any of us, any of his teachers or counselors, have been able to achieve."

I thought I knew what she was trying to lead me to agree to, so I folded my arms across my chest and hardened my expression. Miss Maxmillian sighed.

"Maybe you should look at this another way," she said. "You want to be a teacher, don't you?"

"Yes, but Pete has no interest in teaching."

"That's correct, at least as far as we know from his trumped-up aptitude test responses. What I'm proposing is that you might think of helping Peter as an opportunity for a unique teaching experience. Oh, I know he's not like the students you hope to deal with in the future. You're interested in teaching young children, and you and Peter are nearly the same age. But don't you see? You understand the importance of getting a good education, and he doesn't. Your backgrounds differ considerably, of course. You are a respected citizen of your community and Amherst High, and he's a rebel. Your writing and speaking skills are outstanding; he deliberately refuses to use the skills he demonstrated when he was doing so well in school. The odds are against my plan. But I'm sure that you can see why I am trying to reach this young man. Will you help me?"

"I really would like to help," I said, shaking my head sadly. "But it would be a waste of my valuable time."

"Okay." Miss Maxmillian sighed heavily. "That's reasonable. But would you do just one little thing?"

"If I can."

"Please don't stop speaking to him altogether. And if he ever should ask you why you spend so much of your time and effort preparing for your future, or why you want to go to college, please tell him your reasons. As I have said, he's an extremely intelligent young man. I believe that, given the right motivation, he might reconsider his choices. I understand why you don't want to hear this, Sandy, but I have reason to believe he admires you."

"If he does, he sure has a funny way of showing it," I laughed.

"I have spies in the halls. They have reported how he looks at you when you're with your boyfriends."

"You have spies?" This was getting intriguing. It was almost like a detective story. "Miss Maxmillian, when I was younger I wanted to be just like Nancy Drew."

She laughed. "Well then, think of yourself as a detective on a secret mission. I have no doubt that Peter has the brains to get accepted to one of the best colleges in the country. It's a complete shame that he refuses to utilize his God-given talents. I believe you'll agree, once you have time to think it over, that giving up on him could lead to a waste of valuable brainpower, a power for possible good in the world."

"Maybe. I admit that you've intrigued me. But I have to be practical. I can't let Pete get in the way of my own aspirations."

"At least you could be an inspiration to help him make something of himself. I can't give up hope on that."

"I'm flattered that you have taken me into your confidence, Miss Maxmillian. But I'm afraid that you overestimate my ability to affect his choices." I sighed. "Talking to him isn't easy for me. He irritates me too much."

"I knew my idea was a long shot when I called you in," she sighed. "But in my business, I must remain optimistic." She stood up and offered me her hand. We shook hands, and she asked her secretary to sign a pass for me to get back into class.

When I returned to the classroom, I felt all eyes staring at me curiously. I raised my hands palms upward, shrugged my shoulders, and shook my head to indicate that nothing made any sense to me. However, I had a difficult time concentrating on my schoolwork after that. This monster that had been complicating my life since he first came to my church was not only acting smart, he really was smart! He was supposed to go to college, not become a truck driver, which he apparently wanted people to accept as his ambition. Miss Maxmillian wanted me to motivate him to change direction? Why me? First my pastor had asked me to get him involved in Luther League, now my school counselor wanted me to make him go to college. I was supposed to become, in effect, his mentor? It wasn't fair. What about me?

I seemed to be riding on an emotional teeter-totter: self-pity balanced against self-congratulation. A professional adult had just taken me into her confidence and trusted me with privileged information. I had a secret mission to save someone from self-destruction. If I succeeded, I would be a heroine. But what if I failed? The teeter-totter hit bottom with a thud.

I was as wound up and time orientated as a wristwatch. When scarce daylight turned to ashes, I burned watts of electricity into the early morning hours. When I finally did get into bed, sleep didn't come easily. *Show Boat* had turned out to involve more work for me than *Desert Song* had, and it wasn't as much fun. The finicky musical director ordered me to do careful research, involving trips to both school and town libraries to learn about Mississippi paddleboats, the levee at Natchez, and Chicago entertainment halls in the early twentieth century. Nothing was ever easy for me. It wasn't fair. Darn it. Darn all my other school assignments. Darn the Luther League. Darn how fast time was getting away from me. Darn everything!

## Chapter 18
## OH, OH, I'M FALLING IN LOVE AGAIN

*The Elf's Photo*

On the Friday of the pageant dress rehearsal at the church, I ran out of school right after the closing bell. Mom was parked out front in her car with my Mary costume, waiting to drive me to the church. I changed in the ladies' room and joined shepherds, angels, innkeepers, Joseph, and two magi in the back of the basement. Pastor French was talking to the choir director, and to my relief, I spotted Pete in a far corner, getting fussed over by Sally's mother, Betty. She was busy winding a shiny gold cloth over his head to create a turban. She fastened it with a maroon rhinestone pin. A red corduroy robe constituted his gown. He looked rather comical, standing there in his stocking feet, trying to get his glasses to fit under the turban.

Mrs. Marsh chided him. "They didn't wear glasses in biblical times, Pete."

"And they had corduroy robes back then?" he quipped. "Sorry, Betty, but I won't make it down the aisle without these specs. A blind wise guy ain't no good in a parade." Mrs. Marsh laughed, pulled his glasses off, and stuck them in her pocket.

The choir members were already in their black robes upstairs, arranging themselves in the stall in the loft of the church. The organist was tuning up.

Cast members lined up at the back of the church, the choir began to sing, and I took Joseph's arm. He escorted me down the aisle to the front. He disappeared behind to the side, and the angel arrived to deliver the announcement. Then Neal and I ducked behind the pews and snuck out the door. We ran down a side hall to the back so we could go down the aisle again. This time I had a pillow tied beneath my gown, and I leaned on Joseph as we went from one inhospitable innkeeper to another, until Mark, the good innkeeper, took us to the stable in the front of the church. A cradle lined with hay was already in place. I replaced the Jesus doll behind the cradle with the pillow and placed the doll in the cradle while Neal blocked me from view. Then all lights shown on us, and with appropriate halleluiahs from the choir, angels and shepherds heralded the newborn messiah. The wise men began to file down the aisle to the hymn of "We Three Kings."

The last of the three kings looked different somehow. It was more than his costume and the absence of his glasses. He was so serious, concentrating on feeling his way down the aisle. When he kneeled beside me to offer me his gift, the script called for me to look at him, smile, and thank him sweetly. He looked hard and directly at me, and I smiled at him. It was a lot easier to smile at Pete when I knew he could barely see me, but I couldn't help wondering what was going on in that powerful brain of his. We went through the entire rehearsal twice. When the pastor congratulated us afterwards, I felt guilty. He didn't know how much help his son had been to me, and I didn't know how to tell him, especially when the tallest wise man was striding toward me with his glasses back on. As he walked, he took off the robe, revealing a black shirt and dungarees underneath. He was still unwinding his turban when he caught up with me.

"Ya need a ride home, Sandy?" he asked, sounding remarkably friendly.

"I guess so, Pete, if you'll wait while I take my costume off and get my coat."

He was climbing into the driver's seat when he noticed that I was still standing outside in the cold, beside the passenger door. I knew he lacked the manners to realize that he should open the car door for me, and I took a perverse delight in watching him figure it out. I could almost see the lightbulb turn on behind his eyes. Quickly, he hopped out and swung around to open my door and then ran around to jump back behind the steering wheel. It was dark out, and I breathed a sigh of relief when I could tell that the lights on that contraption he drove still worked. As we pulled out of the parking lot, I fumbled for something to say to him that wouldn't trigger another spat. "Have you finished your Christmas shopping?" I asked.

"Yeah, I guess," he said unenthusiastically.

"Lucky you," I sighed. "I still have to find something for my brother Mike. Boys are so hard to shop for. You wouldn't have any suggestions, would you?"

"My budget ain't in yer bracket. I know a place, though, where you could find somethin' unusual, perhaps somethin' in the sports line, if ya want ta. It's a place where no one in yer family shops. I could take ya tomorrow, but I s'pose ya ain't interested."

"Ahh, well, that could be ... helpful. What time?"

"I could pick ya up at, say, one?"

"Oosh. I have so much to do. Will it take us long?"

"Nah. Ya need to find somethin', don't ya?"

"Make it twelve thirty, okay? On the dot. I'll clear it with my parents, and I'll be watching for you in my driveway. You know where I live, right?"

"Who don't?"

"Remember, I can't be out long. But, you're right, I might find something different if I go somewhere I haven't been."

At the appointed time, appropriately bundled up for the cold, sunny day, I ran out to his car, my wallet tucked into my coat pocket. Pete jumped out of his car, opened my door with a flourish, and greeted me with a dimpled smile. To my surprise, he was dressed in khaki pants. He wore a dark gray, wool coat with a toggled front closure, which was open down to the second toggle, revealing a refreshingly white shirt.

"Today I'm gonna show ya where ta buy real food in an old-fashioned neighborhood marketplace," he announced confidently.

"Food? I need to find a present for Mike that won't go stale before Christmas Eve."

"Yeah, sure. But this ain't no suburban shopping mall like yer used to. There's everythin' in the city marketplace. Like real bread, 'stead of the Wonder Bread chemical crap I bet yer family eats."

This wasn't starting out well at all. He was changing our plans and criticizing what I ate, and we were hardly out of the driveway. Well, I thought, I got myself into this, now I had to take my punishment. At least if I lived through it, I'd be able to tell Miss Maxmillian that I gave it a try.

Soon he was driving into unfamiliar territory, and I lost my bearings. "Where are you going? I told you I can't be out long."

"I know what I'm doin'. Relax. We'll be there soon."

We were driving away from Snyder, most likely toward the inner city. How could I relax? The side streets looked unfamiliar, and the houses on them were old and rather run down. A few unsavory shops lined the roadway. He told me the names of the areas we were driving through; I didn't recognize any of them. Finally, he pulled his car into an enclosed parking lot and parked it. He opened my door again, and I followed him down an alleyway, which opened into some sort of indoor-outdoor marketplace. Small, well-lit stores lined the walkways, and tables displaying colorful merchandise sat out in front of store windows. Aromas of fresh produce and baked goods pleasantly saturated the air, but the market itself was noisy, crowded, and alien. What was I doing there?

"Ya ever been anywhere like this before?"

"No, I didn't know such a place existed. It has an … old world feeling, I imagine," I said, looking around uncasily.

"Ya ain't scared, are ya?" He sounded concerned.

"No, of course not. Should I be?"

"Ya look … worried. Come over here. Let me show ya what real bread is."

He guided me gently, his hand on my back, toward some stalls outside a bakery that filled the cold air with mouth-watering odors. Long cylindrical loaves of unwrapped bread were neatly stacked one above the other. He picked up a loaf and sniffed the crust appreciatively. "Now this is nothin' like Wonder Bread. It's freshly baked, no chemicals, with a crisp, tough crust. I used to buy bread here all the time. Here, take a whiff."

It certainly did smell good. He picked a bag off the top of a stack of brown bags at the stall and put the long loaf inside it. He pulled out his wallet. "Ya want one?"

"No, thank you. Please remember why we're here, Pete."

"I'm tellin' ya ta relax. We've been here only a couple a minutes. We're headin' to a sports store. There'll be somethin' cool there for yer brother. Look around. Ya might learn somethin'."

Everything about that afternoon felt surreal to me. Pete was so civil to me for starters, and there was so much going on around us, so much for me to look at in that eccentric place. It was scary too. Many of the people buying the merchandise looked poor. Some were dark skinned.

Suddenly, a voice in the crowd called out to Pete. "Hey, man! I ain't seen ya in an age."

A Negro in a Kensington jacket approached us, smiling broadly. Instinctively, I braced my arm against the pocket that held my wallet.

"Luke Gibson!" Pete called out happily. "Sandy Schall, I'd like ya to meet my friend Luke Gibson. His homeroom team was real killers on the football field. I think they beat us every time."

Luke grabbed Pete's hand and shook it heartily. He smiled at me warmly and said, "Glad ta meet ya, Sandy. Any friend of Pete's a friend of mine." I avoided his gaze and didn't respond, pretending to spot something I liked in a nearby store window. Luke said to Pete, "I don't remember that we beat ya *every* time. Yer sneaky run for that first down sho had me fooled. Where ya been, Pete?"

"My ol' man took a job out in Snyder. I miss those games we played, Luke."

The black boy's face fell. "Me too, Pete. Listen, I'd love ta catch up wit ya, but I gotta git some last-minute tings fer the folks. Ya know how it is. Nice to meet ya, Sandy." He smiled at me, and I nodded warily.

The boys shook hands again, smiling at each other. "Glad ta run into ya, Luke. Hope ta see ya again real soon. Merry Christmas."

"Back at ya, Pete. We'll git together real soon."

Pete watched his old friend disappear with a sad look in his eyes. He sighed and we started to walk on when another person of color accosted us. "You two want your photo taken with Santa?" A sprightly green elf had popped up near Santa's throne. The jolly Santa sitting on the golden throne had dark eyebrows that didn't match his long, V-shaped white cotton beard.

"Ya wanna?" Pete asked me, his face brightening.

"Aren't we too old for this sort of thing?"

"Com'mon. Have some fun fer a change. My treat."

I hesitated. This was ridiculous, but no more so than everything else that was happening. The elf told each of us to sit on one of Santa's knees. The hefty young Santa, who "Ho, Ho, Ho'd" and winked at me, said, "Smile for the camera." A flashbulb went off. Pete gave my address to the photographer to have the picture sent to me, and I prayed that I would be able to intercept the envelope before anyone in my family saw it.

Back in the crowded plaza, I had difficulty keeping up with Pete's long strides. Unlike other, even taller boys I had walked with, he moved too fast for me, and I soon grew fearful that I would lose sight of him. He made no effort to match my pace; in fact, he didn't notice that I was falling behind. "Pete," I called out nervously, "will you wait for me?"

"Oh, sorry," he said. He stood still while I caught up to him. After that he tried to stay in step with me, which caused him to look around more. We passed by a jewelry stand, and he asked, "Ya like jewelry?"

"I've always liked rings," I said. I took off my glove. "See, I'm wearing a garnet ring that Tanta, my great aunt, gave to me."

"Let me look at it closer," he said. He took hold of my left hand and studied the ring intently. I thought he had inspected it long enough, but when I tried to pull my hand out of his, he held onto it firmly. Surprised, I looked up at him, and our eyes met. Behind the boy's thick lenses, the big, gray green eyes of a confused man pleaded with me not to let go. Then he blinked, and I saw the hard gaze of a person steeling himself for rejection. A demon deep in my gut did a summersault. Realizing that if I pulled away, I'd hurt his feelings, I squeezed Pete's hand instead. Eventually I put my glove in my pocket with my right hand, and we held hands until we got to the sporting goods store, where I purchased a beaded quiver for Mike's collection of arrows. Afterwards, he grabbed my hand again, and I let him hold it. I clung to him like a little kid depending on her big brother for guidance. Overwhelmed by our surroundings, I lost sense of the time. Pete ended up reminding me that I needed to get home. On our drive back, he asked me for my opinion of his part of town.

"That market was fascinating! I must admit that I liked it."

A grin dimpled his cheeks. "I thought ya might."

I remembered to ask him if he planned to be at the church to help decorate it for Christmas Eve candlelight service.

"When is that again?"

"6:30 Wednesday night."

"Ya gonna be there?"

"I said I would be there at the meeting, remember?"

"I'll be there, too."

He turned on his car radio. Some strange-sounding disc jockey on WKBW introduced a song by the Dell Vikings. "Come Go with Me" filled the clumsy silence between us, followed by unfamiliar renditions of songs I thought I recognized, although they sounded strange to me. Finally, he pulled his car into my driveway, jumped out, and opened my door. "See ya, sweetie," he said, smiling broadly.

"Please don't call me that. But thanks for ... the ride."

His car rocketed off, filling the air with his music and leaving me with the bizarre sensation that I had just been let off at my home by an extraterrestrial creature after a spin in another galaxy. What had happened? This afternoon had been one big, dreadful mistake, and I had only myself to blame. How stupid could I get? I let him drag me into a world full of green and black aliens. I had never even mentioned my plans for college. He had held my hand! It was ridiculous. What had I been thinking? Had I been thinking at all? I reviewed the escapade in my mind, and that confusing visceral sensation that I felt when he looked into my eyes came back. It lingered just long enough for me to take an odd pleasure in it before I hated myself for doing so. I hung up my coat and walked toward my room when Mom passed by. She asked me why I looked so gloomy.

"I went Christmas shopping with Pete."

"Whatever for? Why with him, of all people? He obviously has no taste. I thought you hated him. Did he trick you into it?"

"No, no, nothing like that. He didn't do anything wrong. I

got myself into it because … someone asked me to be nice to him. We talked about Christmas shopping, and I asked him for ideas about what to get Mike. He said he'd take me somewhere different to find something special for him. That part actually worked out well. But, otherwise, it was a huge mistake. He is so … I don't know. Impossible?"

Mom looked puzzled. She shrugged her shoulders and walked toward the kitchen. I spent the rest of the day wrapping presents, addressing labels, and kicking myself.

## Chapter 19
## KISSES SWEETER THAN WINE

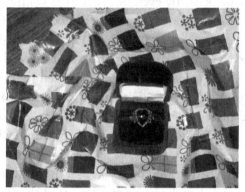

*The Heart Ring*

The Christmas pageant went off without a hitch. Afterwards, the cast and choir gathered in the back of the nave to receive congratulations. I circulated through the crowd in my Mary costume spreading goodwill like a nun. Out of the corner of my eye, I saw Pete tearing off his costume as he raced out the back door. I looked around for Pastor French and spotted him chatting happily with the parents of Neal. Pete's sister Judy hung close to her father's side; her oversized wings flopping downward. She beamed proudly.

On the following Tuesday, around sundown, I walked across the snow-dusted pathway worn in the dead grass between our house and the Beckers'. I found Shirley and her father George loading boxes full of Christmas decorations into their long sedan. George was like a peacock, all puffed up over his position as chairman of the most important decoration project on the church calendar. I helped them finish packing his car, while George bragged about his plan to make a poinsettia Christmas tree like the one Betty had found pictured in her December *Woman's Day* magazine. When his crew gathered at the back of the church, he doled out assignments. Shirley, who had never taught Sunday school nor gone to a Luther League meeting, acted like a bigwig. She handed me a box full of red bows, gave Joyce a carton of pine sprigs, and ordered us to cut the sprigs and tie them together carefully, "with perfectly even bows." Other volunteers lined the window frames with garlands of pine or decorated the choir loft, the pulpit, lectern, and altar with pine sprigs and bows. Some people helped George with his poinsettia tree or decorated the pews. Soon the sweet smell of pine permeated the nave, chancel, and narthex, and George's poinsettia tree became a spectacular scarlet centerpiece near the main altar. The nave was abuzz with people working, gossiping, and stopping to admire what they had accomplished.

When I finished my tedious task, I sat in a middle pew to rest and look around. For the first time, I noticed that Pete had been working in the back. He seemed engrossed in hanging a garland on a high arch. Shirley Becker steadied his ladder. The two of them were laughing.

I slumped down into the pew, feeling a bit sorry for myself. I had helped organize a crew of kids and had given of my own precious time and effort, yet no one except Joyce and that bossy Susie had spoken to me. The troublesome person who had paid so much attention to me a couple of days ago now seemed quite enamored with my young blonde neighbor. Why did that matter anyway? Silently I sulked up at the ceiling, not noticing I was no longer alone in the pew.

"Somethin' botherin' ya?"

"Ah, no." I thought fast. "I guess I was just wishing my family wasn't planning to go to the early service on Christmas Eve."

"Why don't ya go ta the midnight service if ya want ta?"

"I never drive out alone that late at night. It can be dangerous for a girl to drive out alone in the dark."

"Ya want I should take ya?"

"Did you say, 'Would you like to go to the late service with me?'"

"Somethin' like that," he grinned.

"Were you planning to go?"

"Nope. But I'll take ya, if you want me ta."

I sat up straight. "I wouldn't dream of asking you to go out of your way for me."

"Yer bein' stupid again, ain't ya?"

"Why do you use such terrible grammar?"

"Why not?"

"Because it makes you sound so stupid. At least I'm trying to make the best of the gifts God gave me. You should too."

"Shit! What bought that on? Look, if ya don't want ta go ta the late service, just say so, and cut the crap."

"I'm thinking about it. And don't swear in church." I sat and stewed at the ceiling for about two minutes. He didn't move, and I didn't look at him. "Okay, I'd like to go to the late service with you," I grumbled. "But no holding my hand, okay? I don't want anyone to get the wrong idea about us."

"Oh, heaven forbid." He looked up at the church ceiling too, gesturing toward it as if he were imploring the heavens to agree with his opinion of females. "Don't worry, baby, I'll pretend like I don't know ya."

"I didn't ask you to do that. Just act like a gentleman. Is that too much to ask? You do understand what I mean by 'act like a gentleman,' don't you?"

"I'll pick ya up at 10:30," he snarled.

"I'll come out to your car," I said bossily, trying to mask my uncertainty about the whole idea. No wonder I had never been any good at chess. When would I learn to think things out more carefully when I was unsure of the next move?

My parents were bewildered when I told them that I wasn't

going with them to the regular family time Christmas Eve service, but with Pete French to the midnight service instead. Both of them eyed me suspiciously. "For the life of me, I can't understand why you're doing this," Mom complained. "Wasn't going shopping with that boy enough? I thought you acted a bit strange after you got home. Have you forgotten all the terrible things you've said in the past about Pete? Are you sure he's not after you? He could be dangerous for all you know, Sandy."

"Oh, Marie," Dad piped in. "I think she knows what she's doing."

"Well, she has to get dressed at the same time as everyone else. I want a photograph of the four kids dressed in their church Christmas clothing in front of our tree to use on next year's Christmas cards."

"Sure, Mom, I'll be happy to do that."

"And you must promise to come home right after the service," Dad said firmly.

While my family was at church, I finished wrapping their gifts. I distributed them under the tree among the early gifts we had already gotten from friends and neighbors. I knew that my parents would scatter the bulk of the packages under the tree when the other kids had gone off to bed, while I was still out.

Pete picked me up at the driveway at the appointed time. Had he gotten his hair trimmed? It was still too long for my taste, and he had combed it in place with too much Vaseline, but it looked slightly better that night for some reason. I noticed that he wore a white shirt and black tie under his coat.

"I ain't myself tonight, if that's what yer look means. Excuse me, but I *am* a stranger and a gentleman like *you* said ya wanted me *to* be." His partially corrected speech pattern amused me, but unsure of my footing, I refrained from commenting.

We drove in silence to the church, where we were lucky to find a parking space. It surprised me to see how many people were out at midnight. Although both of us almost tiptoed in, settling quickly down into a back pew, Betty Marsh spotted us together and gaped at us with a look of … what was it? Consternation?

The service was beautiful in every way. When Pete didn't pick up a hymnal, I offered to share mine at an appropriate distance. Most of the time he barely moved his lips, but I belted out the familiar carols with gusto. Although we sat in the back of the church, I distinctly felt that Pastor French was aware of the two of us there together. I thought I saw him smile our way once. As soon as the last amen was sung, Pete whispered, "Let's get outta here now, okay?" I hastily followed him out, whispering "Merry Christmas" to Betty.

When he opened the car door, I slid onto the front bench. I was thankful that his convertible, flame-covered top was up, because it was cold. He got in behind the wheel and said, "Well, did I act okay?"

"Yes, thank you."

With his right hand he patted the part of the bench that was closest to him. "Com'mon, move over. You'll be warmer over here."

I eyed him distrustfully.

"Sandy, I ain't gonna bite ya."

I moved toward him, about three inches.

He pulled the car out, and we headed in a direction that would take us farther away from my house.

"Where are you taking me?" My voice rose in alarm. "I promised my parents I'd be home right after the service."

"Calm down, will ya? I have somethin' fer ya."

That's when he gave me the red rhinestone heart ring and then told me it meant nothing. Nothing? What would my friends think if they were to see me wearing it? What would my parents think? He couldn't have chosen a worse gift! And I had nothing to offer him in return. I was in deep trouble. And the evening wasn't over yet.

"You knew it would fit, didn't you?" I asked him, staring at the heart on my finger and trying to appear grateful.

He looked into my eyes searchingly, seemed satisfied, and restarted the engine. This time he drove directly to my house. He turned on his car radio to WKBW, which was playing Patsy Cline's "Walkin' after Midnight." Although it wasn't a Christmas carol, it seemed somehow appropriate to me. As we approached my driveway, I asked him to turn off the radio. It was time for me to warn him about King, the killer guard dog.

"You can just drop me off like you've done before. If you see me to the door, King, our German shepherd, will attack you. He's extremely protective of me."

"Naw, I'm not gonna let ya go ta yer door alone in the dark. Not at this hour. It ain't right. Not fer a gentleman like me."

"I'm warning you, Pete; King will try to kill you. He has attacked people before. When he bit our mailman once—"

He interrupted me. "Shut up, baby," he grinned. "No arguments. A lady has ta do what a gentleman asks. I'm goin' ta walk you to your door, and you ain't gonna stop me."

"All right, but don't say I didn't warn you."

Pete walked me to the side door. As I began to open it, King bounded toward us, barking at full bark, aiming straight for Pete's leg.

"Hi ya, King," Pete said. To my amazement, he whacked the silly animal sharply on the top of his head with the flat of his hand. King looked stunned. Did I detect the seeds of admiration sprouting in his brown eyes? Silently, he followed Pete inside behind me, neither of them uttering a sound. I was at a loss. Nothing was going as expected, including what I said to Pete next.

"Do you want to come into the living room to see our tree? How about a glass of Coke and some of our homemade Christmas cookies?"

"Ya sure yer ... *your* ... folks wouldn't mind?"

"Not as long as we're quiet."

We walked in through the kitchen, King prancing along at Pete's side, his tongue wagging happily.

"Let me help you off with yer coat," Pete said after I had unbuttoned it. I could sense his warmth as he stood behind me and slowly removed my coat. He took off his own coat, and I asked him to hang both of them on the hooks in the hallway.

I poured two glasses of Coke, gave one to Pete, and offered him a choice of our frosted homemade Christmas cookies.

"Everyone helped to decorate them, even Mike, although he ate more than he decorated."

"They look great," he said appreciatively. "Very colorful."

He chose a green angel that Jerry frosted and a ball-shaped blue and red cookie that I had decorated myself. I took one of Patty's purple Santas. Pete broke off a piece of one of his cookies and tossed it to King as I led him into the living room and turned on one of the side lamps. When I plugged the tree lights on, the tinsel-laden, heavily ornamented, ceiling-high spruce dazzled me. The mound of wrapped presents of various shapes and sizes created a perfect Christmas picture. I sat down on the couch, and Pete seated himself beside me.

The Coke gave me a buzzy feeling. "Isn't everything beautiful?" I sighed happily.

"Ya think so, do ya? I think it's a gaudy monument to conspicuous consumption." Those were his exact words.

"What do you mean by that?" I asked him archly.

"Obviously yer family likes to show off its dough."

"That's nasty, Pete. I thought you would find it as beautiful as I think it is. I didn't invite you here for a critical evaluation."

"Is this what you think Christmas is for?"

"I know the true meaning of Christmas as well as you do, Peter French. But people give each other gifts because it's one way to express our love for each other." His ring suddenly stung my finger. "Uh, I mean, it's just a family custom, of course. For us. People give presents for all sorts of reasons." I became painfully aware that my face was flushing.

"Do you think ya need all them ... those ... things?"

"We don't *need* them, no. But Dad works hard because he wants us to enjoy what his hard-earned money can buy."

"It looks to me like all a ya are very impressed with your own money, and maybe ya like ta show everyone what your money can buy."

"What a horrible thing to say! Don't you give presents in your family?"

"I ain't never seen this many presents at one time in my life."

"Oh. I'm sorry, Pete. It was thoughtless of me to invite you inside. Honestly, I didn't intend to show off or make you feel badly. I just love Christmas, that's all."

"I can see why, baby."

"Please, no more arguing, okay?" We finished our cookies in silence, sharing some pieces with King. When I had sipped the last drop of my Coke, I noticed that the tree lights caused a blurry kaleidoscope of colors in the bottom of the glass. "Look at the tree through the bottom of your glass, Pete. Isn't it pretty?"

"Yeah, it's pretty," he agreed. "But not as pretty as you are."

My face felt hot. I jumped up from the couch.

"Well," I said, "it has been a … nice Christmas Eve, but I'm getting tired, and tomorrow will be a big day."

We walked into the kitchen. In front of the refrigerator, I stopped to thank him again for the ring. He leaned toward me, and before I could stop him, his dry, firm lips pressed mine gently. Without thinking, I kissed him back. Then I looked deeply into his questioning eyes. They registered that unsettling look that I had seen in them at the market. Suddenly they turned inscrutable, and I smiled at him uncertainly

"I can git my coat," he said gruffly. "G'night."

"Good night. And Merry Christmas."

King barked at Pete just once, as if he too were wishing him a Merry Christmas.

I turned off all the lights. As I walked to my bedroom, I sensed movement behind my parents' door. Patty was sound asleep, as usual. I put the heart ring into its case, hid it in the bottom of my jewelry box, got into my pajamas, climbed into bed, and counted three slow-moving shadows on the wall, caused by passing car lights. I couldn't sleep. Like old Ebenezer Scrooge, a Christmas ghost haunted me. She had a face that looked like Miss Maxmillian's.

When I finally did get to sleep, I was harshly awakened about a half hour later, or so it seemed, by the eager voices of my brothers and sister urging me to come see what's in the living room. "Get up, sleepy head. It's Christmas!"

I blamed Pete for making me feel tired and irritable on that of all days. Darn him. The grave digger had managed to put a pall on my favorite holiday. As I watched the other kids tear open the wrappings of their gifts, I couldn't help but notice that in their haste to see what they got, they paid no attention to the work that had gone into the wrappings. Even Mom and Dad opened their presents with disregard for the work that had gone into their preparation. I thanked everyone for each gift, but they hardly paid me any attention.

In less than half an hour, all the presents had been unwrapped, except a few of mine. Games, Jerry's elaborate new train set, planes, cars, dolls, numerous other toys, clothes, boxes of jewelry, books, and various items of sporting equipment were scattered all over the living room floor. After I finished opening my gifts, Mom and Dad took their presents to the back of the house and told everyone else to do the same. Then Dad began collecting wrapping paper and ribbons into a big bag intended for the garbage can.

Pete's extraordinary description of our stack of presents as a symbol of conspicuous consumption gnawed at me. Ironically, Einstein was wrong about one thing: our pile of presents was not conspicuous long enough for anyone other than the six of us to notice. He was the only outsider to have seen them; the mirage had vanished. But his disapproving words wouldn't go away. I asked myself why I should feel guilty about my presents. Why am I letting his ideas get to me anyway? Don't I deserve these things? No one, not even Pete, could possibly take objection to the books I received; or would he? He'd probably find something about them to criticize.

Dad, who was enjoying a beer and a cigarette after sitting down to rest from his work and the general excitement, asked me to model the expensive silver fox fur-collared, silk-lined, maroon-dyed camel's hair dress coat he and Mom had given me. He tipped his glass to me and told me it looked elegant. He thanked me for the plaid woolen sweater vest I had bought him. Mom, who also seemed to be in a good mood, pinned on the rhinestone flower brooch that I had so carefully selected for her, and Dad complimented her on how smart it looked. Mike seemed genuinely happy with the quiver I had bought him at that weird city market. Pat and Jerry went off to play with their new toys by themselves. Pete's bleak attitude is simply twisted, I thought as I watched them engaged in such harmless pleasures.

Suddenly Mom popped up out of her chair and asked me come with her into the kitchen. Her demeanor looked alarmingly stern.

"I saw you kiss Pete French right here last night," she said, pointing to the refrigerator.

"Oh. Well, yes. But it was just a little peck."

"Don't beat around the bush with me, Sandy. I want to know the truth. What's going on between you two? I thought you hated that boy. Have you been lying to your father and me about him for some reason?"

"No. Honestly, that little peck was meaningless. Earlier he gave me a surprise gift: a heart-shaped rhinestone ring, of all things. I didn't want to accept it, but giving it back would have been too impolite, wouldn't it?"

"Heart-shaped? Oh, no!" Mom exclaimed.

"Don't worry. It's just a bauble, Mom. I let him kiss me only because I felt badly that I had nothing for him. That's all there is to it." She looked skeptical, so I added, "It's not as if he's even a friend, not really."

"I would like to believe you, but it looked to me as if you two were getting along quite well. For the life of me, I can't understand why you felt obliged to kiss that unattractive boy."

"I'm sorry if it worried you. Please don't let it spoil our day, Mom, okay?"

Darn that PK, I thought to myself. He's managed to make me feel as if I'm wearing a scarlet letter.

The rest of the day went better, in spite of my lack of pep and occasional irritability. We exchanged gifts with Grandma, Grandpa, and Tanta, and the nine of us enjoyed a hearty holiday dinner on our dining room table. The lingering good spirits of everyone else masked my silence.

During the rest of Christmas vacation, I finished up my school projects, drew up my music-themed mural for the Luther League dance, and shopped with Barb at post-holiday sales for clothes to add to our respective college wardrobes.

On the day before New Year's Eve, Pete picked me up and helped me carry the party supplies into the church basement. He looked cranky and hardly said a word. I couldn't attribute his mood to anything I had done. He drove in silence to the church, where we got busy hanging and distributing pink and white decorations. Susie and Carol helped me tape my mural up on one wall. We covered small tables with white cloths. In the center of each tablecloth, we set an empty Chianti bottle dripping with candle wax from a pink candle stuck in its gap. I realized that Sally and her parents had spent a good deal of time creating those centerpieces. I was alone, distributing hats and noisemakers around the tables, when Pete sidled up behind me.

"Ya ain't gittin' me ta wear one a them dumb hats," he grumped.

"Why would I do that? As far as I'm concerned, you can wear a black fedora and trench coat and sit in a corner and sulk all night like a big thug."

He skulked off, and I surveyed the results of our work. The final effect was that of a make-believe nightclub, more for kids than for grown-ups, which seemed appropriate for a Luther League event. Pete reappeared and asked me if I would mind if we stopped by the Marshes' house on our way home, just for a short visit.

"I ain't been there since a few weeks before Christmas, and I promised Betty I'd drop in. Will ya come with me?"

"I'd rather not. Can't you just drop me off on your way there? I have things to do."

"Aw, com'mon. If you're there, I can git away faster. *Please*, Sandy?"

Reluctantly, I agreed and then mentally kicked myself again. After we got in his car, he turned on the radio, so there was no need for us to talk. When he rang the Marshes' doorbell, Betty greeted us, holding a glass of wine, looking somewhat askance at me. She warmly hugged Pete, and he kissed her cheek. The home was small, but it felt warm and cozy. The sweet odor of dying pine permeated the air. Betty offered us lemonade and Christmas cookies; then she handed Pete a wrapped present. Obviously surprised, he chided her for having wasted money on him, but he perked up and remarked about how prettily she had wrapped it. He opened it with care. The box contained a striped tie in various shades of blue. He thanked her with such earnest gratefulness that I regretted not having gotten him anything. Sally Marsh edged shyly into the room, dressed in a white cardigan sweater set and full pink and white poodle skirt.

"Ah, Sally," her mother said, "I'm glad to see that your new outfit looks so lovely on you. Don't you agree, Pete?"

"Ya look very nice," Pete said to her, with an appreciative smile. Her face turned red.

Betty began to wink at her daughter. Sally looked as confused by her mother's odd behavior as I was. I noticed that Betty seemed to be holding her wine glass at an odd angle, with one of her fingers pointed toward the ceiling and I looked up. A sprig of mistletoe tied with a red ribbon hung from a lamp just above Pete's head. Sally took no notice of the mistletoe, or at least pretended not to see it. Looking frustrated, Betty said, "If you don't kiss him, I will. Come on, Sally." Sally obeyed her mother by shyly planting a peck on Pete's cheek.

Pete said "thank you," an appreciative smile dimpling his cheeks. He looked over at me, expectantly. I stepped under the mistletoe and kissed him on his lips, an act that shocked me as much as everyone else in the room. Perhaps I did it to frustrate Betty, or maybe I wanted to see if a second kiss would feel as good as that first one had. It did.

"Well!" Betty exclaimed. "It looks to me as if you two have done that before." Pete deftly changed the subject, they chatted briefly, and then he asked her to excuse us, making a big deal about having to get me back home before my parents started to worry. "Pete, you can come back later," Betty said, enticingly. "You're welcome here anytime. We have plenty of good leftovers to eat." She patted his cheeks. Pete winked at Sally, thanked Betty again for the tie, and promised her he'd be back "real soon."

He had his radio on as he drove me home, its dial tuned to his favorite music station. A boisterous disk jockey calling himself the "Hound Dog of WKBW" introduced a song by the Monotones called "Who Wrote the Book of Love?" Then a man with the incredible name of Bo Diddley sang something unfamiliar, in a voice that sounded Negro to me. Pete pulled his car into my driveway.

"Ya want I should pick you up for the dance?" he asked me offhandedly.

"I guess so. What time?"

"Quarter to nine okay?"

"I guess so," I shrugged. "Don't bother to open my door for me now. I can go in myself this time. See you later."

As his is car squealed off, a Negro voice singing "Ain't That a Shame" filled the air.

## Chapter 20
## ALL SHOOK UP

Pete removed his outer coat as we walked down the church stairs toward the basement. He was wearing one of his churchy outfits that seemed more appropriate for spring than for January: white shirt, the blue striped tie that the Marshes had given him, a dark blue jacket, and tan pants. He carried a box containing a white orchid for me. I hadn't expected an orchid; I had gotten him a rather measly white carnation.

I spotted sprigs of mistletoe scattered among the decorations. My committee hadn't hung them, so I suspected they were the work of Sally's parents, one of two sets of chaperones. Mr. and Mrs. Adolf, Neal's parents, constituted the second set. Most of the kids brought dates. For many of them, it was a first date. When the music began, Pete moved among them, encouraging everyone to relax. Neal asked me to dance; Pete didn't seem to care. He chatted amiably with Betty and then danced with Sally. As the night wore on, however, he monopolized my dance card. The first time he kissed me on the dance floor, I protested that he wasn't supposed to do that until midnight. He pointed up at the mistletoe. As the night progressed, he repeatedly maneuvered me back under the mistletoe, and a strange euphoria swept over me. Each of his kisses felt better than the last: warm, dry, and sensual.

The obvious disapproval of the entire Adolf family didn't faze me. In fact, it may have heightened my mood.

Occasionally, I took a few jabs at Pete, harping about his lack of seriousness about his future and bragging about my own plans. He always managed to change the subject or silence me with another kiss. When he finally mumbled about how he'd like to drive big trucks all over the continent, I said, "You can't be serious, Pete. Come upstairs with me. God will tell you what to do."

"*What?*"

I grabbed his hand, led him up into the dark nave, and asked him to sit beside me in a pew. Reluctantly, he plopped down. "I want to say a New Year's prayer."

"Yer nuts. I came ta dance, not pray."

"Please, just listen."

I folded my hands. "Dear Heavenly Father, bless Pete tonight. Guide him to make the most of the gifts that you have given him. Thank you. Amen." Since my eyes were closed, I couldn't see Pete's reaction, but his sudden coughing fit was hard to ignore.

I nearly fell out of the pew when a deep voice boomed out from the back of the church. "Get out of there, you two. No necking in the church."

Apparently, Neal's father had followed us and had totally misconstrued what was going on. I looked for a sign of empathy from Pete, but he looked amused. "We're outta here, sir," he shouted to the chaperone. We scurried back down the stairs.

After midnight, when the noise making, hugging, and kissing were over, Pete drove me home and parked in my driveway. He told me he was seriously thinking of taking off for Florida. When I began to chide him, he silenced me with kisses and eventually walked me to the side door. Before falling asleep that night, I suffered more pangs of doubt. Why was I allowing this guy to take such liberty with me? I needed to control myself, and fast.

Mom and Dad made their dislike of Pete painfully obvious. They said they hated his looks, the way he talked, and his mysterious power over me. In their eyes, I was a naïve innocent, and he was a wily villain determined to ruin me. Looking back, I realize that those early months of 1959 were a bewildering time for both Pete and me. He fascinated me, but I sensed he was hiding something from me, and I thought his talk of leaving for Florida was just a bunch of malarkey.

"I just wanna go far away, see? My ol' man would be better off if I was outta his hair."

"You're just saying that to make me feel sorry for you."

"What would I do that for? That's nuts. Don't ya, ah, you, get it? Anything's better for me than this damn town."

He always seemed halfway out the door. I imagine that the feelings I awoke in him had thrown the proverbial monkey wrench into his plans. They confused and bothered him just as much my feelings for him disturbed and worried me.

To my astonishment, I learned that Mike knew more about Pete's secret life than I did. I hadn't even been aware that he and Pete had been going places together, so when he told me what happened at Our Place, I was stunned and somewhat jealous.

"Once when we were together at Our Place, Pete nearly went ape," my brother said, obviously savoring the distress his words were causing me. "He had a bad case of smog in his noggin."

"What?"

"Get with the picture, Sis. Pete couldn't remember where he had been the night before. He asked the bartender if he had been there. When the guy said no, I thought Pete was going to lose his supper."

"Did he ever find out?"

"Yeah. He figured out that he had fallen asleep in his car."

While this was going on, I was engulfed in school projects, including extensive research for an English paper on Ralph Waldo Emerson's essays. Emerson's ideas unsettled me because most of them clashed with the beliefs of the church.

"I can't agree with Emerson's one Over-Soul, self-reliant theories," I said to Pete one day. "I believe all truth comes through faith in God."

He laughed at me. "Define faith or truth or God. Geez, Sandy, things ain't as simple as you want 'em to be."

"What gives you the right to laugh? What do you know about this?"

"Enough not to make black and white statements. But I don't wanna argue, babe."

My parents couldn't help me. Transcendentalism was not on their vocabulary list. "Nothing with that many syllables ever makes any sense," Dad told me.

One day in January, Susie called me to tell me that when Pete phoned her to say he wouldn't be around to give her more of his poetry to type, he slurred his words and sounded muddled. Her news made sick. To ease my confusion, I wrote some heavy-handed iambs of my own, ending with the couplet:

Such strife to find the keys to life.
Does he need help, or is it I?

Pete was nothing but a waste of my precious time, I told myself. I should let him drive a truck to Florida and be done with him. I concluded once and for all that Pete was not my kind of person. However, when he called to ask me out to a movie with him, I accepted him on the spot, hung up, and gorged myself on Milky Way candy bars. I hadn't heard about teenage eating disorders back then; I just knew that Dr. Irwin would chastise me for taking in all those calories. The thought of vomiting them back up never occurred to me. Nobody threw up on purpose, as far as I knew. I didn't know about sugar highs either. I just knew that the candy made me feel happy. The next day I told Paul he looked gorgeous when I passed by his seat in English, and in chemistry lab, I got a kick out of convincing Vivian that she was working with explosive acid. After school that day, I tackled the scenery work vigorously with Barb and a mutual friend of ours, Sylvia Zimmer, a Jewish doctor's daughter. With the help of the stage crew tsar, Glenn Ackart, we finished an entire set that afternoon, only taking a break long enough to pay homage to Elvis's birthday.

I was full of sugar-primed energy all that week. On Friday, I painted a whole set by myself after school. That evening after dinner, the rest of the family took off for a basketball game. I was in the bathroom, applying fresh lipstick for my date with Pete, when Ken phoned to ask me out to a play at the university on the following night. He apologized for the late invitation; his dad had just given him the tickets. I agreed to go with him, thinking he might offer a calm break from my stormy, overwrought velocity. After I hung up, Pete rang the bell and staggered inside, nearly tripping over King. It was obvious that he had been drinking.

"Pete, you're drunk," I declared disgustedly. "Go home."

"Com'mon, Sandy, I ain't drunk. I may have had a shot or two, but that ain't nothin' fer me."

"*Nothing*? I'm not going out with you. Get out of here!"

"Please, baby, ya gotta. I need ya." He gently grabbed my shoulders from behind, his cheek touching mine.

"No," I said, with less conviction, melting at his touch and his need.

"Look, I swear to God." He faced me squarely, looking into my eyes. "Ya got a Bible? I'll swear on it. I'll drive like I was Saint Pete hisself. Gimme this chance, baby. If ya don't like how I drive, I'll git ya, you, a taxi, okay? I really need you, Sandy; *please* don't do this to me."

I caved in, and he drove like Saint Peter without wings, never once taking his eyes off the road. We saw *Some Came Running*. The main character of the movie is a writer played by Frank Sinatra who falls in love with a classy English teacher. His friend, played by Dean Martin, has a lethal drinking problem. A needy, loose woman played by Shirley MacLaine is his tragic love interest. As I watched the film, I felt increasingly uneasy about the parallels between what was happening on the screen and what was going on between Pete and me. Once or twice during the film, I felt Pete's eyes on me. By the time the movie ended, Pete appeared to be quite sober. He took me to Santori's, where we had pizza and argued.

I told him I didn't like the movie. The characters were too sinister. Pete raved about the film and Vincent Minelli, its director. He told me he suspected that the Hays Code had restricted Minelli from making the movie even more explicit. When I asked him what the Hays Code was, he sighed and mumbled something about my whole family living under the Hays Code. I had no idea what he meant, but I knew he was criticizing us. I also hated the fact that I knew nothing about movie directing, and Pete did. We argued on the way home; we parted on a sour note, and I had difficulty getting to sleep.

One the following day, I looked forward to my date with Ken, but when he arrived, he acted like a stranger, as if he was annoyed with me too. His mood lasted throughout a long and rather silly eighteenth-century comedy of manners, even during the intermission. Afterwards I begged him to tell me what was bothering him.

"Sandy, I can't figure you out at all. You've been so involved with that greasy kid with the DA. I've seen you together. You sparkle when he's around. I'm sorry, but he appears to be a slob. He can't even speak English. What you see in him eludes me totally. But he's got some sort of hold over you. Frankly, I was amazed when you accepted this date with me. What's going on?"

"Ken, you do know that I think of you as a friend, don't you?"

He looked crestfallen. "Nothing more than a friend?"

"No, Ken, I thought you understood that. I don't feel any … this is trite, I know, but at the moment, I can't think of any other way to put it … any chemical reaction between us."

"And you feel one with that guy?" He stared at me blankly, stone-faced.

"I don't know how I feel about Pete. Most of the time he's nothing but trouble. But I really do want to be your friend, Ken.

You have many admirable qualities. I sincerely wish I felt more of a spark when I'm with you."

He remained stone-faced. Then he said bitterly, "I shall never bother you again."

He drove me directly home in silence, and we parted without saying another word.

That night in bed, I wondered if I had just made a terrible mistake. Ken was a kind, sensitive soul. I had been honest with him. I hadn't meant to hurt him. Why did I always end up feeling badly when I tried to do the right thing?

At Luther League the next night, Susie slipped me a carbon copy of something that Pete had written. I put it in my purse and read it alone at home. It appeared to be some form of a song lyric titled "Poor Drunk Fool."

> I lost all my money in a poker game,
> And I think my left leg's goin' lame.
> My father asked me to change my name,
> And that's what I think I'll do.
> My doctor told me not to smoke.
> My gal says drink nothin' stronger than Coke.
> I'm not even supposed to hear a dirty joke.
> If I laugh it'll strain my heart.
> I don't know much, but I'll tell you right now,
> I'm milkin' the wrong end of this old cow,
> And there's too many wrinkles in this guy's brow.
> Seems liquor'll have to go.

"My gal" was me; Pete felt unwanted by his father, and he drank too much. It was all there. I had lost the respect of a sensitive person like Ken because of a guy who wrote country lyrics? What was the matter with me?

In mid-January, Dad sent Gettysburg College a sizable check to seal the deal for my college education. Pete was writing more lyrics and a book, apparently a tale based upon his experiences at

Kensington, his reform school buddies, and his former girlfriends. Susie said he had a lot of girlfriends back in Kensington. I caught myself feeling jealous of them. Ken was right: he did have some sort of hold on me. I wasn't clueless. I knew we had a sexual thing going on. After our dates, we usually necked shamelessly in his car in my driveway before I went indoors. I excused this to myself as a learning experience. After all, most of my friends had been necking with their boyfriends for years.

When first semester report cards came out, I literally beamed in the glow of my straight A's, not knowing that Pete was drinking whiskey at the Cross Roads bar with some guy I didn't know. Sue called to warn me that he was drunk before he arrived to pick me up for our date. I met him at the door and sent him packing. He returned seemingly sober in an hour, and we went to see *Bell, Book, and Candle,* a movie about a witch, played by Kim Novak, who allows love to take away her magical powers. I found the theme oddly disturbing. Afterwards, I asked him to take me straight home. On the way, he repeatedly apologized for his drinking. After he parked his car in my driveway, he grabbed my right hand, took my heart ring off, and moved it to the third finger of my left hand.

"Please go steady with me, Sandy. I hate thinkin' about you bein' with other guys."

"Why would I do that, Pete? Most of the time you drive me crazy."

"Good crazy?"

"No!" I stared out the window thinking. Finally, I said, "I'll make a deal with you, Pete. I won't date anyone else if you agree to stop drinking. Is it a deal?"

"Deal."

Sealed with a genuine French kiss.

I told myself that everything I did with him was for the greater cause of getting him to go to college. But while January slipped away, my weight kept increasing. At my pre-college physical, Dr. Irwin warned me about my weight gain. "I've seen this problem in many teenagers, Sandy, especially girls. They either overeat or skip meals because of problems related to boys, scholastic demands, or uncertainty about the future. I'm no psychiatrist, but I'm warning you to be careful. I don't want to have to put you on a diet again."

I tried to heed his orders, but the conflicting feelings I suffered when I was with Pete only made my Milky Way binges more difficult to control. In the spring semester, we ended up in the same sociology class. His seat was directly behind mine. It made me feel even more uncomfortable than Paul's similar position in English had done at the beginning of the previous semester. Soon Pete began to skip school again, and on the days that he was there, he seemed despondent and unresponsive to my attempts to cheer him up.

Paul Hartmann, on the other hand, appeared to be a veritable font of positive energy. He never stopped flirting with me, along with every other girl on the planet. I thought he was kidding me when he told me one day, out of the blue, that his mother thought I was beautiful. When I mentioned his comment to Mom, she replied that Grandma Schall had liked her before Dad did. That threw me for a loop. She had told me before that she had to work hard to win over both Grandma and Grandpa Schall. I knew that Grandma wasn't a thoughtful or critical sort of woman, but she was friendly to everyone. She scarcely said a bad word about anyone other than Roosevelt, the Japs, the Jews, all Democrats, and anyone who was not well-to-do and white. Of course she liked Mom. She just didn't want Mom to marry her son.

I worked hard on my English thesis, consumed too much coffee in order to keep myself up working late at night, smoked at home, went on candy binges, and worried about Pete. One night, I had a scary dream about him getting hurt. I told Susie about it, and she told me that he had been driving out alone late almost every school night.

"He isn't drinking again, is he?"

"I don't think so. But a few nights ago, some rival city gang members knifed him in the arm during a fight at a soda shop on Baily Avenue. Sandy, you must swear not to tell Pete you know about this."

The next week, Pete took me to a church potluck supper and watched silently while Neal hugged me and then asked me out on Friday. Pete just stood there. His lack of jealousy hurt me, and I said so.

"I wanted to hit Neal, Sandy, but I coulda hurt him really bad."

I asked Pete to take me to *Show Boat* on Valentine's Day. Afterwards, he complimented me on the sets and said the musical production was fine, for a high school play. But he criticized Amherst for using white kids in black face paint to portray black characters and called the acting insipid and stereotypical. When I complained that he was spoiling the evening, he dropped the subject. We made brief appearances at the cast party and then went to a stage crew celebration. Afterwards, I lingered in his car in my driveway until around four in the morning, when I snuck inside.

By then, Pete and I were into heavy petting: long, lingering kisses, hands underneath clothing, carnal exploration. I kept telling myself that I was probably just catching up with what most of my friends had been doing for years. We never went "all the way," although there were times when I wanted to, and I had every reason to believe that he was more than eager to do so too. But I refused to risk losing everything that I'd worked so hard for. Would it have been different if the pill had been available then? Perhaps. Would I have been too embarrassed to ask a doctor for it? Probably. I suppose I could have gotten a diaphragm, but I knew enough about those devices to suspect that they were awkward and messy to insert, especially for a technical virgin like me. Pete could have gotten a condom, but I probably wouldn't have trusted it, and just seeing that he had it with him would have worried me. Anyway, for whatever reason, somehow, we remained like careful babes discovering a cache of Easter candies on Good Friday and saving it for Sunday. I wanted Pete, but I knew when to stop. When I insisted, he stopped. It wasn't easy.

Mom and Dad suspected the worst. They knew I had been sneaking in late, and they spoke to Pastor French about it. All three of them warned us that our "carrying-on" had to stop. I was embarrassed, but that didn't change anything. I clung to the belief that my determination to go to college would overpower and outlast the emotional fling that Pete and I were caught up in.

Incredibly, I asked Pete to talk to my dad about his problems with the pastor.

"Where would that get me, Sandy? I'm only a burden on my ol' man. Nothin' can change that."

"You're still planning to leave home for your dad's sake? What about me, Pete?"

"And four years ain't a long time? Com'mon, Sandy."

I knew what four years he meant. Nothing made any sense to me anymore. Finally, after taking me to see Disney's *Sleeping Beauty*, Pete told me that he loved me. I cried and burbled that I wished time would stop, that there'd be no future. I blurted out the terrible truth. I had plans for my life that didn't include him.

"Ya think I don't know that, Sandy? I love you, but we're doomed to part."

"*Why?*"

"That's the way it's gotta be."

# Chapter 21
## FIBBIN'

Near the beginning of March, for some reason, I asked Pete when his birthday was. For a moment, he seemed slightly thrown by the question, but he shrugged it off. "Jus' call me Joe. I was born on St. Joseph's Day."

"So, you're not even one month older than I am." He changed the subject, but I made a note to myself to try to wrinkle out whether or not he'd be pleased if I organized a party in honor of his eighteenth birthday. I assumed he wouldn't want anyone to make a fuss, but remembering how I badly I had felt about not getting him a Christmas present, I needed to know for sure.

Just a few days later, after a committee meeting at the church, I was walking alone down the center aisle, heading toward the front door, when Betty, the pastor's secretary, stopped me. "Sandy, may I speak to you about something personal?"

The expression on her face was difficult for me to read; it made me strangely uneasy. Nevertheless, I smiled politely and replied, "Of course, Mrs. Marsh."

She lowered her voice to a conspiratorial level and said, "I feel obliged to tell you something about Pete that I don't think you know."

"What is that, Betty?" I asked her edgily.

"Do you know how old he is?" she asked.

"Of course. He'll turn eighteen this month."

"I knew it! You're quite mistaken, my dear." The inscrutable look in her eyes caused me to take a step backward. She zeroed in closer to my face before she struck me with her fangs loaded. "He turns seventeen this month."

"*No!*" The sheer volume of my denial startled me. Her eyes told me that she knew her venom was strong. Mine was still rising.

"I'm sorry, Mrs. Marsh, but Pete couldn't legally drive alone at night if he weren't seventeen."

"Nonetheless, it *is* true. I'm only telling you this for your own good, not to get Pete into trouble. You think that you know that boy, Sandy, and anyone with two eyes can see you two are, well, shall I say pretty tightly hooked? But if he led you to believe that he's seventeen, he was lying to you, and it's about time you knew the truth, for his good as well as for yours."

"*You* are the one who is lying, Mrs. Marsh. I don't know why, except that you probably want Pete to date Sally. This is a ridiculous allegation. I never thought as badly of anyone as I do of you right now." I skirted quickly around her and continued on down the aisle, feeling as angry as a jilted bride. My heart pounded, and I was shaking all over. I had just accused an adult of lying, right to her face!

"If you won't believe me, ask his father," Betty cried out. "He's still in his office."

"I'm on my way there now," I responded archly over my shoulder, my back to her face.

I knocked gently on his closed door. "Betty?" he asked.

"No, Dr. French. It's Sandy Schall. Can I talk to you?"

"Of course."

He opened the door for me and offered me the chair opposite his desk. He smiled warmly and returned to his chair.

"How are you, Sandy?"

"Not too good at the moment, Pastor. Something ... strange ... has just upset me very much."

"Oh, I'm sorry to hear that. How can I be of help?" His words sounded uncomfortably hollow to me. Didn't he care?

"This is serious, Dr. French. Mrs. Marsh just told me a lie! Right in the church, too. I don't want to get her into any trouble or anything, but well, she *is* your secretary. She lied to me about Pete, Pastor."

Dr. French's expression altered. Now he looked concerned.

"Take a deep breath, Sandy, and tell me exactly what Betty said."

I recounted the incident. When I was done, he sat with his elbows on his desk and his fingers pressed together, seemingly lost in thought. "This just happened?" he asked me, cocking one eyebrow and eyeing me sympathetically.

I nodded. He excused himself, arose from his desk chair, opened his door, and called out, "Betty, please come here at once."

She popped in straight away, as if she had been waiting outside his door. I expected him to give her a tongue-lashing. Instead, he asked her if she knew where Pete was.

"I do," I volunteered. "He should be on his way here right now, to pick me up. He's going to drive me home this afternoon."

"I think I hear him coming into the church," Betty observed.

"Tell him to come directly into my office, please, Betty, and 'close my door after he's inside." She looked disappointed, as if she had hoped to stay. This wasn't going as I had expected. Wiggling in my chair, my eyes settled on a framed picture of Jesus, and a bizarre thought popped into my head: God must be a blond.

Pete's appearance in the office doorway interrupted my wacky train of thought. One glimpse at me would have told him I was irritated. He looked at his father, whose blue eyes were shooting darts at him. To my astonishment, Pete looked scared. He began to retreat from the doorway.

His father's commanding voice sounded brutal. "Come in here, Peter, and sit down." Pete slumped down into the chair next to the pastor's desk.

"How old are you, Peter?" The tone of the question was cruel.

Pete looked like a wounded animal. I had never seen such a beaten expression in his eyes. He slouched down into the chair, took a comb out of his pocket, and nervously began to comb it through his hair. He wouldn't look at me. I gaped at him in disbelief.

"Peter, answer my question," Dr. French said sternly.

"Don't you know when my birthday is?" Pete mumbled.

"Answer my question."

"It's a stupid question."

"Answer me."

Pete continued to run the comb through his hair. His eyes shifted around the room.

"How old are you?"

"Almost seventeen." Pete sighed out his answer like a dying soldier's last gasp.

"*No!*" I screamed. "*Liar!* You *must* be my age! You have … I have let you drive me out, everywhere *late at night*. You drive alone after dark all the time. You were breaking the law? You were, weren't you?" I gasped.

He wouldn't look me in the eye.

"You're in my *senior* sociology class. I had every reason to think you're a senior like me. You talked about becoming a truck driver *next year*!"

Pete looked as if he were going to be sick. Avoiding my eyes, he muttered, "I felt like I was your age. But I never told ya I was."

"You let me believe it. That's the same thing. Mom and Dad warned me you were no good. They were right all along! You're nothing but a liar and a lawbreaker. I was just plain stupid to have trusted you."

He stared miserably down at the floor, saying nothing.

"Peter French, I'm so disgusted with you. I never, ever want to see you again. Do you understand me?"

He continued to stare at the floor.

"I'm not your girl; I'm not your steady. I hate you! You've totally ruined my senior year. Because of you, I broke off with a perfectly decent guy. What a fool I was! I agreed to go steady with you because I *believed* your promises. I'll never make a mistake like that again. In fact, I never want to see you again, Peter French. Not ever!"

I started to cry uncontrollably, vaguely aware of Dr. French ordering Pete to wait outside. I couldn't look at Pete, but I heard him slump out of his father's office. Pastor offered me a Kleenex and a glass of water. I felt powerless; I couldn't control my ridiculous bawling. Then Dr. French excused himself and told me he would be back in a few minutes. He left the room, probably to order Pete to go home. When he returned, he offered to give me a ride. I nodded through my tears.

I stopped bawling, but I kept a Kleenex near my eyes when we were in his car. Dr. French spoke to me gently. "Fatherhood has not been easy for me, Sandy. Given my regrettable circumstances, Peter has often had to fend for himself. He has a habit of hanging around with older kids. Good or bad, they seemed to accept him as one of them." Pastor sighed. "Actually, Pete comes and goes pretty much as he pleases. I can't control him. I knew he liked you, of course, and I felt that was a good thing." He sighed again. "I knew he shouldn't be driving at night, but ... I couldn't stop him. Maybe I didn't want to stop him from being with you. You've been good for him."

"What about me? If I had known the truth ... you should have told me, Pastor."

"Sandy, I feel badly about this. But I believe that you need more time to think. Try to understand that our family circumstances are different from yours."

"I think I already grasp what're trying to tell me, Pastor," I managed say. "But there is no possible excuse for Pete's lying. And he was breaking the law too! I'm sorry to have to ask you this, but why didn't you stop him? You knew it was illegal; he was committing a crime every time he drove off alone at night."

"Perhaps your accusations are justified, Sandy. I wish I knew how to be stricter with Peter. But, please, don't be too hard on him. You have been a very good influence on his life. His behavior has improved a good deal since he has known you. I am so very, very sorry that you two have had this misunderstanding."

"*Misunderstanding*? Our whole time together has been based on a lie! I can't forgive him for that. He tricked me into caring for him. I thought he was my age. He knew that, and he never told me the truth."

"Now, now. Give this a little time. All will seem better in the morning."

"I'm sorry, but no it won't, Dr. French. I resent having been lied to. Please tell Pete that I don't want him to call me anymore. I don't want to see him again. *I'm being honest.* I mean what I'm saying."

We drove into my driveway. As I got out of his car, Dr. French patted my hand, looked into my eyes, and told me how sorry he was that his son had hurt me so badly. I began to sniffle again. He pleaded with me not to allow myself to get so upset. Between sniffles, I thanked him for the ride and reminded him to tell Pete I would *not* answer his calls.

I ran into my room, pulled the heart ring off my finger and threw it into the wastebasket. I flung myself on my bedspread and wailed.

Everybody in the house and probably everyone two doors down heard me. When my parents came into my room to ask me why I was so unhappy, I just shook my head and asked them to leave me alone for a while, *please*. When Mike popped his head in to ask me to come to dinner, I said, "Tell everyone I didn't feel like eating. But don't worry about me. Nothing's physically wrong, okay?"

"Everyone knows you're crazy, Sandy. We all understand," Mike said, not unkindly.

Later that evening, when it was time for the little kids to go to bed, I went out into the living room, lit a cigarette, and calmly told my parents what had happened. Dad admitted that he had called Ernie to find out what Pete had done to make me so upset. He knew the whole story, he said. Mom railed against Pete. "I tried to tell you that he's an ugly, no-good liar. Now maybe you'll believe me."

Dad just kept shaking his head, giving me his all-knowing look. "This is all for the best," he declared repeatedly.

"Pete lied to me. I won't forgive him for that. But I blame Miss Maxmillian and Pastor French too. They told me to be nice to him, to help him fit in at Luther League, to make him see his potential to become more than a truck driver. But they never told me he's not a senior." I teared up but controlled myself. I didn't want to break down again.

"This is my fault too, I suppose. I stupidly believed that I could help him. I should have known better. I even started to care about him. He told me he loved me. I didn't know that he was just *a kid*, a whole year younger than me! If I'd known that, I might have realized that he was going through a phase or something. I might have bribed him to be good with comic books and candy bars like the kids I babysat. What a fool I've been!"

"Don't be so hard on yourself, Sandy. It's not the end of the world," Dad said kindly.

"I just hope all the other kids won't make fun of me when they know." I sighed. "Girls never date younger boys. Not a *whole year* younger."

"Why did you like him at all?" Mom asked. "He certainly isn't good looking."

"He's so darn smart," I whined, still fighting to stave off the tears. "But he isn't a total egghead. He amused me, and he knew about sports and music and movies and books and … just about everything. He's not like the other bright guys I know like Glenn and Ken, who know a lot about science or poetry but don't seem to care about much else. He was fun to be with. He acted years older than someone like Paul."

I paused. Age was defined by years, wasn't it? Anyway, Pete lied to me. That was all that mattered. He lied!

"I don't want to speak to that creep again. That's final!"

My parents didn't argue with me; they simply urged me not to fuss. In different ways, each told me I was right to forget Pete. I needed to think about college instead. After they retired, I ate four candy bars and smoked six cigarettes, one after the other. I would beat this devil, I decided. I never should have given in to the flattery of the pastor and the counselor in the first place.

Patty was asleep when I went back to my bedroom. I fumbled through the Kleenex in the wastebasket in the dark until I felt the ring. I decided to save it to give to Goodwill and tossed it into the bottom dresser drawer where I kept old clothes that I intended to get rid of. Then I got ready for bed, watched the shadows on the wall, and tried to imagine what it would be like to live with sensible girls in a college dorm, miles away from this adolescent stupidity.

The next time I saw Pete, in sociology class a couple of days later, I barely looked at him, and we never spoke. I glanced at his eyes only once, when he wasn't looking at me. They had dark rings around them, and the whites surrounding his gray green irises had a pinkish cast. He didn't come to class for the rest of the week. I didn't care.

When I ran into her in the cafeteria, Claire remarked upon how I didn't appear to be "dripping with cheer" that day, so I asked her to tell me a joke. I had to fake a laugh. "Well, that helped," she said sarcastically. "One of my horror tales would have had the same effect." I knew Barb would be interested. My attachment to Pete had always baffled her. But it was too hard for me to admit to her that her negative intuitions about him had been right.

Three times that week, Pete called my house asking to speak

with me. I refused to answer the telephone myself, and I left strict instructions with everyone in the family to tell him I wouldn't talk to him. If answering machines had been in common use back then, ours would have said, "If this is Pete French calling, hang up and don't call again. If you're anyone else, please leave a message after the beep."

I immersed myself in school-related work all week. Around four thirty on Friday afternoon, I left Amherst through the back stage crew door and was surprised to see my father sitting nearby in our car, signaling to me. I opened the passenger door and settled wearily down beside him on the front seat. "Hi, Dad. I'm surprised to find you here. Nothing's wrong at home, I hope?"

"Ernie called me, and we had a talk. He asked for my help."

"Oh, boy! This is Friday the thirteenth, isn't it? What did he want?"

"It's about Pete."

"I knew it. This is an unlucky day, Dad."

"Don't be funny, Sandy. Apparently, Ernie's concerns are legitimate. Pete has hardly eaten anything all week; he doesn't sleep, and he wanders around looking like a ghost. Ernie wants me to ask you to speak to him."

"I already told Pastor that I never want to speak to that liar again."

"Yes, you have made that perfectly clear to the whole town. And believe me, I'm on your side. I understand. You feel betrayed, and I don't blame you one bit. But it's not the end of the world. I trust that you haven't lost your virtue or your good sense, and it won't be that long before you'll be off to college. Next week we'll be leaving on our spring vacation. That gives you a good deal to look forward to, and Ernie's kid has nothing. Look, I'm on your side, but I told Ernie I'd ask you to speak to him. Say anything that will get it through his thick head that he doesn't matter to you anymore. He'll try to trick you into forgiving him, but I know you won't fall for that."

"I can't do that, Dad. I'm sorry, but I can't. If I were to speak to him now, that would make me feel like a liar too."

"It's not the same thing. No one is going to think you're a liar if you just try to make him understand how you feel. Come on. Ernie's concerned that Pete will make himself sick, or even do something worse to himself, the way he's acting. Couldn't you just say a few words to the kid? Help him to understand that you need to go your separate ways?"

"Dad, forgive me for saying this, but I fear you're being used. Pete is a survivor. He'll be okay. His dad doesn't know him at all."

"But Ernie is really worried. He's not asking that much, is he?"

"Dad, you don't know what you're asking me to do."

"Sure I do, Sandy. What I'm asking isn't that much. What's the big deal?"

"I ... I don't know. Maybe if I start talking to him again, I won't be able to stop."

"Now, that's just plain ridiculous. You have more sense than that. You're a strong-willed girl. Just talk to him for a few minutes. That's all. Will you do it for me? It'll get Ernie off my back."

"I am absolutely certain it's going to be a mistake. I don't know why, but I am."

"I don't think so. Can I tell Ernie you'll talk to Pete?"

"Dad, I can't say no to you. I'll do it, but only because you're asking me to. I'm sincerely worried that I'll let you down though. It might not turn out the way you want it to."

"I trust you, Sandy. You need to trust yourself."

"Pete is smarter than I am, Dad. He knows how to get to me. I'm worried about this."

"Just remember that he lied to you. Remember how it made you feel to learn the truth from someone else."

"Okay, Dad. I can do that."

"That's my girl. As soon as we get home, I'll call Ernie, and you can get it over and done with."

## Chapter 22
## SINGING THE BLUES

Pete called shortly after Dad and I had our talk. I answered the phone myself. My voice sounded flat-affected, even to me, but Pete sounded like someone else. He apologized politely for bothering me and said he would appreciate it very much if I would let him take me for a short drive in his new car. "It won't be for long. I'm sorry to disturb your day, but honest, I'll get you right back. Tomorrow afternoon at two, okay? It won't be for long."

"Okay," I said unenthusiastically. "But it must be brief. Saturday looks busy for me."

"Sandy, I … never mind. I'll be there at two. I'll be watchin' the clock. See ya at two?"

"Yes, for a *short* ride."

When I sidled out onto our driveway, deliberately late, he was standing beside an odd-shaped, ugly, old brown car. When his hand reached toward the car handle to open the passenger door, I said I could open it myself, and I did. I found myself sitting on the off-brown, half-torn upholstery of a jalopy that smelled as if it had recently been sprayed with Lysol. It was a 1948 DeSoto, Pete said, the only car that he could afford. What he didn't tell me then was that the vehicle was neither registered nor insured. These were luxuries he couldn't afford, since he had quit his irregular job at the A&P weeks ago in order to spend more time with me.

"I know she's not pretty, but my other car finally broke down. It would take more dough to fix her than this car cost me. I've checked out her motor. She's okay. I call her Dizzie."

"Am I risking my life going anywhere with you in this Dizzie thing?"

"I'll be very careful," he said soberly.

"Can I believe that?"

"Come *on*! Give me a break, okay? I understand yer mad at me. I just want to talk. Ah, thank you for agreein' to see me."

"Remember, I only agreed to talk." I sat close to the door, as far away from him as was possible on the battered old bench.

He drove off in silence. He looked so miserable that I searched my brain for something to talk about that was totally unrelated to what was bothering us. "You never told me why you once said you had trouble finding your house here on Walton Drive."

"Nobody ever told me we was movin,'" he answered with a shrug of his shoulders.

"Yes, somebody else told me that happened, so I know it's true. But please elaborate."

He winced at my implication. "Well, last year and over the summer, I worked as a janitor at Resurrection and made enough dough to buy the blue Ford. Then me and one of the boys in the gang drove to Ontario for about two weeks to fish for walleyes. It was quiet and pretty up there on Big Gull Lake. We had a good time. When we returned, ya gotta try to imagine this, I discovered that my house on Pembroke was deserted. Cleared out. No people, no car, no furniture, nothin.' I went next door to ask the neighbors if they could tell me what was goin' on. All they knew was that my father had moved out, which was obvious. They didn't know where, so I stayed that night at my friend's house.

"The next day I called the church. The secretary told me that Dad had resigned a month earlier. She sounded surprised that I didn't know. Heh!" He chortled bitterly. "He had officiated over his last service there, and I never knew it 'cause I never went to church. She gave me vague directions to Dad's new church in Snyder. Drivin' around Snyder, I found the church, and that's where I met Betty, who treated me kindly. You know how she is."

"Oh, I know *that* all too well."

He looked at me quizzically, but continued, "She took me to the house on Walton and invited me to come visit her house whenever I wanted to."

"I'm sure she did. Did you drive this friend of yours up to the fishing place in Ontario?"

"Yeah, in the Ford, like I said."

"Did you ever drive at night up there?"

"'S'pose so."

"So, you not only drive illegally here, you drove illegally in a foreign country?"

"I never said I was no saint. Ya know that. Look, I am very, very sorry that I did whatever it was that made ya so mad at me."

"Don't play dumb with me. And try harder to speak correctly. You know the real reason why I'm angry with you. I wouldn't be here now if our dads hadn't asked me to."

"You hate me that much?" He sounded desolate. "Look, I didn't know I was tellin' a lie. I was so used to tellin' everyone that I was seventeen that I believed it myself. Can you understand that?"

"No. Not unless you're crazy."

"Maybe I am. Maybe I had a lapse o' memory."

"And you expect me to believe that? How are you able to get served at bars? You're *way* underage for whiskey."

"No one ever carded me," he shrugged. "I guess I look and act older. I just walked up to the bar at Our Place one day and ordered a seven an' seven, ya know? That's a Seagram's 7, whiskey, and 7-Up. Mark, the bartender, and I got to be buddies. We talk sports and cars together. What can I say? One time a substitute bar tender asked to see my ID, so I just left. I said I'd come back later with it. As I hoped, Mark was there when I went back, and he vouched for me. I like, uh, *liked* to go there to get outta the house and away from the sissy boys at Amherst."

"I know how you feel about my school and my friends. You're telling the truth about that, at least. Tell me about what your life was like when you were a little kid. Talk to me about your relatives. What was your mother's family like?"

"It's a complicated story. You said you wouldn't stay out with me long. We need to talk about somethin' more important."

"No. I just said I'd let you talk to me. Anyway, it might help me to understand you if I knew more about you. Just the plain and simple truth, please."

"What're ya Sergeant Friday? Look, it really ain't, no, it *isn't* that easy to remember, okay, Joe? I got moved around. Some of the time I lived with the Schilkes."

"That's your mother's family?"

"Umm. I lived at Uncle George's off and on, both before and after she died. He's my mother's older brother. He's a neat guy. Quite wealthy."

"Wealthy? What do you mean?" This sounded suspicious. It was difficult to imagine that Pete had a rich uncle.

"He has a fortune and five kids to give it to. In fact, I was a ring bearer at George Junior's big fancy wedding at George Senior's farm when I was about five, I guess. Ugh." He grimaced. "I had to wear a white suit with a big black bow at my neck." He looked as if he were trying to shake the memory of it out of his head. I pictured him as that uncomfortable little boy, and for the first time since I had become so angry with him, I had to struggle to suppress a grin.

"Where is this farm?" I asked, straight-faced.

"Uncle George owns three homes in Connecticut: a mansion, the farm, and a big city apartment. Aunt Lillian raised my sister Judy in the mansion. I usually stayed at the farm. As I got older, I worked with farm kids who were older 'an me. We hayed, and I learned to drive a tractor. I had to work the chickens. Have I told ya I hate chickens?"

"Why? They're harmless."

"They pecked at me when I fed them or got their eggs. But the worst thing was when they were slaughtered. The heads of the fryers were chopped off, but the severed parts still moved and bled all over. It wasn't a pretty sight."

"I can imagine. Talk about something else. Please."

"Like us?"

"No. Tell me more about your rich uncle."

"He's a real estate entrepreneur."

"A what?"

"A developer with big ideas. He's a funny guy. Liked to hang around with other cool rich guys. They spoke Yiddish a lot. George opened the first strip mall in Connecticut, in a suburb of Hartford, and put a movie theater in it. I went to its big opening in 1950 and saw *The Eagle and the Hawk* with John Payne and Rhonda Fleming and *Kill the Umpire* with William Bendix."

"You would have been eight then."

"Whatever ya say," he grumped.

"What does that mean?"

"Sorry." He watched the road. "George has an office building in Hartford with big glass windows overlooking the city. In his mansion he's got an Olympic-size swimming pool, a real one, not one like yours."

"What do you mean by that crack?"

"It's tiled and heated, and it has a regular drainage system."

"Humph. You're making all this up, aren't you?"

"Want me ta drive ya ... you, to my father's office, so's you can ask him?"

"It's not necessary right now. Please make more effort to speak correctly."

"Geez! Sorry."

"So you spent summers with your Uncle George. And you were in Newburgh, New York, the rest of the time?"

"That's how I remember it. My mother died when I was five. After that I lived on the farm, then with my French grandparents in Hartford. I also spent time with Uncle Eugene and Aunt Helen in Wethersford, not too far from there."

"Schilkes?"

"No. Eugene is one of Dad's older brothers."

"Okay. Stop. This is a weird story. Your French grandfather was an Irish butcher, right? He chopped up meat, and the Schilkes chopped up chickens? Lots of blood and guts there, Shakespeare." I *really* had to work to stifle a grin this time.

"Do you want me to tell the truth or not?"

"What sort of a place did they live in? The Frenchs?"

"It was in a poor immigrant neighborhood; I guess that's how *you* would characterize it anyway. They had an apartment in a wood frame building, over some shops. There was a dairy down the street, where Grandpa took me for pistachio ice cream."

"You like pistachio ice cream?"

"I guess I did, back then."

"I love it with strawberry syrup. It's very colorful: red and green." I stopped myself short. I had promised myself not to get friendly. "You got along well with your grandparents?" I asked him in a way that I hoped sounded disinterested.

"Most of the time. I do remember one time when Grammy got really mad at me."

"Only one time?"

"Well, I remember that time because it happened on her birthday. I was maybe five or six. Grammy had expectations of having a special day for herself, some sort of party with us kids, but George's wife decided to take Judy and me to a public outdoor swimming pool. I skinned my legs on the sides of the pool and got delivered back to Grammy, badly bleeding and sunburned. She ended up taking care of me instead of doing anything for herself. She really bitched at me for giving the rich Schilke bastards priority over her."

"Come on. She didn't use those words, did she?"

"She said those words, sometimes in German." While he talked, he drove us farther away from the neighborhood. Suddenly he pulled up to a curb in front of a wooded area and stopped the car.

"What are you doing? You assured me that we would drive for only a little while and then you would take me home."

"I didn't mean for this to be an interrogation period, officer. I want to talk about us, Sandy."

"Don't you understand? There isn't any 'us' now. I'm going away. First I'm going to Florida on a family vacation. Not so very long after that, I'll be off to college in Pennsylvania. I suppose you'll be getting drunk or finding another way to waste away your life." I tried to sound tough, but I couldn't look directly at him.

"Pete, you need to understand that this fling between us was a big mistake."

"Fling?"

"Listen to me. I had my future carefully planned out, and you came along and confused me. I thought you were my age, so I agreed to date you, but then I let it go too far. You must have known, just as I did, that it couldn't last. Now we have to forget each other. Period."

His voice was low and unsteady. "You don't care about me at all. You can't even look me in the eye."

I felt tears welling up. "Stop it! I told Dad this would be a mistake. You know you're making me feel badly, don't you? And you're the one who lied to me. You're trying to trick me again. I won't let you."

"You really don't want nothin' more to do with me?"

"*Anything* to do with you. Ohhh. Stop looking at me that way. You're making me feel terrible."

"I don't mean to hurt you, sweetie. I just want it to be like it was."

"That's the problem; don't you see? What you want is impossible. You're thinking only about today, about now. I am thinking about the future. You don't care about the future. We're just too different."

"What if I told you I'd go to college?"

"I wouldn't believe you."

"I'll study to become a minister like my dad."

"A minister has to have a calling from God."

"I did! The other night, I was sitting in the basement, and I saw a strange light. It was like a miracle. Like God spoke to me."

"What? A burning bush in your basement? I gave you credit for more originality than that. Take me home."

"Aww, come on, Sandy. I'm sorry. Honestly, I'll pass those stupid Regents and the SATs and all the tests, and I'll get to college if that's what you want. And what God wants, of course," he added lamely. "Sandy, please, just look at me like you used to."

"How long is this reformation going to last?"

"Look at me."

"No. I know what will happen. You're smarter than I am. You're going to win me over. You don't care about the future."

"I care about you, honest, sweetheart. I need you. I'm so sorry about the age thing. I know you can't accept what happened. But I really did believe I was older. I sure as hell … heck … wish I were older. Give me a chance, okay? We belong together."

I looked into his eyes and started to cry.

"Awww, please, don't do that. Com'mon, baby."

He moved toward me, but I screamed, "*No!*"

"You'd leave me with no hope?"

"Stop that. Please. You'll find someone else."

"Do you really want that?"

"Yes. No. I don't know. Ohh! I wish we had never met."

I opened my purse, groped inside it for a Kleenex, dried my eyes, and checked my watch. "I must get back," I insisted. "Look, you know that I … care. I don't like to hurt people. But this is wrong. In spite of what you said now, we have no future." His look cut right through me. "Pete, you're forcing me to say that I can't trust you anymore. What if by some miracle you did the work necessary for getting accepted to a college? We'd still be apart. We got in over our heads. We're too young for all of this."

"If I got into Gettysburg, couldn't we see each other?"

"You don't want to go there. You wouldn't be happy there."

"If you're there, I will."

"We'd still be apart for a whole year."

He sighed. "I know. Maybe I could visit you. I'd see you at the holidays, wouldn't I?"

"You're serious?"

"Never more serious."

"If you're saying all this just to fool me into—"

"Hey! Give me some hope. It could happen. I ain't ... I'm not incapable of learning. If I have a reason, to do the fuc ... sorry, requisite work to earn a scholarship to Gettysburg, I'll do it."

"I can't think now. Take me home, *please*. I promise that I'll go for another drive with you. Maybe even tomorrow. But if you ever lie to me again, I mean it, no one, not even God himself, will make me talk to you. Do understand me?"

"You'll go for a drive with me again tomorrow?"

"I suppose so. I want you to tell me more about yourself."

"How about a little kiss to seal the deal?"

"Peter! I knew it!"

"Just kidding. Now how about a smile?"

I was not in a mood to smile, but I looked into his eyes. They were smiling.

## Chapter 23
## Hard Headed Woman

It was impossible for me to get more than a wink of sleep that night. I tossed and turned, worrying about what I was doing to both of us. The dangerous game I was playing could backfire in so many ways. If I were trying to be Pete's psychiatrist, I definitely lacked the clinical disinterest of a professional. Just sitting near him affected me in ways I didn't want to admit. Why did I feel obligated to uncover the roots of Pete's behavior anyway? I'd probably end up hurting him worse than I already had. Why couldn't I just stop agreeing to see him? How could I understand his motives when my life had been so normal? He was younger than I was, but he had been forced to deal with situations that would have devastated me. I remembered how casually he had spoken to me about his mother's death. Losing her and dealing with his unhealthy stepmother must have drained him emotionally, whether he could admit it or not.

Darn him! I had vowed to be rid of him forever, and now I was losing sleep over him again. Why did I have this overwhelming desire to understand him? I shouldn't have agreed to see him again. We were going to have to part soon no matter what. I should simply accept that and be done with him. Yes. That was the answer. Tomorrow would be the last time I'd go out alone with him. I'd ask him a few more questions and tell him good-bye. It would be the best solution for both of us.

The next day, I politely asked him to remind me what the "C" of his dad's middle name stood for.

"Chauncey. It's Irish, my Grandfather French's first name."

"He was from the country with the Blarney Stone? That explains a lot."

"Hey! I'm proud of my Irish blood."

"Was Chauncey French wealthy enough to pay for your dad's education?"

"Naw. The ol' man got scholarships to study for the ministry. Went ta ... to ... Wagner Lutheran College. He was an okay student, I guess, and he played on the baseball team. He was a decent left-handed pitcher. Can you imagine that? Him pitchin'? After that he went to Hartwick Seminary in New York. His first job was in New Jersey; then he went to Newburgh."

"Where's that?"

He looked down at me in disbelief. "It's in your home state, baby."

"Don't make fun of my geographical disability."

"Why not? Anyway, why do you want to hear this stuff?" He looked at me searchingly.

"I'm trying to be polite."

"Right, Sergeant Friday. I think yer buildin' up a case against me. I just can't figure out why."

"That's not fair. Well-mannered people act interested in the experiences and backgrounds of the people they talk to, that's all."

"Hum. Yer actin' sucks ... sorry ... needs work. But I'll play along, if *you* want me to. My ol' man worked at a church about thirty miles north of New York City, on the Hudson River, okay?"

I nodded, annoyed.

"That's where I was born. Criminal gangs used Newburgh

in the thirties and early forties as a sort of a harbor, called a 'safe place,' or neutral meeting place for rival criminal gangs."

"Real criminals?"

"Yup, scary guys. They got liquor cheap in Canada and shipped it to New York City without payin' dues or taxes. They sold the liquor for big profits in their restaurants and hotels. Dad was all righteous back then. He became sort of a holy crusader against the bad guys. Preached sermons about how the town should get rid of the criminals and, well, he got the truth about them out in the open. He was virtually lionized by the press for it, but he received death threats at home. Excitin' stuff. He probably never realized how much shit … what danger he was in."

"Oh, he must have. Did he succeed in his crusade?"

"I 'spose so. 'Course the criminals just moved somewhere else."

"This occurred before your birth?"

"Yeah. I can't remember much about Newburgh. That's the truth, ma'am. I only remember that once I used my position as the pastor's kid to charge other kids a penny to spin on the baptismal font. It was a goin' concession for me, until a large chunk of the font broke off. Accidentally, a course. I got in deep shit with Dad for this." He chuckled, and I arched my eyebrow. "Sorry. My confrontation with my father was not an uplifting experience," he said soberly.

Stifling a giggle, I asked him to tell me what he did with his dad. "Did you go fishing together or play ball?"

"He took me to a few baseball games. I don't know how young I was when I went to my first one. Later, in Buffalo, he took me to games at Offerman Stadium. When he had to go back east for church business, he took me to see the New York Giants play at the Polo Grounds. I saw Willie Mays. That must have been after 1951."

"Do you remember when Judy was born?"

"Hell, no. I was only two. And before you ask, I have only a vague memory about my mother gettin' sick. By the time I was five, she was deathly ill, so I was sent off to Hartford to live with my French grandparents. Grammy told me later that the stomach cancer sent her into a painful, rapid decline, and she knew she was dying. She made my dad promise to remarry so that Judy and me would have a mother."

"Grammy and Chauncey raised you up from the time you were five?"

"Not just them. I spent time with other relatives like Uncle Eugene in Wethersfield. I remember playing board games with older girl cousins there. My older cousin Richard, the son of Edward, my ol' man's eldest brother, was a teenager when I was just a kid, but him and I got real friendly. He didn't mind my taggin' along with him. Edward eventually dispossessed Richard because his second wife didn't want him around."

"How could he do such a thing? To his own son?"

"He wanted to make his wife happy, I guess." Pete shrugged. "Richard did okay. Grammy raised him with me until he joined the navy."

"It sounds as if Grammy ended up raising a lot of boys. Who taught you about right and wrong? Chauncey or Grammy?"

"Ya stump me there, baby."

"Watch it."

"You have posed a problematic question, ma'am. People called Chauncey a man of integrity. They respected both him and Grammy, but maybe he was kinder? She could be tough."

"Can you give a specific example of what you learned from either of them about right and wrong?"

"That's a difficult question to answer, ma'am. Grammy led by example. She was always kind to me, and she kept tellin' me to be kind to others."

"You wouldn't have felt badly about ruining Grammy's birthday if you didn't have a conscience. Was Chauncey mostly responsible for that?"

"I suppose I learned somethin' from him. Are you done yet? I don't like your line of questioning." Pete looked embarrassed.

"When did you come to Buffalo?"

Sighing, he told me that in 1948 his dad answered the call to serve at Resurrection Church. He and Judy were left with various relatives while the pastor got settled, and then Grammy and Chauncey moved into the parsonage with the two children. Pete began second grade at PS 61, learned to read music, and took piano lessons. Somewhere around that time, he said, he and his sister both had their tonsils removed.

"How odd. You and your sister got tonsillitis at the same time?"

"We weren't sick. My ol' man just got a special deal from some hospital big shot who belonged to his church."

"I find that difficult to believe."

"It's nothin' but the truth, ma'am. Lots a kids have their tonsils removed. Didn't you?"

"No. There has never been anything wrong with my tonsils."

"Like I said, there was nothin' wrong with mine either."

"No father would make his kids suffer for no reason."

"You don't know all fathers." I eyed him scornfully. He said, "I didn't suffer anyway. It was fun. I got wheeled into the operating room and then all's I remember is wakin' up and gittin' ta eat lots a ice cream."

"So it wasn't that bad?"

"Course not. I bet you get treated well *whenever* you get sick."

"Mother serves me food on a tray in my bedroom when I don't feel well, if that's what you mean. Of course, she calls the doctor if I have a temperature."

"Uh, well, I don't remember nothin' like that. Just the mustard plaster and caster oil. That stuff tastes rotten."

"What? Is that all your doctor ordered, even for a temperature?"

"We didn't ever see no doctor. Grammy took care of us. That was her universal cure. It always worked."

"I never heard of such a thing. It's positively primitive."

"And that's wrong because?"

I wouldn't fall into his trap. I was asking the questions, not him.

"Tell me about Tommy's mom, please. I know she's very sick now. Do you like her?"

"Ottilie got dealt a bum hand, that's all. She was an unmarried childhood friend of my ol' man, and he needed a wife. His parishioners expected him to remarry, and he wanted to honor his promise to Gretchen. He wrote to her, they started seein' each other, and one thing led to another. In 1950 they got married. It wasn't no match made in heaven," Pete said grimly.

"Poor Tilly got thrust into a new family with kids that she had no idea how to care for. Grammy sorta resented her too. She thought she was stupid, and she didn't like her. When Tommy was born in 1951, Grammy and Chauncey moved to Mexico City to live with Edward, who had become quite wealthy and was runnin' some toothpaste company there."

"Why did you say 'poor Tilly' the way you did?"

Pete sighed. "I don't git yer question."

"Okay. I'll try to make it easier for you. What did Tilly look like?"

"I ain't no good at describin' women."

"Was she tall or short?"

"Geez! She was sorta short. Her hair was dark, her face was plain, and she had ugly moles, okay?"

"And she rode a broomstick? Com'mon."

"Cut it out. I'm sick a this."

"Did you like Tilly?"

"Sandra Schall, you're a nag."

"So hate me."

"Heh! I couldn't even hate poor Tilly. She got kinda mean though, after Tommy was born and she got so sick."

"You were in school then?"

"Yeah. I got good grades, and my teachers seemed to like

me okay. I remember only one time when I sassed off one of my favorite teachers in front of the class by saying somethin' funny that made my buddies laugh but annoyed her. She couldn't let me get away with it, so she made me copy every word starting with 's' in the whole damn … sorry … in the entire dictionary."

"That sounds like an old one-room schoolhouse punishment to me. Did you have to do it on a chalk slate?"

"Com'mon. Those sissy boys at yer school probably sat in the corners and cried when they got yelled at."

He wasn't far off the mark there, but I didn't give him the satisfaction of telling him so.

He told me his dad tried to make a normal life for his family. It was around that time, he reminded me, that he and his dad went to baseball games together. He liked the game so much that he would sometimes skip school and hop on a trolley to see one.

"I see. What happened to Tilly? That's probably more interesting."

The first disaster happened when Pete was eleven. Ernest planned a summer trip with his young family, a drive to the western states, hoping that a family adventure would bring them all together and smooth things over between his wife and her stepchildren. When the family was touring the Grand Tetons in Wyoming, Ernest stopped his car at a local store, and Tilly went inside to buy supplies. When she failed to return to the car, Pastor left Pete in charge of the younger kids and went in to find out what was keeping his wife. He nearly tripped over Tilly lying on the floor, not far from the door, surrounded by dumbfounded strangers. They told him that she had suffered some sort of fit. Pastor assumed that the demands of the long trip and the changes in altitude had somehow triggered the strange seizure. He hoped things would get better, so he drove on to Salt Lake City, Utah, but Tilly still felt unwell. Ernest gave up, cut the excursion short, and they returned to Buffalo.

"She had a couple more seizures. One at church. The ol' man's parishioners began to gossip about possible causes. I didn't understand what was going on, only that there was somethin' wrong with Tilly. To me, she was just sick and strange. Finally, Dad sought serious medical attention for her, and she had some kind of therapy, but nothing seemed to relieve her unstable condition. Eventually doctors diagnosed the brain tumor."

"Yes, I heard that she is very sick now. That is so horrible. *Two* wives with cancer."

"That's life, I guess." He shrugged. He told me that Ottilie had two operations, but the illness kept recurring. Meanwhile, her behavior grew more and more erratic. Pete was home when his father wasn't, so he was a frequent target of Tilly's irrational behavior. He told me this with no self-pity, as if it were a mere fact of life. Once, he said, Tilly threw something hard directly at him that left him black and blue.

"I never told my ol' man, a course, 'cause I knew the poor woman wasn't well."

His heartrending story came dangerously close to melting my resolve. I wanted to console him, to hug him. But he wasn't seeking sympathy. He never would have told me any of this if I hadn't insisted. What he did want, I refused to give him.

"Of course, Tilly's illness had a deleterious effect upon the marriage," he said.

Again, I said nothing, but I hung onto every word, noting his rarely exposed command of the language. Reluctantly, Pete continued his halfhearted narration. His dangerously unstable stepmother couldn't sustain her wifely commitments to Ernest, nor could she mother the three children. She was hospitalized intermittently for extended periods. Pete was not privy to his father's life and feelings, but later he learned that at some point Ernest began to develop a romantic interest in a younger unmarried member of his congregation, Anne Diefendorf, the director of the church choir. Insisting again that he was not good at physical descriptions, Pete said Anne was a plain, pleasant, caring spinster.

"How much younger than your dad is she?" I asked.

"About twenty years."

"Wow! That's quite an age difference."

"Yeah, I guess so. Not that it mattered to them. Age difference didn't matter. They were in love." He looked at me pointedly.

I stared out the car window and hastily inquired if Anne had a job. Her line of work was physical therapy, he said. Ernest began to meet Anne secretly, in locations distant from his parish. Pete guessed that it was possible that Tilly sensed that something like this was going on or, more likely still, someone from the congregation spotted Anne and Ernest out together and told her.

"When Tilly was in the hospital, Dad began taking us to the Diefendorfs' house in Clarence Center, where Anne served us hearty homemade dinners. We played board games 'n ping-pong, stuff like that. I don't know how much Tilly knew about this, but it's conceivable that she was so mean to me because she was acting out her frustration about Dad's mistress."

"Did your dad ever talk to you about his relationship with Anne?"

"I remember only one time, when we were driving to the hospital to visit Tilly. I 'spose the ol' man told me about the affair then because he had to warn me not to mention Anne to Tilly. That was the closest we ever got to those 'man-to-man' discussions some dads have with their sons, or so's I've been told. It was kind a strange. He said I should understand that a man has his needs. Heh! Then he told me that Anne means a good deal to him, but I must never tell Tilly about her. I'm 'sposed to understand and keep his secret."

Pete shrugged. "It's is no problem, far as I'm concerned. Hell … heck, Anne is not that much older'n me. She cooks good food. She gave me a few drivin' lessons. She's like a big sister to me, I s'pose."

"Well, I'm sure that some of what you've been telling me is true, because Dad told me about Tilly and Anne and asked me to keep it a secret. But he didn't mention that Tilly's illness had caused her to become so cruel. I don't think I could have taken the abuse you say you put up with. I'm sorry you had to."

"Don't go feelin' sorry for me, Sandy. She never really hurt me. Her brother was scary, though. You had enough? Can we talk about somethin' else?" He parked his car near a woody area. I knew that he wanted to talk about us. I wasn't ready for that.

"Tell me about Tilly's brother."

He protested with a loud groan and a stifled "damn." I froze my determined expression until he gave in and, in his matter-of-fact way, told me that early in 1958, he overheard Tilly's end of a telephone call to her brother in Connecticut. She spewed out a torrent of vile language and ill feelings toward Ernest and his whole family. Tilly's brother dropped everything and drove from Hartford to Buffalo to rescue his sister. Pete described the brother as a macho, uneducated tough guy who owned a gun. He turned up at Ernest's doorstep and roughly announced that he had come for Tilly and he'd return again later to "take care of" Ernest and Pete for mistreating her. He told Tilly to pack her things and ordered Pete to help him load her belongings into the car.

The brother softened up a bit to him while the two of them were working together moving Tilly out. Nevertheless, the distraught brother made it clear to Pete that he thought Ernest had been somehow systematically killing Tilly. Brother and sister drove off, leaving all the children, including Tommy, in Buffalo. Later, Pete heard that Tilly's brother, after having his own doctors examine his sister, arrived at the same conclusion that Ernest had about Tilly's hopeless condition. Her family entrusted her care to a sanatorium. Pete said he never saw her again. And his father continued to see Anne.

When he finished his story, I sat in stunned silence. The tale was incredible. It was almost a convoluted version of some of the nineteenth-century fiction that I had read. Pete's dad was in many ways like Charlotte Bronte's Mr. Rochester, the intelligent man married to an insane wife, who falls in love with the caring Jane Eyre, while he keeps the existence of his crazy wife secret. Some of Pete's youth, according to his accounts, was almost as bad as Dickens's foundling, Oliver Twist. Pete had a creative mind and a vast knowledge of literature. Had he contrived this whole story? On the other hand, if it were true, I couldn't let Pete know how much it affected me. I was determined not to break down again.

"Sandy?" The way he said my name dented my shield.

He reached his hand over toward mine. Not thinking, I put my hand into his. I moved slightly closer to him, but when he tried to pull me to him, I pushed him away. He sighed and shrugged his shoulders. I pleaded with him to give me time to digest what he had just told me. Looking sad and frustrated, he nodded and started up his car. It took every last iota of self-discipline that I possessed for me to hold myself back from moving over and hugging him.

On our way to my house, I told him our plans for Easter vacation. We would leave on Wednesday, despite the fact that school would still be in session, and return to Snyder on April third, the day before my eighteenth birthday. Pete drove in silence, seemingly lost in his own thoughts. Finally, he broke the silence to ask where we would be staying on our trip. All I knew was that we'd be in a motel in Harrisburg, Pennsylvania, on the first night and in a motel in Aiken, South Carolina, on the second night. For two weeks after that, we'd be at the Lido Beach Motel in Miami.

I could almost hear his brain ticking. "Would ya ... you mind if I was ta see you in Miami?"

"Tell me you're kidding."

"Burt and me have been plannin' to go to Florida anyway."

"You and some other guy are going to Florida in what? Not this contraption of yours?"

"Sure. We're chippin' in. He'll buy the gas and most of the food. No fancy motels."

I shook my head. "Now I'm sure you're crazy."

"Ya ... *you* like me this way, though, don't you?" His devilish eyes forced me to smile.

"You're interesting, Peter French. I'll say that for you. But I wish you'd stop doing things like this that worry your father."

"Aw, he ain't ... isn't worried about me. He just wants me to stop embarrassin' him. I'll be okay, *if* you'll promise to see me when I come to visit you in Miami. Deal?"

"You'll be risking your life if you try to get all the way down to Miami in this junk heap. I sincerely doubt you'll make it."

"Are ya worrin' about me?"

"Just be careful while I'm gone, okay?"

As he pulled his car into our drive, he asked, "Are you goin' to Luther League tonight?"

"No. I have to help pack and get ready for school."

"How about a little good-bye kiss?"

"I'll give you a happy birthday kiss instead."

He studied me if he was trying to gauge if I was being sarcastic. I smiled hesitantly and gave his cheek a quick peck before jumping out of the car.

As soon as I stepped inside the door, Mom ordered me to get the rest of my clothes ready for the trip and chided me for slowing things up.

"You aren't seeing that Pete French again, are you?"

"Dad asked me to have a talk with Pete, so I did. That's all."

"Well, I certainly hope that's the end of it. Now get your things ready for packing, and be quick about it."

## Chapter 24

## JAILHOUSE ROCK

Pete didn't show up in sociology before I left; he didn't call me at home either. I couldn't help wondering if he had actually been serious about driving to Florida. Anxious to go there myself, I babbled about our plans to my friends, who told me they begrudged my parents' willingness to let me play hooky in Florida. You guys should meet a champion hooky player, I thought. Compared to Pete, I'm nothing but an amateur. I wondered how far south he'd get before Dizzie gave up the ghost. Until that happened, he'd get to travel more comfortably than I expected to. I'd end up squashed in the back of the station wagon with my sister and our squirmy, long-legged brothers. Early Wednesday morning, we headed south. As usual, I hugged a window near Patty, and our gangly brothers stretched out and buried their faces in comic books.

Our visit with our relatives in Aiken was brief. I didn't care since my older cousins were away at college. Dad and Uncle Jim clowned around like they always did, Aunt Bea had casseroles ready to feed the whole bunch of us, and no tears were shed when we left.

As we drove south from Aiken, Pat and I tried to recall the names of the lush subtropical vegetation along the roadside, and

I looked for road signs indicating how many miles we still had to go. When Dad finally pulled up to the front of the Lido Beach Motel, he and Mom let us take a short run on the beach. It was late, but the air felt like a warm moisturizer on my skin. The sea smelled salty, and the waves looked inviting, but Mom and Dad called us back to help unload the car and get settled. The boys grabbed everything Dad handed them, threw their clothes in their room, and raced outside to run in the sand. Patty and I hung our blouses and sundresses in the closet and filled our dresser drawers while Mom and Dad unpacked their stuff in the largest room, the one with a small living room, a kitchenette, and a television set. Before Patty and I could scoot back outside, Mom ordered me to call the boys in, supervise the showers, and make sure everyone got tucked into bed. She and Dad drove to a nearby market to buy food for breakfast.

The next day after breakfast, we kids headed for the water. Dad designated me to act as the family lifeguard. The official lifeguard, a darkly tanned, muscular fellow, told me that sharks hadn't been seen near our motel in ages. The only other sea creature I feared was the Portuguese man-of-war, a blue jelly fish that had once painfully zapped my baby finger. The lifeguard said he hadn't seen any of them recently either, so I waded in to where the waves were deep enough for me to dive into them like a dolphin. Riding on salty, buoyant, sun-warmed waves, I felt lazy and forgetful. Almost. What was happening to Pete? Later, as I stretched out on my blanket in the sand, I imagined him behind the wheel of Dizzie, stuck somewhere between Buffalo and Miami, waiting for a tow truck. I couldn't even begin to guess what had really been going on. I learned that later.

Since my brothers weren't satisfied for long with just playing in the water or building sand castles, Dad bought tickets for a blimp ride along the Miami seacoast. He went up with the rest of us, turning green so we could enjoy the view. He and Mom took us to a marine exhibition, where the boys admired only the ugliest fish. They took us to a gorgeous tropical parrot garden, where Patty and I ogled the floral beauties and marveled at the colorful talking birds, while the boys tried to get make them say "you stink." Back at the motel, the boys found other boys to play with on the beach, and Pat and I took long walks together. On Palm Sunday, we went to a Lutheran church where they gave each of us a miniature cross of dried palm leaves. Occasionally, a mailman brought mail to our motel unit. I received a sympathy card from my chemistry class. Everyone signed it, including our teacher, Mr. Long. The printed formal sentiment was, "To express sincere sympathy to you in your sorrow." Some kids wrote, "It must be awful for you," or "We are taking a test now. Our only consolation is that hooky players like you have to take harder tests." My teacher wrote, "You'll walk the plank when I see you again," and signed it Long John Silver. That card was my first surprise. The next one arrived late Friday morning. I was lazing alone in my pajamas in the girls' room after breakfast, when Dad knocked loudly on the door. "You better be decently dressed, Sandy." He sounded irritated.

"Just a minute, please, Dad. Do you need me to watch the kids on the beach?"

"No. A bad penny has turned up. He wants to see you."

"What? Oh! It isn't Pete French, is it?"

"You knew he was coming?" Dad sounded doubly annoyed. "Hurry up, will you, Sandy? I don't want to talk to him."

"I'll meet him out back. On the beach."

Quickly, I tugged my bathing suit on, threw a towel over my shoulders, and walked out toward the beach. There he was, standing on the sand, his hair blowing in the breeze, looking tanned and jaunty. He wasn't wearing swimming trunks or bright shorts and a flowered shirt like a typical tourist. He just wore dark dungarees, a black shirt with the sleeves rolled up, and penny loafers. When he spotted me, his face dimpled into a boyish grin.

"Hi, sweetheart. How's your vacation been?" He grabbed my hand.

"You crazy jerk! I never thought I'd see you here."

"Good to see you too, Sandy," he said, his voice dropping.

"Did you really drive down all this way in Dizzie? Just to see me?"

"You sure do look terrific." He eyed me up and down appreciatively. "You don't need to hide under that towel though. Show me yer bathin' suit."

"I'm not hiding. I'm a bit chilly." I loosened my tight grip on the beach towel, but I kept it around my shoulders.

"Ya can't hide from me forever, ya know. Ya gotta trust me now, right? Ya gotta, rather, *you must* believe me, because seein' is believing. I told you I would come down here, didn't I?"

He was so tan, so cocky, so irritatingly charming. I tried to hide how deeply his sudden appearance affected me. He seemed to sense my confusion. He stared into my eyes, and I held his gaze. He took a deep breath.

"Me being here doesn't bug you, does it?"

"No, no." I squeezed his hand. "Walk down the beach with me and tell me about your drive. Who is this guy you're with?"

"Are ya writin' a book? Can't we just talk like we once used to?"

"Don't have a cow, Pete." He looked at me as if I had flipped, and I giggled. "Mike is always saying that. Please tell me about your trip and the guy you're with, okay?"

"Okay, babe. I'm with Burt Platzel, a senior. He says he knows you, but not well."

"Is he a dark-haired guy who wrestles?"

"That's him. He's in the German Club too, but he's not in one of those sissy boy fraternities. And that's not due to him bein' a Jew, although I suppose the frats at yer school don't allow Jews. He's just smart, so's he never wanted to join one. I got to know him because his locker's near mine, and he saw me sneakin' out of school a couple a times. Burt 'n I started to play hooky together. When I told him about my plans to drive to Florida, he said he'd like to come along. He's a fun guy, happy-go-lucky. He shares my admiration for teachers and my undying loyalty to Amherst High. He's not too crazy about rules either, or his folks fer that matter. Burt don't, ah, doesn't have a lotta money, but he's got more of it than I do, so we made a deal. I'd supply the wheels, and—"

"Wheels?"

"You remember: Dizzie. Burt doesn't know how to drive a shift, but he agreed to pay for the gas and some of our food. We packed up and took off from Snyder in that ol' chariot on the same day you did. We slept in Dizzie beside the road when I got too tired to drive on." He chuckled. "No one woulda bet old Dizzie could make it outta New York State, and here we are."

"I can't believe my eyes! Oops. Sorry. I do believe my eyes. You look quite tanned and, well, happier than you've been in while." I desperately wanted to hug him.

"You stopped yer first night at the Family Motel in Harrisburg, didn't you?"

"Don't tell me you stayed there too."

"Ya kiddin'? I saw your car there when we drove through, but I just kept drivin' on."

"Of course you did," I said, rolling my eyes. "Do continue."

"On the first night, we slept in Dizzie in North Carolina. Then we hauled ass ... sorry, drove down to Ormond Beach, Florida."

"I'm a bit foggy about where that is."

"Only a bit? Sweetheart, you get lost three miles from your own house."

"Humph. Tell me anyway."

"It's north of Daytona Beach, if that means anything to you. I'll show you on a map sometime, okay? Anyway, we slept in the car in residential neighborhoods. We crunched ourselves down below the windows to make the car look deserted from the outside. Then we just hung around and reconnoitered. I noticed some cars drivin' out onto the long drivin' beaches at Ormond and Daytona. Unfortunately," he shook his head, "I forgot to ask about the tide schedules. Me and Burt ... ah, Burt and I drove

Dizzie way out onto the farthest sands. We got pretty shook up when the tidewaters suddenly rose. They were above her runnin' boards before we knew it. Her wheels began to spin. I rocked her from first to reverse, only I got nowhere. Dizzie's wheels were in the grip of the wet sand. Then her transmission cracked."

"That doesn't sound good. Everything you say amazes me, the chances you've been taking, the crazy things you've been up to, all this mechanical jargon."

"I'll make it easy fer ya. We were stuck in the sand, the car's driving mechanism was disabled, and the water was about to come in and sink us."

"Did you panic? I would have abandoned ship, to coin a phrase."

"Heh! Well, lucky for us," he said, with a sheepish grin, "this sort of thing happens with some regularity on the driving beaches. Traffic boats out in the deeper waters patrol the area routinely, equipped to summon towboats for stranded vehicles. A rescue boat spun over to Dizzie, dislodged her wheels, and towed her to a garage for repair. We spent the night there, chatting with the owner and his workers, nice guys. The catch was that we couldn't afford to replace Dizzie's old transmission, not on our shoestring budget. So they had to send out a gofer to look for one in the junkyards. They told us they couldn't do the job for less than fifty bucks, and they insisted on half down to send the guy to the junkyard. We had to give them just about all of our remainin' cash for the down payment."

"Then how did you manage to get the job done?"

"I'm gittin' to that, baby. We scrounged up enough guys at the garage for a poker game."

"Oh, no!"

"Yup. We not only won the fifty bucks we needed for the transmission, we made some extra cash to boot. A course, we were lucky, but Burt and me also happen to be good at poker."

"That I can believe."

"You can believe everythin' I'm tellin' ya. Understand?"

"Don't bring that up again, okay?"

"Um, so Dizzie was fixed, and we drove south to Boynton Beach and spent the night in another residential neighborhood. Unfortunately, this time we got noticed. Just before daylight, we were … how shall I put this so it won't bother your sensitive little ears? We were rudely awakened by tapping noises: two police officers knocking the butts of their guns on the car windows, one on each side of the car so that we two dangerous desperados couldn't escape out either door. Uh, oh." He looked a bit sheepish. "Did I tell you that I never attained a registration or car insurance for Dizzie?"

"*What?*" I exclaimed. "You haven't registered your car?"

"Sweetie, I could barely afford to buy her, let alone worry about the details. I sort of neglected to tell Burt about that too."

"*Details?* You could have been arrested in Amherst, when we were out together. Peter French, you're—"

"Sandy, are you going to be mean? Or are ya interested in what happened?"

"Oh, go on," I sighed.

"Well, we were not about to argue with armed cops. So I drove Dizzie behind their car to the police station. The cops roughly escorted us inside and locked us in a cell."

"I can't take this. I'm talking to a jailbird."

"Do I scare ya, baby?" he asked menacingly.

"Yes, but I'm tough. Go on."

"Yeah, you're real tough, babe," he grinned. "Well, these cops turned out not to be as tough as you think you are. They gave us a hearty breakfast. It was more food than we had had in two days. We didn't leave a crumb. The cops ate their own breakfasts, and then they began to make a pitiful attempt to hassle us. The bad cop went on about how it's against the law to sleep in a car in a residential area. He threatened to arrest us for vagrancy. The good cop reminded him that the city judge was off work for Holy Week. The bad cop told us that, as sheriff, he had the authority to make us work on the local chain gang until the judge returned.

At that point, Burt and I both put on long, contrite faces. We could tell that the bad cop was really not very hard-hearted, and he certainly was no whiz kid. The good cop shook his head and asked us if we wanted to take advantage of our right to make one phone call."

"This is just like in the movies!"

"Life is better than art, baby." He smiled. "I'm proud of what happened next. I had a brilliant inspiration. I told the sheriff that I would like to call my dad, but that he's a minister, and he would be very busy during Holy Week, too busy to take calls. This got to the sheriff, as I hoped it would. 'Yer dad's a minister?' he asked me, obviously impressed.

"'Oh, yes, sir,' I said. 'But, I'm sorry, sir, he's just too busy now. I could never reach him back home in Buffalo, sir. He'll be flooded with Holy Week duties.'"

"I can imagine how you enjoyed calling him 'sir' like that," I remarked facetiously.

"Heh! It worked. The sheriff softened right up. 'Okay,' he sighed. 'I'm gonna let you two go because I'm a good Baptist, and it's Holy Week. But I don't want to see you two in my town ever again, not for the rest of your lives. Is that understood?' We nodded solemnly, and said, 'Yes, sir,' simultaneously."

Pete mimicked the bad cop's harsh tone and southern accent. "'And ya'all are to go back North, where ya'all came from. I'm gonna have my deputy, Billy Bob here, escort ya'all in that rattletrap of yours out of town, headin' north. He'll take ya'all right up to the northern boundary of Boynton Beach and watch you drive on. No turnin' back, now. Is that clear?'"

"So how did you end up here? We're south of there, aren't we?"

"Easy. I figured there must be some other road going south around Boynton Beach, and sure enough, I found a back road."

"You continue to amaze me. Do you realize the danger you were in?"

"What danger? I knew where I was going."

"Ohh. You're impossible. You left Snyder when we did, right? So, what did you do the rest of the time? You didn't continue to sleep in your car, did you? What did you eat?"

"Do I detect an interest in what happens to me?"

"I can't begin to tell you," I said, shaking my head and rolling my eyes.

He told me that Burt wanted to follow the hordes of college students heading for Fort Lauderdale on spring break. For a while, they inveigled their way into the crowd, but Pete felt uncomfortable living with drunken Ivy Leaguers. Then he remembered an older couple that had once belonged to Resurrection Church but now lived in Fort Lauderdale. Once they had tried to get Pete's father interested in taking a position in their Fort Lauderdale church. Ernest liked the idea, but in the end, he decided that a move with Anne in tow would involve too many dangers to his reputation, and the plan fell through. The Florida couple often revisited Resurrection, and Pete overheard them inviting Ernest and his family to stay with them at their place down south. When the two boys showed up at their door, the couple recognized Pete and invited them to stay awhile. He said he hated to impose upon their kindness, especially since he felt that he and Burt made them feel uneasy. So they made their own beds, did their own laundry, and helped with kitchen chores, but saved their winnings so they could check in at the motel across from ours.

"And here I am," he said, flashing his dimpled grin again.

"Oooh," I groaned, covering my eyes with my free hand, shaking my head.

"Ya gotta learn to trust me, baby. Will you go out with me tonight?" His eyes again looked intently into mine.

It was impossible to say no. "My folks won't be thrilled, but they'll let me. I hope."

"Good." His dimples returned.

"Do you have a bathing suit?"

"Why?" Suddenly, he seemed defensive.

"You're not afraid to go into the ocean with me, are you? After lunch?"

"I'll come see ya this afternoon, but I don't like wearin' a bathin' suit."

"Why? You must have brought one."

"Maybe ... if I wear a shirt over it."

"Why are you suddenly acting so modest, Pete?"

"I don't like people ... seein' my scar."

"Uh, oh. We'd better turn around. You can tell me about the scar on our walk back."

"Why should I tell you?"

"Please?"

"Fer a kiss." His lips were extra warm in the sun; I responded eagerly. Part of me couldn't resist his tightening embrace, but my stronger self told me to pull back. I held hands with him, however, on our return toward the Lido Beach Motel.

# Chapter 25
## WAYWARD WIND

"Ya sure ya want to know?" I nodded. "Geez! Women! Sorry, sweetie, but when guys asked me how I got it, in gym showers, ya know? All I had to say was that some doc had to sew me up fer somethin'. The truth is, I was born with a rare condition that was supposed ta kill me. I don't know the tech lingo, but ya can look it up if ya want to. It involved some sort of tissue bands that were wrapped around my intestines. They made me throw up milk 'n baby stuff. I wasn't a pretty sight: a skinny-lookin' kid who was supposed to die sometime before I hit one."

"I've never heard of such a thing!" I exclaimed.

"You don't read the medical journals?"

"I avoid them religiously. I'd end up believing I have every disease in the book."

"Well, this is a rare, sorta male baby thing, so don't worry about that. Oh, they think it's transmitted through females lines, so don't worry about that either."

"Go on," I said, avoiding his implication.

"Well, as I understand it, the condition still exists, but it gets treated different now. Remember, I'm warnin' ya ... my scar is ugly. As to how I got it, all I know is what Grammy told me, because I was so young when it happened. Grammy says my ol' man and my mother were highly distraught when the doctor revealed his prognosis, me bein' their firstborn and all."

"They must have been devastated. You can understand how they would feel, I hope?"

"Sure, why wouldn't I?"

"Sorry, Pete, but you talk about this in such a blasé manner."

"I was too young to care then. Anyway, I got lucky. I'm here to prove it." He smiled. I squeezed his hand.

"Go on," I said.

"My pediatrician was distantly related to an unlicensed immigrant doctor, a Jew from Belgium, who had escaped the Nazis and was being harbored in New York. In Belgium, he had devised a procedure for removing intestinal bands like I had, and he wanted to get a special dispensation to practice pediatric surgery in New York. I guess I was the first case to come along that he could demonstrate his skills on."

"Will you show me that scar or not?"

"Ya don't want to see it. I'm warning you, it ain't … *isn't* pretty."

"Show me."

He lifted up his shirt to reveal a three-inch long, deep, vertical scar almost in the middle of his abdomen, which had two or more long scars running horizontally across it.

"Ugly, ain't it?" he said, apologetically.

"Ugly, isn't it?" I corrected him. "Well, it's not as pretty as my appendix scar, I grant you that. But the operation saved your life, so I don't think you should be embarrassed about the scar."

"It caused me embarrassment in another way, too," he murmured.

"What do you mean?"

He looked down, kicked at the sand, and sighed. "I shouldn't a mentioned it. It's another male thing."

"Can you give me a hint?"

"Oooee! It's just that, since they didn't think I was going to live, I wasn't circumcised like the other boys I knew."

"Oh." He was right. It *was* a delicate subject.

"They finally did it when I was in second grade. When I had to tell my teacher why I had been absent, she seemed shocked. Talk about being embarrassed! Okay, I told you what you wanted to know, so now can I see your appendix scar?"

"No, you may not. In the first place, this is not a bikini I'm wearing, and in the second place, it's a little scar compared to yours. I'm jealous."

"Can I see your bathing suit?"

I dropped the towel. He said, "I like it a lot, Sandy, but I still think you need a bikini."

"Why am I not surprised to hear you say that? Nope, not a chance. Respectable girls don't wear bikinis."

"It's more fun *not* bein' respectable."

I laughed. "I don't doubt that for a moment. But life is about more than just having fun."

"Yeah. Maybe that's what that old Belgium doctor wanted to tell me. When I turned sixteen, I received a mysterious, brown wrapped package in the mail sent by the doctor's attorneys. It contained two books, and they're not exactly comedies. Have you heard of Franz Kafka? The Austrian novelist?"

"No, Professor, I'm sorry."

"Oh, I wouldn't expect you, or most people, to have read him. The books I got from the doctor are Kafka's *The Trial* and *The Castle*. The trial one is sort of an allegory about man's struggles against bureaucracy. *The Castle* is mainly about that too, 'cept it revolves around a man's attempts to enter a castle. It has many possible interpretations. I guess the books are more like philosophy than literature. I'm not sure why he sent them to me."

"Why don't you ask him?"

"He's dead."

"Oh, I'm sorry. I have a theory though. I believe there must be a reason why your life was saved. You're meant to do something important. Perhaps in some strange way the doctor knew you would be smart enough to understand those books."

"You're being very sweet, sweetie. I don't want to discourage you from feelin' that way, but this idea of someone being able to see into the future is weird. He was just a surgeon doin' his job."

"He didn't have to send you those books, did he?"

"No. That's puzzling, I admit. It was an unusual gift. I think the books are cool."

"Maybe the doctor predicted how smart you'd be because he knew your family. The counselors at Amherst believe that you're special too."

"What do you think? That's all I care about."

We were almost up to our motel. I let go of his hand and ran toward the water, shouting, "Come on, take off your shoes. You should at least wade in the water, big baby."

"Baby? Did you call *me* baby?"

"Why not? Don't you believe in equality for women?"

Pete shook his head at me as if he thought I was crazy. But he took off his shoes, rolled up his jeans, and walked beside me along the shore. After we kicked about in the water for a while, I told him I'd better get back or my folks would wonder. Dad was planning to take us to a fried chicken restaurant that night.

"I'm afraid they wouldn't be too happy if I invited you along. You don't like chicken much, do you?" He shook his head, looking as if he were trying to figure out his next move. I beat him to it. "If you would like me to, I think I could meet you afterwards, say out in the front of the motel at eight, okay?"

"I'd love that, baby," he grinned.

"See ya, baby."

"Women!"

Just before eight, Pete drove up to our motel in Dizzie, and I hopped right in. When I asked him where we were going, he said there was a good movie at the Hallandale Drive-In, *Gunfight at the O.K. Corral*, with Kirk Douglas and Burt Lancaster. I stiffened.

Kids didn't watch movies at drive-ins. The kids at school called them "passion pits." Was I about to make another big mistake?

"Have you seen the movie?" I asked him uncertainly.

"Sure, it's great. You'll like it."

I thought fast. I wanted to know if he intended to return to Amherst and if he'd let me tutor him. Could we just talk at a drive-in?

"What's the matter? You got another idea?"

"No. No. It's just that it sounds like a boy's kind of movie. Is it a double feature?"

"I'm not sure. I should have checked the local rag. I'm sorry."

He looked so crestfallen that I agreed to go with him. The A movie was engrossing enough for both of us, but we began to talk during the B feature. He almost sounded happy. He told me he intended to drive Burt back to Buffalo; in fact, that was part of their deal. He insisted that he wanted to go to college, and he agreed to let me help him with his grammar. He expressed confidence that he could pass the New York State Regents Exams, even the English one. He seemed ready to agree to anything, so I told him I would make a "supreme sacrifice" and let him kiss me again.

"I don't want no 'supreme sacrifice.' Fergit it," he growled.

"I'm kidding, dummy," I giggled. "I just realized that for the next few days we're actually the same age." He embraced me. I was hungry for his touch, and one thing led to another. We ended up doing what just about every other seventeen-year-old couple was doing at that drive-in, within limits, and we got back to the motel with my virtue technically intact before midnight. Before I got out of his car, he told me that he and Burt had to leave their motel in the morning, before they ran out of money.

"Please *drive carefully*," I said, sincerely worried. I kissed him again, tenderly. "I'll be praying for you. Please don't get caught in any more high tides, sweetheart."

"So long, sweetheart. I love you. See you soon." As he drove off into the night, my spirits sank. I went into the motel, tapped on my parents' door, and whispered that Pete had left for home. Dad whispered back, "That's good. Now go to sleep."

The final surprise arrived in the mail on the last day of our stay at the Lido Beach Motel. Dad handed me a postcard. "This is for you," he growled, shaking his head. I knew Pete had sent it to me as soon as I saw the picture of a blonde girl clad in a revealing bikini. The message on the other side was in his hand.

"Hi," it began. "The swamp is real swampy. We didn't get any alligators though. We didn't even see any. Dizzie is no more. We're stranded. We were traveling along the road about 50 when the engine caught fire and through (sic) a rod through the block. Then—we're walking. I found a kind soul who gave me 20 bucks for her tires. Will we stay in Florida or will we take the bus? That is the question. Hope to see you soon. Pete"

"Oh, no!" I exclaimed. "Pete is asking a 'to be or not to be' question!"

Dad must have read the card before he gave it to me.

"Crazy kids. Do they have any more money than what he got for the tires? That bus ride won't be free, you know. And they have to eat."

"Should we call his father?" I asked.

"Let *him* call Ernie. It is *not* our business. Ernie was nuts to let the boy go off like that in the first place in that run-down excuse for a car."

"But what if they never make it back home?"

"Sandy, listen to me. He's none of your concern. He's just a dumb, undisciplined kid, and he has to learn to pay for his own mistakes. Now get on with your packing and be grateful that you will be in a safe car with a family that cares for you and travels sensibly."

I wanted to believe that Dad was right. But he didn't know Pete. The boys' predicament sounded hopeless. What were they going to do? Would I ever see Pete again? Silently, I cried myself to sleep.

After we arrived home, on the evening of April third, I called Pete's house. Judy answered the phone. When I asked her if Pete could come to the phone, she said she hadn't seen her brother "for weeks." I couldn't bring myself to tell her why I had called or what I knew.

No sooner had I hung up the phone when it rang. I answered it immediately, hoping it was Pete or someone with news about him. But it was Susie Ogden, calling to invite me to her house the next day for lunch. I walked into a surprise party, planned by Susie. Sally Marsh and Joyce Hecker had been in on the planning too. I pretended to be thrilled and fussed over each card and gift, as if those scarves and pieces of fashion jewelry were things I desperately needed.

That evening Grandma, Grandpa, and Tanta came by to bring me presents that I appreciated, items from my list of things I needed for college. I went to my bedroom early, sat at my desk, tried to get into a novel, and hoped desperately for the call that never came.

On Sunday, Pete was not at church, nor at Luther League, where the kids celebrated my birthday with a cake. Sue pulled me aside to pry for reasons why Pete wasn't there. Obviously, she had expected him to return for the party. I didn't want to tell her that Pete and I had met in Florida. That would set plenty of tongues wagging.

On Monday at school, my girlfriends gave me a surprise birthday cake in the cafeteria and cards riddled with hilarious excuses for being late for my actual birthday. We grew so rowdy that the lunch monitor threatened to kick us out. When I arrived home late from school that afternoon, the first thing I spotted on the kitchen table was a long, thin box with a card attached to it with my name on it that said in his handwriting, "To Sandy: A little late, maybe." Inside the box were a half dozen red roses and a smaller note with "Birthday Greetings" in formal print and, in his own hand: "Happy Birthday, Sweetheart—Pete."

Scurrying around like a mouse that had uncovered a huge

stash of cheese, I hastily put the roses into water, picked up the phone, and dialed his number. Pete answered.

"When did you get back?" I asked him breathlessly.

"Ya mad at me?"

"No! I was worried."

"I got here late on Saturday." He sounded short-tempered.

"I'm sorry. I should have thanked you at once for the beautiful roses and your lovely card. I can't tell you how happy I was to see your handwriting, Pete. I've been so worried! You weren't at the League meeting or in school. No one knew where you were."

"So you got the flowers?"

"Oh, I was so happy to see that they were from you! They're lovely! How did you get them here?"

"Never mind about that. I wish I could get you much, much more, sweetheart."

I pelted him with questions: How did you and Burt manage to survive all this time? How did you get back? Why didn't you contact me sooner? How could you afford the roses?

Gruffly, he told me to shut up and let him explain. He sounded low spirited and exhausted, and he mumbled that he wasn't sure he wanted to tell me anyway.

"Please, Pete, you owe me that. You worried me so much."

His account was barely coherent. That day, apparently, he had borrowed money from Grammy to buy the roses, walked to a flower shop, and then walked to my house to drop them off.

"Oh, Pete, I'm sorry. You must be exhausted. Get some rest, okay? We can talk later."

"Thanks. I love you. I'll call you real soon." He hung up. He called me later that evening to say he just wanted to hear my voice.

"Are you up to telling me about your trip yet?"

Reluctantly, he told me that he and Burt had hitchhiked out of the Everglades area south of Lake Okeechobee, where Dizzie "blew up." Truck drivers picked them up twice. One drove them east; another drove them north to Melbourne, where Pete mailed me the bikini postcard. They didn't have enough money to stay anywhere, but they managed to hitch to a bus station, where they phoned home for ticket money for the trip back. The long-distance phone calls were expensive, and they used up their last coins making them. After locating their respective parents, they had to do a lot of fast talk to explain their hopeless situation. Their fathers were angry; both boys were roundly chewed out before their parents finally settled the logistics of their trip home. Then Burt and Pete had to figure out how to retrieve the money their fathers telegraphed them: meager funds in amounts limited to, and designated specifically for, bus tickets.

"After the long lectures we each had to put up with, Burt and I debated hitching all the way home."

"No! You didn't, did you?"

"We sure wanted to, but we knew we'd starve. No one hitches fifteen hundred miles with no food and lives to tell about it."

Pete sighed heavily. "It was a god-awful, sorry, horrendous trip. I hope I never see another bus station again. Those damn bus seats must have been made for midgets. My muscles are still cramped, everything hurts; I was fuck … um, sorry … incredibly uncomfortable."

They made their way through dirty, crowded bus stations from Savannah, Georgia, to Virginia, to Erie, Pennsylvania, and eventually into downtown Buffalo. From there, they had to solicit rides home from relatives who didn't exactly welcome them back with open arms. That, he confessed with another sigh, was the censored version of a long, miserable ordeal.

I listened quietly, uttering scant, sympathetic sounds, eager for more details, but afraid he might stop talking if I were to interrupt. After he finished his self-censored account, he sighed again and asked me, "What else did you want to know? I ferget."

"You were gone *so long*. You said that the money that they sent you was earmarked for bus tickets. How did you get food?"

"Thanks for thinkin' of that, sweetheart. Our old men never did. But if I tell ya, *you*, you'll get mad at me again."

"Oh, no! You didn't steal food? Tell me you didn't."

The line seemed to have gone dead.

"Pete? Are you still there?"

"You won't report me to Inspector Javert, will you?"

"Who is that? What are you saying?"

"*Les Miserables.* It's a story about a guy who gets put in prison for almost two decades for stealing a loaf of bread."

"How can you be such an intellectual show-off when you're in that condition? You are incorrigible. You deserve prison. Well, did you rob the money?"

"You have a criminal mind."

"Either you did or you didn't. Don't keep me in suspense, Pete."

"We didn't eat for two or three days. We lived on water and squirts from bottles of ketchup. Then we got, well, desperate. Nobody missed what we took."

"Not money? What then? Jewelry?"

"Com'mon. I told you, I'm no crook, exactly. Look, they have these, what, plastic? I don't know, some kind of see-through, wrapped, shit-awful, sorry, tasteless cardboard sandwiches at the bus stops, for a buck, probably. We were starvin', so one of us took turns divertin' the clerk's attention, while the other guy grabbed the sandwiches. We didn't take nothin' else, honest."

"It's not only in fiction that people get put into prison for stealing."

"They gotta catch ya first."

"Oooh. I suppose I've become an accomplice or something, just by listening to this."

"Yup."

"Please get some rest. Listen to the wisdom of an older woman, baby."

"Yes'm, old lady."

"Pete, I'm serious, even if you aren't. Get some decent food from Grammy and some sleep. You could get really sick if you don't make up for the sleep you lost."

"Oh, Sandy, what's the use? I've got no wheels. How can I see you when I got no car? I shoulda ... *have* ... stayed in Florida. Gotten a job."

"I'm glad you didn't."

"Really? You really worried about me?"

"You know I did. I want to help you. I ... care ... about you. You know that. Please get some rest. When you're thinking clearly, we'll work something out. For starters, I'll help you with your grammar so you'll get a decent grade on the English Regents. You'll need good grades in all your classes."

"It ain't gonna do no good," he said despondently.

"Yes, it is. Things always look worse than they are when you're as tired as you must be. Just remember that if you make an effort, with your intelligence, you can do anything."

"Like get a car? I need down payment money, Sandy."

"Right now, you need to rest. We'll talk tomorrow, okay?"

"Bye, sweetheart."

"I really am glad you're back, Pete. Please get some sleep, for my sake, if you won't do it for yourself."

## Chapter 26
## WHAT IS LOVE?

The fact that I had been fretful ever since I got the bikini postcard had not been lost on Mom and Dad. When they asked about the roses, I told them they were a late birthday present from Pete, because he had missed my Luther League birthday party. Dad arched an eyebrow at that, and Mom scowled. They hadn't read the card Pete attached to the rose box, had they? It had appeared to be sealed when I opened it.

Pete's predicament gnawed at me. Darn him! In spite of my determination never to speak to him, to forget him completely, I wanted to help him, and I needed to see more of him. But how could we get together if he didn't have a car? He was flat broke. I didn't want him to go back to work, but how else could he ever get money for a car loan? None of his friends had ready money. I had saved up a small amount for college, but not enough for a down payment on a car. Grammy was poor. As far as I knew, no one at church would lend him money. My dad wouldn't lend him a dime; he wanted Pete out of my life. But Pete's dad had money. I needed to think of a way to spin Pastor's guilt into gold. Rumpelstiltskin could handle the job, but he was annoyingly demanding and totally fictional.

I thought about what my dad might do if Mike were

desperately in need of a loan. Mike had no record of buying cars or handling money wisely like Pete did, but Dad would give him the loan anyway. Could I ask my dad to convince Pete's dad to do what he would do? That's it, I thought. If anyone could persuade Pastor, Dad could. But, knowing how Dad felt about Pete, how would I convince him to do it? He knew Pete would use a car to see me, and he didn't want that to happen. In order to alter his mindset, I'd have to be both "sweet and cunning," words used by Shakespeare in *Twelfth Night*. Except this was real life.

I found Dad outside in the driveway, shining the top of his car. I grabbed a rag and rubbed the fender. As we worked side by side, I told Dad the sad details of Pete's harrowing journey home after his car had exploded in the swamp, omitting the part about how he and Burt managed to grab some food. Dad listened to me silently, shaking his head.

"Ernie never should have allowed that kid to drive to Florida in the first place. I could tell that car of his was on its last legs. Boys like Pete need strong parental guidance."

"You're so right, Dad. Pete's father should be more like you. Poor Pete," I sighed. "Now he needs to find a way to get a down payment for another used car."

"Why? So he can take you out? You don't expect me to be a party to that, do you?"

"I didn't say that, Dad. It's just that, well, I wish you knew Pete better. He's really not as bad as some people think. I thought he was nothing but a hooligan at first, but I was wrong. He's had to endure all those family problems. You know about that, and you probably also know that Pete used to get good grades in school. It wasn't until his stepmother got so sick that he fell in with a bad crowd at Kensington and stopped caring about school. Now that he goes to Amherst, he's changed. He has ambitions, good ambitions. He even wants to go to college when he graduates, a *whole year* from now."

"Hah! That's just what he tells you. He'd say anything to take advantage of your ... generosity."

This tactic wasn't getting me anywhere. I was down to my last idea. Recently, Dad had asked me for a favor, and I had complied. It was when I wasn't speaking to Pete, and Pastor got worried about him and sought help from Dad, who convinced me to talk to Pete. I had been more than reluctant to obey Dad, but I yielded to his wishes. Could I turn the tables on Dad now? I knew I couldn't sound like I was asking him for a payback, but that's what it would be: I wanted a payback from him for doing the favor he once asked of me. It was risky. He might still refuse to do it on the grounds that my renewed concern for Pete was payback enough.

"Dad, all I want you to do is to talk to Dr. French on Pete's behalf. Suggest to him that he should lend Pete the money he needs to make a down payment on a used car. You would lend money to Mike if he needed it, wouldn't you? Isn't that what a good father does? Help his kids out in their times of need? Pete is desperate. Eventually he'll get a job and pay his dad back. He has gotten jobs before to pay for his cars. Please, Dad? I know you can do it."

Dad's expression was impossible for me to fathom, so I pressed him a bit further. "Dad, a counselor at Amherst told me about Pete and swore me to secrecy. Because of my promise to her, I can't tell you what she said, except that she asked for my assistance in guiding Pete onto the right track so he could pass the junior English Regents in June. Dad, she believes Pete has the ability to do quite well at college, if he would only try."

"Why would a counselor tell *you* that?"

"She saw me with Pete in the school halls. She admitted to me that she couldn't get through to him. I guess she thought Pete would listen to me."

"Pete's a junior at Amherst, right? Do you really believe that he could, or would, go away to college if he graduates?"

"He tells me that he wants to. He'll need to be tutored in English, of course. I said I'd help him with that. I want to be a teacher anyway. The counselor said it would be good practice for me. Believe me, Dad; I balked at the idea at first. But the counselor pleaded with me to do it. Don't you see? I'm trying to do the right thing by helping Pete out. You taught me to do the right thing."

I was walking on land charged with mines, and I knew it. Would I be able to persuade the great persuader? Or would it all blow up in my face? I had to take one more step, cross my fingers and hope it wouldn't blast my scheme to smithereens. "You're always helping others, Dad. You do it through the Shrine and your civil projects: the Little League fields, your church work, the charitable clubs you run. I admire you for what you believe in. I'm trying to be like you."

"I don't know, Sandy. I think Pete is just using you."

"How? You know I wouldn't let him get away with anything, Dad. I'm your daughter. I have big plans for myself. I'm going away to college."

"Well, I guess it wouldn't do any harm to talk to Ernie on the kid's behalf. Remember though, I'll only do this because your counselor told you that Pete needs help. I still worry that you're way too fond of that kid. I don't want to have to hear from someone else that you two have been engaged in anything … shameful. Is that clear?"

"Perfectly clear." I nodded solemnly.

"You need to be seeing other guys who are more … I don't know, more normal than Pete: good-looking guys who have two good parents and play in high school sports."

"Pete played football at Kensington, Dad."

"No, Sandy, I'm talking about young men like the students at Gettysburg. I'll offer you a deal; take it or leave it. If I agree to speak to Ernie, you must promise me you'll go out with boys at Gettysburg. Will you agree to that?"

"I promise I'll date the nicest guys at Gettysburg, Dad. And thank you so much. I just knew I could count on you."

"I'm counting on you too, Sandy."

"Don't worry, Dad. I'll keep my promise."

Dad would keep his word. Now I needed to figure out how I was going to teach Pete the English skills he needed to pass the Regents exam with a high enough grade to get accepted to a college like Gettysburg. To that end, I made an appointment to see Mrs. Meese after school. She listened to me outline my intentions to tutor Pete. But, contrary to the supportive encouragement that I had expected from her, she reacted negatively. "You're not going to be able to change that boy. He's incorrigible. It's in your best interest to do well in your own work. Period. Let Peter French fend for himself."

When I told her that Miss Maxmillian had asked me to mentor Pete, she grumpily agreed to lend me an old copy of an earlier English Regents Exam, along with the answer key. But she made it clear that she had reservations about my chances for accomplishing anything.

"Peter French is a lost cause. A leopard can't be made to change his spots." I couldn't believe that she had just uttered such a banal platitude. The sour expression on her usually cheerful face was a side of her that I had never seen. She had always seemed so interested in me; I thought she treated all students that way. Had Pete been on target when he alleged that she favored me only because she was looking out for herself, because I was both well motivated and politically connected? Didn't she know that Pete was smarter than any of her supposedly advanced chosen followers?

While I was doing my best to help him, Pete rested up from his ordeal, forced himself to eat what Grammy prepared for him, and took long walks around the neighborhood. He phoned me in the evenings. He didn't have a positive thing to say about himself; he just seemed to want to hear about my day. I didn't want to reveal what I had been up to, so our phone time was relatively brief. The reticence didn't last long. My dad kept his word and talked to Pastor about the money Pete needed, and the pastor advanced Pete the loan. After that, our phone lines buzzed with renewed electricity.

"I can't believe it, Sandy! My father actually offered me a loan to cover a down payment on a car, enough to get a good one! I'm sorry that you weren't the first person I called about it, sweetie. I had ta make a date with my Kensington buddy. He's gonna take me round to all the used car lots, startin' tomorrow."

"Not that Negro kid, I hope."

"What did ya have ta go and say that for? Luke knows where to get deals; he knows a lot about cars."

"Right. You'll end up with an old purple Cadillac."

"Cute, baby. Stereotype much?"

Two nights later, he called to announce that he and Luke had located a "real beauty," another '53 Ford convertible, or as he put it, "a red rag top."

"Does it have flames on it?"

"Sadly, no," he laughed, "but she's a real beaut."

When he drove it into our driveway, I had to admit that his car was handsome. Mike came out and congratulated Pete for finding such "well-kept-up, lady-killer wheels."

"You'll have to fight off Pete's women now, Sandy. The chicks will love this chariot."

"You're welcome to take them all for yourself, bro."

"It's a deal, sis." He winked at me. Mike could be so charming when he wanted to.

The next morning, Pete showed up at school dressed in black, but he gave me a dimpled smile in sociology class. "Hi, teach. Ya ready ta start lessons tomorrow night?"

"I hope you're serious about this," I said sternly. "We have a good deal of work to do and a short time to do it in. You're not the only item on my schedule, you know."

"I understand. I don't like it, but I understand. Just as long as ya … you … aren't seeing other guys," he said cheerfully. "Where does this class meet, teach?"

"Come to my house at seven tonight. We'll work in the basement. Be prepared to buckle down to work. No excuses accepted."

When Pete sat beside me on the couch in my basement "classroom," I could tell that he had other ideas about how we should spend the time together. But I meant business. I shoved him away and laid down the law: either get serious, or get out. In addition to the sample exam and answer key that Mrs. Meese reluctantly lent me, I borrowed a grammar book from the school library. Warning Pete to keep his hands to himself, I reviewed the grammar rules, emphasizing that he was forbidden to say "ain't" or to use double negatives.

"You've convinced yourself you're such a tough guy that you've locked yourself into a lazy speech pattern. You have a multitude of bad habits that you need to free yourself from in a very short time. I'm certain you can do it, Pete."

"I'm damned sure I can, teach," he grinned.

"Peter French, this is no joke."

I assigned him to write a paragraph about his favorite animal, and he wrote about an Irish Setter that he had once found as a stray. His father named the dog Trouble. He wrote a touching account about how much he had loved Trouble, ending the paragraph with a sentence about how much he hated cats.

"You love trouble, all right, there's no question about it, Pete. Do you know the meaning of a double entendre?"

"Heh! Scout's honor, that was his name."

"Did you say 'Scout's honor'?"

"Hey! I was one badge short of being an Eagle Scout before I quit."

"Why did you quit?"

"I don't know. I just said fuck it."

"Use that 'F' word again and you're out of here. Understand?"

"Yes, ma'am."

I picked up my red pencil and corrected his poor grammar and the loose sentence structure of his paragraph.

"Aw," he said as he watched me pencil in my corrections. "I thought it was beautiful." I explained his mistakes to him, including the inappropriate diversion about cats, and ordered him to memorize the correct spellings of the words he had misspelled. Then I added another long list of words he needed to be able to spell correctly. I assigned him to rewrite the paragraph; he accomplished it perfectly in a split second. When I assigned him to give me an oral report about Trouble, he raised his hand and asked me for a bathroom break.

"You're dismissed. You can use the one by the garage," I proclaimed bossily. "It's the one Queenie uses, but I guess it's okay. Patty says it is."

"It isn't dirty, is it?" He looked worried.

"No, and it won't matter to you that Queenie is a Negress."

Before I realized what was happening, he grabbed me and pulled me, bottom up, across his lap.

"*What are you doing?*" I yelled in a whisper.

He slapped me three times with the flat of his hand, hard spanks across the butt of my Bermuda shorts.

"You prejudiced [slap], spoiled [slap] brat [slap]." He let go of his tight grip on me.

"I didn't hurt you," he said, letting go of me. "So don't pretend I did. You deserved a whipping for even thinking what you just said. Queenie is no different from any other human being, except she works harder."

I stared at him incredulously.

"But she's a Negress. She smells funny."

"She's a *what?* Sandy, you're the one who needs more learnin' than I do. Where did you pick up that term Negress? Your parents? If Queenie does smell funny to your delicate snobby nose, what you probably detect is good, honest sweat." He rose from the couch, shaking his head like a disappointed grandfather. When he returned, I was in a bad mood. He ignored my pouty expression and told me about his dog in flawless English. I was amazed at how well he spoke when he concentrated. I was disappointed too. I wanted to criticize him.

"So, what other groups of humanity have your good parents taught you to despise?" he asked.

"You're being unfair to me, Pete. I don't despise anyone. I just don't ... I don't socialize with some ... types of people."

"Like who? Catholics? Jews? Indians? Polish people? I'm part Irish. Maybe you ought to refuse to socialize with me."

"Don't be so hard on me. You have no right to act as if you're so darn superior. I ... dated ... a boy with Indian blood whom I still admire very much."

"Yeah. That big dumb jock you go goo-goo over. I know all about him, but you're avoiding the bigger question."

"I can't change the way I was brought up, can I?"

"Why not? You want me to change. What you learned was wrong. So unlearn it."

We argued a good deal. And we worked well together. When we disagreed, we never resorted to physical abuse of any kind; in fact, he never even tried to spank me again. I grew verbally feisty when he criticized my ideas, and he used devious means to avoid facing up to his feelings. When I blew up at him, he stoically endured my tirades and patiently suffered my fumbling remorse after I had calmed down. When I sensed that he was starting to dive deep inside himself to take refuge from his feelings, I knew how to rile the waters and reel him to the surface. Because we listened to each other and we cared, we always reached a compromise before parting for the night.

We dated every weekend, often alone, sometimes with couples we both liked. My parents griped every time I went out with him. I grew tired of reminding them that I would soon be at Gettysburg, and I did all I could to assure them that they need not worry. But I approached my obligations at school in a halfhearted way. My friends mocked me about my inscrutable younger boyfriend. I protested to them, to my parents, and to myself that Pete was my protégé, just a final fling before college.

Barb complained that I never had time for her anymore, so I finally agreed to a Friday overnight at her house. When he dropped me off there, Pete accused me of cheating us out of a Friday night together and promised to pick me up at two the following afternoon. I kissed him good-bye and told him I'd be looking for him at two. But as soon as I was inside Barb's familiar house, we slipped into our old routine of gossiping about friends, film stars, and clothing styles, avoiding the sticky issue of my relationship with Pete. We stayed up talking late, slept in, enjoyed a late brunch, and then lazed about some more. The upshot of our indolence was that when Pete's car pulled into Barb's driveway promptly at two, I wasn't ready. Thoughtlessly, I left him sitting out there. Later, I noticed that he had driven away. I didn't worry until about four. Then I realized how callously I had acted. How long had I left him waiting? No wonder he had gone away. He had every right to be angry with me.

Meanwhile, Barb was annoyed at me for fretting about Pete. In no uncertain terms, she finally told me the truth about how she felt about him. "You're letting that creepy guy run your life. Why? He's younger than you are, and he's no dream catch by any stretch of the imagination. He's stupid and ugly and way beneath you. I always admired you for being so independent, Sandy. Ever since you got involved with that greaser, you've changed. I'm not the only one who thinks so either."

"What do you mean? What have you heard?"

"Oh, you know, people say that you've not been yourself lately. I defend you, of course, as well as I can. But frankly, Sandy, I'm worried. Remember how much fun we used to have? You're so eager to get away from school now, even when you're having fun, and you're always worrying about that guy. In my opinion, Pete would make anyone turn morbid. Why are you letting him do this to you? It makes no sense. Why do you let him monopolize your time? He's dragging you down with him. I'm sorry to say it, but I liked the old you better."

"I can't seem to satisfy anyone anymore, Barb. I'm simply not at liberty to tell you all the reasons why I spend so much time with Pete. All I can say is that I made secret promises to important grown-ups to help him out."

"Gee, I wonder if it has anything to do with your church stuff," she said sarcastically. "I don't get that either."

"I can't say. All I can tell you is that, honestly, Pete gets to me. I can't explain it, even to myself. I don't think you'd understand anyway. Your life is different. Someday maybe something like this will happen to you."

"Boy, if that doesn't sound condescending, I don't know what does! I'm not your little sister, Sandy."

"I'm sorry. Let's just be friends again, okay? We've had a good time together, haven't we? But now I really need to call Pete."

Barb threw her hands up. "I give up. Just don't forget I told you so when you're finally sorry that you've let him take over your life."

By the tone of his voice when he answered the phone, I knew Pete was angry. He barely said hi and told me to make it fast because he had to get off the phone. He was busy. "Find your own way home. You can't treat me that way, Sandy. I waited for you longer than I should have, stuck in the driveway of that dumb broad's house. What were you trying to prove? That I'm yer lapdog? No way, baby. I won't be used by no woman."

"You're right, Pete, okay? Your grammar stinks, on purpose, I assume, but you're right. I'm so *very sorry* for treating you badly. I was wrong. It was thoughtless of me. I need to make it up to you. Do you really want me to find another ride home?"

"Be on the corner of Main and Burbank in five minutes. If you're not there—just be there." He slammed down the phone.

I gathered up my things, thanked my disgruntled friend, and was on the street corner in four minutes. I had one minute to think about how I would have reacted if he had treated me the way I had treated him. After I hopped into his car, we quickly and pleasurably made up. Nothing I did with my girlfriends was ever that much fun.

One Sunday afternoon, not long after that, I asked Pete to

drive me over to my grandparents' home because I owed them a visit, and I wanted to see how they got along with Pete. He was deferential and polite to all three of the elders living there, and his grammar suddenly turned flawless. He spotted Grandpa's leather-bound copy of Stevenson's *The Master of Ballantrae,* and he and Grandpa had a lengthy discussion about Stevenson's life and his works. When we were having refreshments, Tanta pulled Pete aside and led him into a back room, where I couldn't hear what they were saying. Later, I asked Pete to tell me.

"Your great aunt and I have a little secret," he said, grinning mysteriously.

"Tell me."

"Nope."

"Please?"

"I'll just give you a hint. It's about a diamond."

"For you? That is ... *oh no!*"

Tanta had no right to presume that Pete and I had a commitment like that.

A few days later, Pete startled me by stopping in his tracks as he was walking me to his car. He bowed stiffly before me, and I exclaimed, "Pete! What are you doing?" I could tell by the twinkle in his eyes that he expected me to react that way. "May I have the honor and extreme pleasure of escorting you to the junior prom, Miss Schall?"

Hoping he didn't notice my sigh of relief that he wasn't about to ask me anything more serious, I responded with a more crucial question. "Are you aware of the dress code?"

"I never go to anything that requires me to rent my own clothing," he responded, mimicking Groucho Marx.

"Well, you'll have to, if you're going to escort me, sir," I laughed.

He told me that he and Burt Platzel were going to get measured at a clothing rental place for the requisite white coat, black pants, bow tie, and cummerbund. They planned to make it a triple date. Burt already had a date, but he secretly admired my friend, Sylvia

Zimmer, the quiet Jewish girl that had worked with me on stage design. He begged Pete to get me to invite her and her date to come along with us. Sylvia sounded pleased with the idea. After I helped him with the arrangement, Pete confessed that his strategy was to let the other two couples drive in a separate car, so he and I could have more time alone.

When I told Mom who would be on our triple date, she asked me point blank if I really wanted to associate with "that sort of people."

"What sort, Mom? Our pastor's son and four other kids?" I walked out of the room, wary of getting into an argument about Jews. Back in my own room, I realized how much Pete had already influenced my thinking. Was Barb right? Was he controlling my mind? In this particular instance, however, I knew that Barb would agree with Pete.

No one seemed surprised to see me with Pete at the dance. After Paul and Cal asked me to dance, Pete restricted our movements to an outside corner of the dance floor. He led me out of the gym as soon as possible, and we drove in his car to a big nightclub in downtown Buffalo. The other two couples followed in their car. The McGuire Sisters were featured that night. I was thrilled to see Dorothy, Christine, and my favorite, Phyllis, in person. They told jokes and sang familiar songs: "Sincerely," "He," "Something's Gotta Give," and others. I thought they looked better in person than they did on TV. But Pete wasn't impressed. He criticized their performance so loudly that he embarrassed me, and I had to shush him. He mocked their music for what he called their lack of soul. "You're weird," I whispered. "Most people like their romantic themes. I sure do."

"That's not the same thing, baby. I'm talkin' about depth of feeling, sincerity. Anyone can say something romantic and not mean it. Take your brother Mike. He knows how to talk romantic, but do you think he's sincere?"

When the main act left the stage, he asked me to join him for a slow dance on the club floor. He held me so close that I felt that sweet 'Yul Bryner kind of sexy' all over. I told myself I had a right to feel that way; after all, it was prom night.

Adhering to his original plan, Pete split away from the other two couples as soon as he could. Around four in the morning, we were parked in my driveway, seriously petting, when he uttered the unforgettable words: "Sandy, I love you so much it hurts. Please, marry me."

And how did this passionate, sensitive girl respond to such a heartfelt plea? I laughed; I actually laughed.

He pushed me away.

"Forgive me, Pete. I'm not laughing at you. This is just too much. I'm losing my grip."

"Then let me take care of you."

"Thank you, dear, with all my heart."

"Is that a 'yes'?"

"No! And stop making me be the reasonable one. It's not fair. It's been a wonderful night. I wish it didn't have to end, but it does."

"You don't want to marry me?" he asked, softly.

"I didn't say that. I'm saying that we *can't* get married, and you know it. If I were to give up my hopes for a college degree, and we did elope, which is what we'd have to do, considering how my parents feel about you; and then somehow we did manage to find someplace where we could live on nothing, you'd have to go off driving a big truck to Alaska or somewhere, and I'd have to find work doing a dumb menial job that I'd hate, or, worse still, I'd be stuck home, yelling at our kids. Is that what you want?"

"Hey, who said anything about children?"

"Oh, oh! Did you see the garage lights flick on and off? They know we're out here. I've got to go in."

"No. They can wait a minute. At least tell me you love me. You've never even said that to me, Sandy."

He tried to fondle me, and I pushed him away. "Let me think, Pete, please."

Would any other girl have stopped to ponder, feeling the way that I did? What was wrong with me? I felt as if I were being asked to commit myself to a nunnery, except the other way around. The words "I love you" were the most important words in the world to me. Mike said them to a different girl every weekend. Why hadn't he been cursed with my problem? Everyone loved *him* no matter what he said or did. I loved Mike. It wouldn't be difficult for me to tell him that I loved him. I loved everyone in my family. Did I love Pete? He meant as much to me as they did. That wasn't true. He meant more.

"Do you love me? *Say it!*"

"Yes, God help me, I love you," I sighed.

After one final passionate kiss, I ran indoors.

## Chapter 27
## Why Don't They Understand

June 1959: graduation month. It was a season of parties and a time for good-byes. I had high expectations for the graduation ceremony itself. I saw it as the culmination of years of hard work, a major milestone in my life. But the evening didn't start out well. After I donned my white gown and mortarboard, Mom took a picture of Vinnie and me. He wore a black cap and gown, because he was a boy. Mom fawned over him every bit as much as she did me, as if the only difference between us was the color of our gowns. Yet he had had hardly lifted pen to paper since we had begun going to school.

As we lined up for the procession into the gymnasium, I opened the program eagerly, looking for my name in the list of award winners. My heart pounding, I discovered that I was about to get the best prize a girl could receive: the PTA Award for Highest Ranking Girl in my class of four hundred. I could hardly breathe. I prayed that I wouldn't trip on the way up the stairs to the award podium. My friend Glenn Ackart was a high ranking boy, and Russ Meyer won a Regents Scholarship in science and math. Cal Campbell earned a scholarship to Amherst College, and Paul Hartmann got two awards: the U.S. Air Force Academy scholarship and the annual Rotary Club Award for All-Around

Boy. Below these listings, I found my name among those who had won State Regents scholarships.

Pete didn't go to the ceremony, but he seemed genuinely happy for me when I showed him what I had won. He urged me to enjoy the graduation parties and festivities and expressed neither jealousy nor regret when he wasn't invited to my pool party for the Meese gang on Saturday. In my mind, the party was as much for my parents as it was for me. The kids seemed to think that Dad was a card, and they enjoyed it when Mom laughed at their antics and took photographs of everyone. She posed Paul next to me, making a big deal about the fact that the annual yearbook paired us together under the letter "V" for Versatile in the Senior Alphabet.

As she snapped the camera, she exclaimed, "You two versatile kids sure make a handsome couple." This embarrassed me. I couldn't tell how Paul felt about it. He just laughed and said, "Thank you, ma'am," as if he were already standing at attention at the Air Force Academy. Throughout the party, I sensed that Mom and Dad kept pushing us together, and they encouraged Paul to stay after the other guests left. Wrapped in our towels, we stretched out and leaned back on parallel lounge chairs. I admired Paul's handsome features as he enthused about how much he was looking forward to the academy. "And afterwards, I plan to become a member of SAC," he boasted.

"What is sack?"

"Sorry. We use professional acronyms in the military. It's the Strategic Air Command, the guys who keep the skies of America safe from communist attacks and such. So you can sleep better at night."

"That's a truly noble goal. It sounds dangerous though. Please take care, okay?"

"I'll do my best, ma'am," he said cheerfully. He seemed like a fairy-tale prince: charming, handsome, and sincere. He would make some girl very happy, I thought.

At church the next morning, I was alarmed by the fact that

Pete's forehead looked moist and his skin didn't look right. He had done a poor job shaving his face, and his clothes were disheveled. I asked him if he felt okay, and he nodded despondently. We settled into a pew near the back of the church, and I reached into the pocket of the pew in front of ours to pick up a hymnal. After we stood up for the entrance hymn, I felt the weight of his body against mine. He was slowly dropping down, toward the floor, as if falling into a faint. It took a good deal of effort for me to brace him up; he helped me by grasping onto the back of the pew in front of ours. He looked dazed and barely conscious. I realized I had to get him out of there.

"Lean on me," I whispered, and we staggered out the back of the church. We escaped into his father's office, where I ordered him to sit down and put his head between his legs. After resting a while, he protested that he felt okay and insisted that he was ready to drive himself home.

"You're not going to drive home alone," I insisted, deeply concerned.

I watched him carefully as he drove, wishing I knew how to operate a stick shift. No one was at his house when we got there; they all were at church. We descended into the basement, where he threw himself on the sofa with a muted moan. I let him lie down there for a few minutes. Suddenly, he sat up. "Look, I'm okay now. Let me just rest for a couple of minutes more, then I'll take you home."

"No. Not until you explain. What's the matter with you?"

"It's confidential, okay?"

"Absolutely not."

"You're not going to let me keep this to myself, are you?"

"Absolutely not."

"Anne … oh, I can't talk about this. It's wrong for me to be telling you."

"Out with it. What did Anne say to you?"

He wouldn't meet my eyes. So I waited. Finally, hesitantly, he opened up. While I was having my party, he had gone to see

Anne Diefendorf at her invitation. She told him she wanted to have a serious talk. He assumed it was about her and his dad, so he agreed to come. She greeted him in the friendly way she always did and offered him a piece of her homemade cake.

"That damn cake was the last piece of food I've eaten. And I'm afraid that it didn't stay down."

"Go on," I urged.

"After I ate her damn cake, she told me—" He stopped and dropped his head into his hands. "I can't do this, Sandy. She said it was just between her and me. Right now I can't think straight anyway."

"This is about us, isn't it? If you love me, you'll tell me."

"If I love you, we shouldn't be together now."

"That's ridiculous. What is this all about? Out with it."

"I give up," he sighed. "As I remember it, Anne sat down next to me on her couch, real friendly like. Then she convinced me that I have to stop seeing you."

"What? Why?" I tried to keep my voice calm.

"For your sake, Sandy," he said loudly, looking right at me.

I shook my head but managed to remain silent.

In a softer tone he added, "She made me see, for the first time, how selfish and blind I've been. My love is only going to hurt you."

"Pete, that doesn't make any sense."

He nodded miserably, his eyes avoiding mine. "Anne pointed out that when you go off to Gettysburg, you'll have to make new friends; new girlfriends *and* boyfriends. She reminded me of the time when one of the guys at Resurrection went to college, just to UB here in Buffalo, for Christ's sake. He found a new girlfriend there and dumped his old steady who was still at Kensington. Broke her heart. Anne said it happens all the time. So the sooner we stop seeing each other, the better it'll be for both of us."

He hid his face in his hands, so I couldn't read his eyes.

"It sounds to me that she predicted that I was going hurt you, not the other way around," I said angrily. "So she scared you?"

"No!" He dropped his hands and looked into my eyes intently, almost angrily. "You've got it all wrong. By loving you, I'm making you feel obligated to, how did she put it? Stay loyal to me. Shit! How dumb could I be?" He put his face in his hands again. "She's right, Sandy. I've been a jerk. Of course you'll find someone better. I accept that now, and so I'm letting you go. You're free of me. You'll thank me for this someday, Sandy."

"Do you even know what you're saying?"

"Don't worry about me. I'm fine."

"You're lying again, and ... oooh! I'm so mad, I could spit! I need to talk to that woman!"

"No. I'm telling you, I'm okay with this. You're upset now, but soon you'll see the wisdom in what she told me."

"Have you forgotten that I love you?"

He sighed. "How could I?"

I rose up from the couch and began to pace. "Anne had no right to say those things to you."

"She's trying to help us, Sandy."

"Maybe, maybe not."

"She is! She's my friend."

"Really? I see her differently."

"You don't know her."

"Okay. But I know that she loves your dad."

"What's that got to do with this?"

"You're not thinking straight, dear. Can't I get you to eat something? You'll understand this more clearly if you get something in your stomach."

"I don't feel like eating."

"Well, then shut up and listen to me, sweetheart. First of all, I think Anne is speaking for your father, who admits he can't communicate with you, right?"

"You don't think she really believes what she said? You're wrong there. She meant it."

"That's not my point. What I'm trying to say is that, first and foremost, she loves your dad. She's your friend only because she loves him. She knows you well enough now to know that the best way to manipulate you is to convince you that something you're doing will hurt someone else."

"Huh?"

"Your dad thinks you're too … close to me, and he's probably said so to Anne more than once. So she's doing his dirty work for him. She's trying to get you to give me up by telling you that you're not good for me."

"Aw, she's not that underhanded. She's not mean."

"Maybe not. I don't know. But she doesn't understand what we mean to each other."

He nodded silently.

"My good friend Barb doesn't approve of us being together either. She has warned me to stay away from you. She thinks it's your fault that I've changed, as she puts it. Both Anne and Barb undoubtedly mean well. But neither of them understands how we feel about each other. *Nobody* does. Look at me, now, Pete, please?"

He looked so unhappy. I kissed his sweaty lips, suddenly feeling miserable too.

"My parents are the same way," I sighed, hugging him. "Dad got me to promise to date boys when I'm at Gettysburg. He and Mom both think the guys there are more respectable than you are."

"They would say that. Those guys at Gettysburg *are* more respectable than I am, that's for damn sure."

"As you once said, respectable is boring. But you have never bored me. Not for a minute. That's one of the many reasons that I love you."

He sat up straighter, grabbed my hand, and touched the heart ring. "You really do love me, Sandy?"

"I *do not* tell lies. Do you, honestly, love me?"

He groaned, dropped my hand, and looked away. "You still don't trust me."

I felt tears welling up. Crying wouldn't help. "I'll trust you if you'll trust me, Pete. I hate the thought of having to leave you. But we have the whole summer ahead."

"Then you'll leave me. You say you always keep your promises. So you'll date those respectable squares at Gettysburg, and you'll find some cube who's better than me, Sandy."

"Oh, there will be a lot of good, nice boys at Gettysburg. But no one like you, I'm absolutely certain of that. I mean this with all my heart, Peter Andrew French. I'll keep that darn promise, and I'll put up with those bores, but trust me, I know how to choose guys who won't try anything. And if they ever do, I'll tell them I have a big, tough boyfriend back home who won't hesitate to kill them."

That finally brought a twinkle to his eyes.

"We're going to have to trust each other. I get jealous more easily than you do, so it's going to be hard for me too. You're cute and sexy. Girls find you attractive."

"I thought you never lied."

"I wish I *were* lying. But I've noticed the way they look at you. Shirley Becker and Sally Marsh will have their claws out to get you as soon as I head for college."

"You're either trying to make me feel good, or you're in danger of being committed, poor girl," he said.

"The latter, for sure. We're both nuts, you know that. We're an oxymoron."

"What do you mean?"

"Don't play dumb with me. You know what an oxymoron is, wise guy. We've become a living contradiction. Alone together: that's us. Just as alone and together contradict each other, we contradict the ideal of a perfect couple. We're too young, we're going to be miles apart, and no one believes we belong together. Life is absurd, isn't it? But I have a feeling."

"What's that?"

"Ours won't be dull."

"You're damn right about that, honey."

## Chapter 28
# Bye Bye Love

*Before We Said Good-bye*

About a week later, Pete arrived to pick me up one evening after everyone else had already left the house. I met him with open arms as he bounded into the dining room. "You look like one of those smug know-it-all guys on the College Bowl, Pete. What's up?"

"I found out that I didn't flunk the English Regents." He whirled me around.

"You know your score?"

"You won't like it."

I stopped spinning. "Well, tell me anyway. Don't keep me in suspense, Pete. You must have passed, you certainly don't look unhappy."

"You might say that. But my score was only 98."

"No! That's better than I did, genius!"

"Yeah. You don't seem to mind that, but ol' lady Meese will be pissed. Sorry. I mean I didn't do it her way."

"I don't understand."

"I answered the multiple choice questions on literature and got every one of them right."

"You weren't supposed to even try that. You're amazing!"

"Good amazing?"

"Of course, good. I love you so much." I hugged him tightly and gave him a heartfelt kiss.

"If I'd known how happy you'd be, I'd have gotten those last two points, sweetheart."

It was a fantastic beginning to a beautiful summer. Except for the abysmal cloud that was stalled on our radar, it couldn't have been better, at least for me. When I told Dad I wanted to make a little money for college incidentals, he said that the head of the town's summer recreation program might hire me to write stories for the *Amherst Bee* about playground activities.

In order to pay back his dad for the car loan and to start his college savings account, Pete needed to earn a lot more money than I could make, so I asked Dad if he knew of anyone in Amherst who would be hiring teenage boys over the summer and paying good wages.

"You aren't asking me to help Pete find work, are you? He can find his own darn job. Well, actually, the boss of the town highway department did ask me if Mike would be interested in doing road repair. The pay is very good, but I told him that no kid of mine is going to risk his life doing that sort of work. Older crew guys hate the summer kids. They can be awfully rough on them."

"If Pete were willing to take the job though, would you put in a word for him?"

"If he's fool enough to want to do it, I'll help him get an interview with the boss. But that's all I'll do."

"Oh, Dad, Pete's not that bad. He got a higher grade on the English Regents than I did, and he really does intend to go to college after he gets out of Amherst next year."

"Huh. Well, I'll get him that job interview, if he's dumb enough to want it."

Pete passed the interview and got the job, but Dad was right about how the regular crew would treat him. They seemed to regard him as a threat because he accomplished his assignments in about a quarter of the time that they took to do the same things. They accused him of trying to show them up in front of their boss, and they made things as hard for him as they could.

"Sandy, you wouldn't believe how long it takes one of those guys just to change out a street sign. I guess they figure they don't need to knock themselves out to make this town look pretty, when it's already so much nicer than where they live."

So Pete slowed down his work pace, and he talked to the men in street language, demonstrating he could be every bit as foul-mouthed as they were. He knew all about sports and local politics, so they grudgingly accepted him. His skin became deeply tanned by spreading gravel and tar in slow motion in the hot summer sun. His brown hair bleached to blond, and his muscles grew firm. After obtaining a truck-driving license, he occasionally drove the heavy crew trucks. One bright day, when I was out driving on my playground rounds in Dad's silver Buick, I spotted Pete's road crew. I pulled the car over to the curb, not far from the section of the road where they were spreading tar. Pete ran up to my dad's car, leaned his head through the window, and gave me a hot, sweaty kiss. His lips tasted salty, and I heard the crew razzing him jealously. "Hey, Pete, introduce us to the Dolly in that tank."

He grinned appreciatively at me and waved me on.

"I thought of a brilliant idea today," I bragged to Pete one evening. "I'm making arrangements for the town to sponsor a Miss Amherst Recreation contest."

"That's stupid."

"Why? It'll be like a junior Miss America pageant. Ellen, the woman I work directly under, will help me judge the little girls on the basis of beauty, poise, and talent. The winner will be crowned Miss Amherst Recreation. The playground girls don't have as much to do as the boys do, so they'll enjoy it, and the contest will attract attention to the summer recreation program. The *Amherst Bee* will eat it up. Mom and Dad think it's the best idea I've had yet."

"They would," he said sarcastically.

"Why are you being so negative again?"

"You think some little girl ought to be turned into a clown just because she's pretty?"

"She has to have poise and talent too," I pouted.

"Oh, right. And you're going to be the judge? You couldn't tell a sour note from a birdcall. What do little girls do in talent contests? Dance in tutus? Twirl batons? Come on, Sandy. The Miss America pageants are a conservative good old boys' political tactic. Has there ever been a black contestant?"

"You never think I have any good ideas. You're mean and critical, and I hate your guts."

"Ooo-eee! What a devastatingly thoughtful comeback. How could I ever argue with that?"

I carried out my idiotic scheme, the contest attracted publicity to the town's summer recreation program, and I felt terrible. Once I had blown off steam at Pete for pointing out how stupid the idea was, I had to reluctantly admit that he was right.

On weekends, he drove me into the country, where he took me to his old haunts, including the summer cabin in which he had stayed alone to plant the baby trees that were now thriving in the fields beyond the cabin. We walked down into Zoar Valley, a woody secluded area beside a stream, where we made out in the grass. I created watercolor paintings, using stream water to lubricate my paint, and Pete did some writing. On the drive back home, we stopped for homemade ice cream cones at Pete's favorite dairy.

One weekend, I suggested taking a trip together to Crystal Beach, a Canadian amusement park with a fast roller coaster and other rides that I had enjoyed as a kid. I couldn't understand why Pete grimaced at the idea.

"You don't want to? I thought everyone liked Crystal Beach." That was when he told me about the race riots that had occurred in 1956 on the Crystal Beach Boat; riots that I hadn't bothered to read about in the newspaper. Every summer I had been taken to the park at various times in the sedans of family or friends. I had no idea that it was a tradition for Buffalo teenage gangs to go there by boat on opening day, Memorial Day, dressed in gang outfits. Pete said that minor gang fights often broke out on opening day, and the police had to keep them in tow.

"Were you on that opening day boat in 1956?"

"Well, yeah. The riot wasn't like the papers said though. It happened on the last ride home. The boat, the *Canadiana,* was packed with nearly a thousand teenagers. It started to rain, and a bunch of us kids went downstairs to stay dry. A few of the girls belonging to a black gang challenged a gang of white girls. That wasn't anything new. It certainly wasn't the big deal the newspapers made of it. The way they told it, it sounded like a gang of black thugs was attacking some poor little white girls. The town fathers, as the papers called the old boys, churned up a huge outrage. My dad was called in to be a member of a ministerial commission to deal with the gangs. As if he would have done any good. I once heard him use the expression 'There's a nigger in the woodpile' when he thought someone was causing trouble. Anyway, the upshot of it all was that the fuss that the newspapers kicked up helped to accelerate white flight to the suburbs."

"White flight? What does that mean?"

"It's the term for the white people moving out to the suburbs to escape from the scary, or so they thought, black folk. White flight eventually made it impossible for Dad to remain at Resurrection. Everyone important in his church moved out to the suburbs."

"Well, I'm glad of that, Peter French."

Pete and I gradually discovered that we had almost identical likes and dislikes, the major exceptions being his interest in sports and my penchant for shopping. We had lengthy discussions about everything, from mystery novels to what parts of the world we hoped to visit someday. Neither of us liked to go to country fairs. I had been wary of crowds since Mom warned me to stay away from them during the polio epidemic, and Pete just didn't like them, period. But we both loved secluded Zoar Valley, so he took me back there several times. Once we drove over the Peace Bridge to enjoy Niagara Falls and envy the honeymooners; another time we found a secluded beach along Lake Erie's Canadian shore, where we played on the sand and made out.

Wherever we went, however, the shadow of that dark cloud loomed. Gettysburg sent me reams of information about Orientation Week and college rules. Pete found it incredible that I would be required to wear a blue and orange freshman beanie. The silly caps were touted as a way for upper classmen to identify us so they could "make us feel welcome," but Pete pointed out that they'd also mark us for hazing. The college had a strict dress code: no denims on the campus, skirts and stockings for ladies, and ties and jackets for gentlemen at sit-down dinners. Students had to attend weekly chapel services, and no one was excused from class without a note from his or her dorm mother and nurse. Boys could only visit girls in their dorm mezzanines until 10:00 pm.

"Are you going to obey all those stupid rules?" Pete asked me dubiously.

"I have no choice."

"Might as well be in prison."

"That's not true. Tradition is important."

"Do you really believe that?"

I laughed. "Honestly, I haven't given it much thought."

"I'd just ignore the rules."

"You'd get in trouble."

"And that would be different because …?"

The day I learned the identity of my assigned dormitory roommate, I complained to Pete that I had hoped she would be a girl from a different state, not somebody called Doris Keller from Buffalo.

"I know her! She played violin next to me in our school orchestra at PS 61."

"You played a violin? No!"

"Is it so hard for that silly brain to imagine?" He gently bonked my head affectionately. "I know a good deal about music."

I rolled my eyes. "You know a good deal about everything, it seems. Who needs an encyclopedia when you're around? Okay, tell me, Heifetz, why have you been hiding your violin from me?"

"It's no longer exactly … in one piece," he said, with that mischievous gleam in his eyes.

"I have to ask."

"When I was, oh, about eight," Pete recalled, "I found a violin while poking around in our old stuff in the attic. My school had an award-winning orchestra, because the orchestra director encouraged kids to bring old family instruments in to school. So I took the violin to school, and he showed me how to play it. Other music teachers supervised my practice for one hour every morning. I already knew how to read music, of course, because of piano lessons. When I reached a decent level of expertise, I auditioned for the orchestra. Doris was older, but I was better than she was, so I had the first chair, and she played next to me. I played solos, and we held concerts in a big hall. I especially enjoyed playing the 'Triumphal March' from *Aida*."

"Your dad must have been proud of you then."

He shook his head. "I don't remember him attending one concert."

"I think that's just … wrong."

"Until my voice changed, I was also in the Buffalo All Boys'

291

Choir. He went to one of those concerts, the one when we sang the 'Rip Van Winkle Suite.' Ugh!"

"I wish I knew something about classical music."

"You have a tin ear, sweetheart."

"Thank you very much."

"I think we should change the subject before I say something else I may regret."

"No. You haven't told me what happened to your violin, or about Doris."

"She's not very pretty, but she's a nice kid."

"Plain and nice. Just my type," I said facetiously. "And the violin?"

"Oh, yeah ... yes. One day I smashed it in half, across my knees, on purpose."

"Why, for heaven's sake?"

"I think I was about fourteen then. It was bad enough having to be a four-eyes with a preacher for a dad. I looked like a real sissy carrying that violin case to school. So I got rid of it."

"It wasn't a tough guy thing. I get it."

"Don't ya fergit it, little lady."

"Ooooh, you terrify me."

"Ya better be afraid of me, kid, if ya know what's good fer ya."

*He* was good for me. I enjoyed every minute of the fleeting time we had together that summer: our drives in the country, our discussions about the movies we saw, even our arguments, and especially our making up. Religion was a touchy subject for us, however. Pete mercilessly heckled me when I told him I had read every page of the Bible.

"And even after that, you insist it's the 'true word'? You never questioned any of it? Have you read about the *Dead Sea Scrolls*?"

"No. What do they have to do with the Bible?"

"If the professor in that Bible course you're required to take at Gettysburg knows what he's talking about, you'll find out. I don't want to spoil his fun."

That sort of comment irritated me, and he knew it. "Look, Sandy, I don't want to get your dander up now. Let's not argue, okay?"

Our last evening together was miserable. He drove us to a secluded area where we parked, petted, and repeated promises we had already made. He told me to call him as soon as possible to give him my dormitory phone number. Individual rooms weren't equipped with phones, and the few phones shared by all the girls were neither private nor easy to come by. Our only recourse would be to write each other daily: small consolation for the long separation. We kissed good-bye over and over, until he finally escorted me to the garage door. Neither of us wanted to be the one to close the screen door. Finally, I closed it for the last time, and we touched our hands together, the screen separating our skin like the barrier of space and time we could no longer avoid.

I remember how he looked, standing on the other side of that screen. His expression mirrored everything that I felt. I shut the inner door for the last time and ran to my room crying. My little sister, who was already in bed, turned her body toward the wall, where she probably kept a world where no one was weeping. Eventually Dad knocked on my partially closed bedroom door.

"Sandy, I refuse to waste any more money on your college education if you're going to carry on this way. I'll save money, time, and effort if we don't go tomorrow. Just say the word."

"What are you suggesting, Harry?" Mom yelled at him angrily from the living room.

I sat up and grabbed for a Kleenex. "No, no, Dad. I'm sorry. I shouldn't blubber on like this. I want to go to Gettysburg. I really do. I'm just being silly. I'll be okay. I'll be fine on the trip. I promise not to put a damper on anything."

I got into my old stay-at-home pajamas and decided to go out to the refrigerator to get a glass of pop. I overheard Mom talking to Dad in the living room as I tiptoed by. They didn't see me.

"Harry, in many ways I'm actually glad she's leaving. I'll miss her, of course, but it will be best for her. Remember when we visited the college? All those handsome young men? She's bound to meet someone there more suited to her than Pete is. Before long she'll have forgotten him altogether."

"Yes, it's all for the best. She'll fit in well at Gettysburg."

I strode softly back past them and then called out in a clear voice, "Good night, Mom, Dad."

"Oh!" Mom exclaimed. "You didn't hear us talking just now, did you?"

"Good night," I said. "Sleep well."

I didn't sleep well. Pete and I had only been apart for a few hours, and I missed his tender touch already. I knew it would be worse for him. The one being left behind always suffered the most. I'd soon be engulfed in work and engaged in meeting new people. Would Pete be busy too? Would he meet someone else? I hated myself for wondering.

*Epilogue*
# GRADUATION DAY

I sensed Tanta smiling down on me as I twisted my diamond ring around the gold band on my left hand. Inhaling a lungful of fragrant spring air, I tried to curb my impatience. Time didn't need to go by any faster than it already had since I received by BA degree there in 1963. At last, I heard the orchestra tuning up for the entry march. I watched the young members of the 2006 graduating class of Gettysburg College, self-conscious in their academic regalia, as they swept down the grassy aisles, golden tassels swinging cockily from their mortarboards. All around me, teary-eyed parents popped out of their white lawn chairs to snap pixels of memory like fish jumping out of a Minnesota lake to snap up insects.

I focused my attention upon my old classmate, the man in the unadorned black academic robe who was about to receive a great honor there. He didn't look as stereotypically professorial as some of the other academics as he walked up the stairs to the podium: several of them were wearing spectacles, and many of the males had beards. He sat in a chair beneath the colossal orange and blue college banners that were wafting lazily in the breeze.

He appeared to be quite composed as he returned the smile of the attractive blonde woman sitting next to him. Her blue satin robe gleamed in the sunlight. The dark blue velvet and orange satin bands on her sleeves signified that she was the college president. Something about her reminded me of Grandma Chrystene. If she were sitting next to me now, I mused, she'd be delighted to see that a woman holds such an important executive position.

President Will stepped up to the lectern. She greeted the guests and graduates. My mind started to wander until I heard her mention his name. She enumerated the reasons Gettysburg was awarding him an honorary doctorate. I couldn't read his expression. Was he amused, embarrassed, or merely bored?

"A multitalented student, you were also on the move: you graduated with departmental honors in 1963—that is, in three years." She emphasized "three."

"You were teaching at the University of Minnesota when your book exploring the question of whether army units or individual members of those units are responsible for military atrocities first came out. This book is widely credited as a founding work for the field of applied ethics. In a glorious and peripatetic academic career, you have held distinguished positions at eight universities, edited two influential journals, and authored nineteen books and dozens of articles in ethics and legal theory. A central, powerful theme of your work has been the analysis of individual and collective responsibility ...

"For sharing and advancing the goal of living ethically in community; for your moral vision, acute intelligence, and ability to illuminate in teaching and writing; for challenging simple answers and simple-mindedness with compelling insight and argument rooted in the real context of our lives, we celebrate your accomplishments and honor you today with our highest award.

"By virtue of the authority invested in me by the Board of Trustees of Gettysburg College and the laws of the Commonwealth, I hereby gladly confer upon you, Dr. Peter A. French, the honorary degree of Doctor of Humane Letters, with all the rights, honors, and privileges pertaining thereto."

The college provost, wearing a deep red robe and matching mortarboard with a golden tassel, stepped forward. He placed a blue and orange satin-lined hood over his head and secured it into place over his black academic gown.

Dr. Will handed him a scrolled diploma, bound with orange and blue ribbons.

When the ceremony ended, he disappeared behind the podium.

I searched the retreating swarm of parents and graduates, watching for him. At last, I spotted him making his way toward me. He had discarded the black robe, and he was pulling off his tie with his right hand as he walked swiftly, his new hood draped over his left arm, his left hand holding his second doctoral diploma. Casually, he tossed the tie, hood, and diploma my way. I almost dropped them.

"What did you think, Sandra? Did I do okay?"

"You couldn't have been more impressive."

"I did it all for you, babe. It would have been fine with me if they had just mailed me the degree."

"I know, and I'm very, very grateful. I'm so proud you! It's a momentous day, even if you refuse to admit it. I hope my photos turn out. The kids will be anxious to see them. Just think: two doctoral degrees, you sexy old devil. I think I'm jealous." I hugged him hard. His face lit up in a dimpled grin.

"When we get back, I hope you'll demonstrate your gratitude in a more … intimate way."

"It's a date, sweetheart."

As we walked toward the car, I reminded him of how extraordinary we were in those days. "After our tiny, but effective, wedding, we were the only married couple at Gettysburg. I've never regretted a moment of our forty-five years of marriage. Have you, Peter Andrew?"

"Sweetie, I hate to spoil your fun."

"Are you saying that you *do* have regrets?"

"Well, there is one thing that I regret."

"No! Really?"

He shook his head sadly. "I could have been a damn good truck driver."

I heaved a sigh. "Ain't that a shame?"

"Sandra, your grammar is atrocious."

I gave him the finger. He laughed at me and grabbed my hand.